An Adve... Unique Eats,

PENNSYLVANIA

going

LOCAL!

VOLUME
2

Cool Pubs & Cozy Cafés of Central Pennsylvania

Ride Far
Eat LOCAL!

Ken Hull

Printed in the United States of America by Nittany Valley Offset, 1015 Benner Pike, State College, PA 16801 **www.nittayvalley.com**

First Edition October 2010

ISBN 978-0-9795842-1-3

Cover design by Rose Ann Hoover
Inside layout design by Bryan Benner
Map design by Michael Hermann - Purple Lizard Maps

The author and publisher encourage all readers to visit and support all the places listed in this book and recommend those who partake of any alcoholic beverage to do so in moderation and travel with a nondrinking driver.

TABLE OF CONTENTS

DEDICATION

Once again, I dedicate this book to Jesus — my Savior and Lord, who has blessed me with all the opportunities, abilities, and adventures in my life; to my wonderful mom and dad who have always believed in me and supported me in all those adventures; to my extended family and friends who encourage me and stand by my side; to all those who helped me along the way; and to you, my readers and fans, who made this second book possible.

PREFACE

Wow, what a ride (literally)! In 2007 while working on my first volume of going LOCAL!, I put over 7,000 miles on The Mighty Steed (my '94 Harley Sportster) exploring the back roads and byways of central PA to find some of the coolest places for you to eat, drink, or just hang out with a cup of coffee. Then, while that book was finding its way into the hands of fellow foodies, beer geeks, café lovers, and adventurers, I realized a second book might be in my future.

That idea was already floating around in my head because many places I wanted to put in the first book I couldn't due to space restrictions. Plus, fans everywhere were telling me of their favorite places (many I had never even heard of) and wanted me to visit them. And with the book selling so well and people asking me when I was going to write a second one, it was clear another volume was needed. I had enough places, in fact I had more than enough places.

It's amazing, once you get out and explore, how many locally owned places you can find doing so many wonderful things. We are so blessed here in central PA. Men, women, and families who have committed their lives, talents, and passions bring you eats and drinks of great taste and freshness. Their businesses are good for the community, and by supporting them you ensure their future. And if you take the time to explore these places and the bounty of central PA, you can even have fun and life-enriching experiences too. Fun and life-enriching experiences? Yes! From my 24-hour odyssey at a VFW in rural Osceola Mills in my first book to the 20 minute paddleboat ferry ride across the Susquehanna River in this book, "fun and life-enriching" is what going local is all about.

As you will read in the pages to come, I've traveled some pretty awesome roads, drunk handcrafted beers (moderately and responsibly) that were so authentic and delicious that I thought I was in Belgium, enjoyed coffees, teas, and pastries from sweet cafés, and eaten some of the best food ever! And I did this without gaining a pound. Kidding! I did this by getting out there, listening to my readers, talking to locals, and just opening myself up to whatever came my way. Sometimes that didn't work out so well, but most of the time it did, and it was wonderful.

The thing is, I found that going local was more than just eating and drinking. Throughout central PA there are many indie businesses that encompass every aspect of life and need, from your local barber shop and hardware store to retail shops and services of all kinds - all owned and operated by our friends and neighbors. I wanted to feature some of these local gems within each region, but as I traveled out from the chain-infested State College area, I noticed most of our smaller towns only have locally owned businesses. Bless you. However, since many of my dear neighbors in the greater State College area are still imprisoned by the box stores I felt it important to unchain them by featuring some other local businesses as well.

This was cool, but as I considered that, I created a dilemma for myself. I was already way over my word count with just the eats, pubs, and cafés; adding locally owned goods and services would put me WAY over! Fortunately I have friends who have more creative brains than I do, and they helped to solve that problem for both. As you will read in the next section we cleverly came up with a way to get some extra places in, plus some of the centre region's local goods and services.

In 2009 our economy hit some really hard times, so this is all the more reason to support all these locally owned businesses. Just since my first book debuted, seven places closed. It's tough, my friends, but we can help by supporting our locals. We'll also be saving gas and resources by sticking close to home - taking a bunch of day trips rather than one big, expensive one. We can do it!

Please use this book not just as a guide to unique eats, cool pubs, and cozy cafés, but as a way to lend a hand to our locally owned businesses and our community. Oh, and to have fun and life-enriching experiences as well. That's how I roll, and look what happened to me.

Only by God's grace and the blessings He provided through folks like you supporting me have I made it to where I am today. I never thought I'd write one book, let alone two. I also thought I'd never hear someone tell me that what I created would change their lives. And I never, ever thought I could support myself by riding around the state on my motorcycle, eating great food, and drinking amazing beers and coffees. But that's how cool life can be, and I can't wait for what's down the road.

Yeah, it's been a great ride. And now the adventure continues!

ABOUT THIS BOOK

As with Volume 1, this is not just a guidebook, and it isn't a critique or review – it's a journal, travel log, memoir, fact, fiction and hopefully a good resource and read as well. In fact, I've written it more like a story about my adventures and experiences as I've traveled around central PA and the places I've discovered.

Most of time these journeys are with my travelling companion and source of transportation, The Mighty Steed, my sweet 1994 Harley Davidson Sportster (inspired by Che Guevara's 1939 Norton 500 called La Poderosa – The Mighty One). Don't be surprised if I write as though I'm with another person sometimes, because when you've logged as many miles together as we have, it's hard not to think of him as a friend. He's always ready to go on an adventure, and never fails to give me all he has (especially when passing minivans).

My purpose on these adventures is to be an advocate, scout, messenger, and just a lover of life – whose experiences and discoveries will be like an adventure and discovery for you. As with my first book, I'm sure I've missed some places, but that's cool because I also want you to find some on your own – using your own map, asking locals, and by just hitting the road to discover what's around the next curve.

My hope with this book is to also inspire and encourage you to break away from the chain gang (chain restaurants, fast food places, and retail box stores), to experience for yourself the rich blessings of indie (independent) owned eating, drinking, retail, and service businesses we have here in central Pennsylvania. I fear that if we don't support our locals and the old-school, mom-and-pop places, they will fall by the wayside and be forgotten.

This book is all about going local and supporting these indie sole proprietors that were the foundation of our country. The chains are a new thing within the past 40+ years, and how in the world did people survive before them? I'll tell you how, by shopping and getting services at locally owned stores, shops, pharmacies, and other businesses, as well as dining at local restaurants, pubs, or cafés. By supporting them you keep your money local and keep that money cycling back through the community (not out of state or off shore). Plus, you ensure their survival, and they will be there for you and appreciate your business.

So there ya go - keep it local and keep it alive! That's what going LOCAL! is all about.

HOW IT WORKS

Since this is somewhat a guide book, I've tried to
set it up in a way that's easy to follow. I've also
started each listing with a section where you'll find
the name of the owners, the address, contact information, and other stuff so you can plan your visit
and know a little about the place before you go.

My good friend Mike Hermann of Purple Lizard Maps
created another cool map inside the book, which
allows you to navigate your way around and find the
places I've listed. The map starts with two small
circles in the center. From there, my area goes
approximately 75 miles (as the crow flies) out, and
360 degrees around, to form a larger circle of about
150 miles in diameter. I then thought of a way to
divide that large circle into twelve regions so that
you could easily picture them in your mind. It's
like a combination clock and dartboard.

I figure everyone can visualize the state of Pennsylvania, a center point, a dartboard, and a clock. I
also think we all understand the concept of directions
according to the numbers of a clock. Here's an example:
If I say something is at 12 o'clock, I mean straight
north. If it's at 6 o'clock, then it would be straight
south. And, if I said to look to 9 o'clock then you
should look directly to the west. Get it? The dartboard part refers to the center circles and lines
that divide the area and create a pie shape for each
region. Within these regions will be towns (in Bold),
next to them will be highlighted numbers, which will
correspond to the pages where the places I've written
about can be found.

I begin the book with two regions, which are the
circles in the center. The (bull's eye) is for a region
titled "Boalsburg, My Home" and is represented in
the Table of Contents as Roman numeral I. Around
that is a larger circle representing about 10 miles.

That region is titled "Happy Valley, My Neighbor,"
with a Roman numeral II. Then, the pie-shaped region
at 1 o'clock will be represented as Chapter 1.
Chapter 2 is the 2 o'clock pie-shaped region and so
on. On the first page of each listing, there is a
little PA state icon indicating the region by a
shaded piece of the pie.

Sound confusing? It's not, just dive in and start
reading, find a place you want to try or region you
would like to visit, unfold the map which is located
between pages 148 and 149, and get going. What are
you waiting for?

Enjoy!

Note: Please keep in mind that the information I'm providing about all the listings is the most current I could
gather prior to printing. In some cases, the establish-
ments may have changed hands, been sold, or even closed.
Menus, prices, and hours may change too. Please check the
"Updates" page of my website **www.goingLOCALpa.com** for any
information I may have discovered since printing this book.

I.
BOALSBURG,
MY HOME

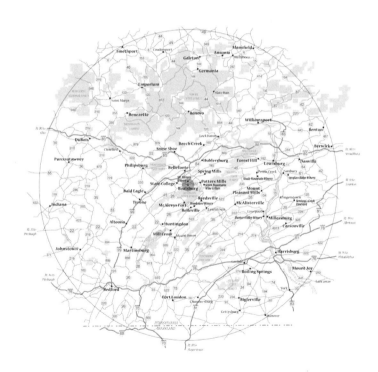

BOALSBURG, MY HOME

I pontificated quite a bit about my sweet little historic village home last time and I'm going to do it again, darn it! If you've been to Boalsburg, you know why I'm so enamored with it. The most recent comments I've heard from visitors are, "It's like a little New Hope," or, "Ahh, its sooo quaint, you must love living here." Well, yes I do. On some occasions, when visitors are standing around my cabin taking pictures and looking around with admiring eyes and smiles, I'll come out and talk with them - sometimes I even invite them in - and sometimes I've even made some friends that way.

One day Ifat and Danny Fitussi, a couple from Tel-Aviv, Israel, who had just arrived at Penn State University, were in the village exploring. I opened the door (to their surprise) and introduced myself and asked if they were interested in my cabin. With heavy accents, they politely introduced themselves and said they were. We talked outside and I showed them all around - how I built it from scratch and all the cool details of the structure.

I got a very good vibe from these guys so I invited them inside for a look (I think they were both taken aback). With more smiles and graciousness, they walked in. I showed them the downstairs as well as upstairs, and their smiles couldn't have been bigger or their compliments more sweet and sincere. As I walked them to the door, we agreed to stay in touch and from that day on we've remained good friends. On other occasions, I didn't have to invite folks in at all, they just walked right in on their own.

One hot, sunny, summer afternoon after I had cut the grass, I retreated to the cool of the cabin for a cold beverage. As if the beer angels blew their trumpets, announcing the opening of a Tröegs ale, my best friend Mike "just happened" to stop by on his way home from the office. While we were hanging out inside enjoying our beers, Mike looked out the window and started chuckling. There at the corner of Main and Academy, was a group of older women all donning red hats. We watched them as they walked down the street and out of sight. I admit we had a good laugh, but the laughter was soon to end. Without a knock or even the standard "Yoo Hoo," my cabin door flung wide open and . . .

Note: Not previously mentioned, I had no shirt on. Hey, it was hot and I had been cutting grass. Plus, I thought I was in the privacy of my own home.

Anyway, the cabin door opened and six members of the Red Hat Society walked right in my house. Walked right in! Mike could hardly contain himself from bursting out laughing and I only wish he had a camera to  take a picture of my face. There I was, no shirt, sweaty, and drinking a beer. The old girls didn't miss a beat or retreat though, they sashayed on in and all eight of us stood there in my little living room (I guess when you get to be of a certain age nothing fazes you). As if this was an everyday occurrence, the leader looked right at me and asked, "What's for sale?" I thought Mike was going to burst. I calmly said this wasn't a store and quickly reached for my shirt.

Now again, when you've traveled that long road of life, you learn many things. And one of them, at least with women, is grace. The six of them very graciously commented on how beautiful my home was and how sorry they were to have assumed it was a store (to their credit, my place had been my art gallery for six years prior and they must have just remembered that). They politely turned around and began to leave. Mike at this point had retreated to the kitchen to try to hide his reaction. As the last red hat left, I saw one of them fanning herself and whispering to the group as the leader looked back to see me buttoning my shirt. I think she had a slight grin. True story.

That, my friends, is one of many "open door" experiences I've had here in Boalsburg. I wonder how many of my neighbors have had the same. So you see, whether shop owner or resident, we here in Boalsburg welcome you to stop by anytime. But, if you don't see a sign reading OPEN or a business name on the door, you might want to knock first. Luckily, the following places in this section, as well of the rest of this book, are all about walk-ins. So without further pontification, I welcome you to the "New Hope" of central PA, Historic Boalsburg Village.

Enjoy!

Boalsburg Chocolate Company

Did you look at the "Cuisine" description for this place? That's right, this isn't just a candy store, it's a chocolate and fudge shop that offers the most delicious and decadent cocoa-based morsels of goodness, AND a wine shop too! Mmm, chocolate, fudge and wine? Are we in heaven? No, but close - we're at the Boalsburg Chocolate Company.

It all started when Bill and Cheryl Speakman decided to "retire" and open a bed & breakfast here in Boalsburg. Actually, it started when Bill dipped his toes in the chocolate biz as his very first job out of college, back home in Pittsburgh. Back then he was hired at The Joseph Horne Company, which was the first department store in downtown Pittsburgh back in 1879. He was originally hired in the cosmetics department (of all places) as an assistant buyer. The office next to him was the department of Candy and Gourmet Foods (much better). The buyer of that department had a heart attack, so the vice president came over to cosmetics looking for a replacement. Bill took the position, not realizing that Horne's actually owned a chocolate company. He was then

JUST A TASTE

Locally Owned By:
Bill & Cheryl Speakman

Cuisine:
Chocolates, Fudge & Wine

Price Range:
Free samples to $12 – $20 per pound

Hours:
Tue. – Sat. 11am to 5pm (Extended holiday hours)

Wi-Fi:
No

Location:
126 E. Main St.

Contact Info:
(814) 466-6290,
www.boalsburgchocolate.com

Vegetarian Offerings:
Yes

Supports Local Farmers:
Yes

Locally Owned Accommodations Nearby:
Springfield House Bed & Breakfast on location

Things To Do Nearby:
Boalsburg Village, PA Military Museum, Boalsburg Heritage Museum, Boal Mansion Museum

taken over to the factory where he met Betsey, the previous owner who taught him the ropes and set his love of chocolate making in motion.

After six years there, he had a bunch of other jobs but ended up in the State College area working for Penn State Public Broadcasting. It was after retiring from there that he became an innkeeper. I guess that wasn't enough for Bill, so he took his experience in chocolate making to open a little shop in a first floor annex of the B&B. It's a quaint and well-appointed shop with wonderful ambiance and a variety of chocolates and fudge that will convince you to dump any diet you're on.

The offerings at BCC are sooo good! You can buy one piece or stock up by the pound if you want. Here are just some of the amazing morsels you can choose from: hand-made truffles, locally crafted creams, nuts, chews, fruits, and seasonal specialties, all using 100% chocolate. The fudge is good too! You're probably thinking, "Fudge is fudge." Wrong. This is hand-mixed and deelicious (even better than my mom's, but please don't tell her).

If Boalsburg weren't sweet enough, this addition puts it over the top! Imagine walking the 200-year-old tree-lined streets and then seeing a beautifully restored, gingerbread-trimmed, wrap-around porch house. As you walk up a wide path next to it, you're greeted by a fountain with cast-iron tables and chairs set out beneath the canopy of maples and oaks. In front of you is a quaint little building with a large glass window, and the words Boalsburg Chocolate Company written on it. Through the window you see glass cases displaying everything chocolate from white to dark, filled to plain, covered to dipped (and you wonder why I love where I live).

When you walk inside, you are greeted by beautiful chocolates, bottles of wine, and the smell of sweet-

ness. Sometimes I just like to look at the chocolates – some are like mini art pieces – colorful and
decorated. For me, it's hard to choose a favorite.
I love the Chocolate Covered Pretzels, the Peanut
Butter Melts and the Clusters (dark chocolate poured
over coconut or raisins or blueberries), but the
Snowballs are really, really good too! Those are
caramel and coconut cream surrounded by milk chocolate and then rolled in coconut. Yum! And it's not
just me, my friends love the place too.

All the chocolates at BCC are locally made and some
are made by Bill, in-house. He uses the kitchen of
the B&B to make goodies that find their way to the
pillows of the guests. He and Cheryl even offer free
wine and chocolate tastings for guests on the weekends.
He's a smart guy, and almost like a drug dealer, who
gives you your first sample for free then you're hooked!
He said that guests rarely leave the B&B without
buying a "stash" of chocolates, fudge, and wine.

Speaking of wine, did I mention that BCC sells Mount
Nittany Wine? Yes they do, and if you can't make it to
the winery just down the road you can stock up here.
Mount Nittany has a special permit which allows them
to sell their wine off-premise. It's a match made in
heaven to be able to have your off-premise place be
a chocolate shop — not to mention a chocolate shop
in the middle of a beautiful historic district.

Now, imagine you and your sweetie have made your choice
of chocolates, you pick a bottle of wine, pay for
it all, walk outside, and sit at a café table beside
the fountain. You then uncork the bottle, set out
the glasses you cleverly brought along, and pour the
wine. Then you unwrap the chocolates, take a bite,
let it melt on your tongue, rinse it down with a sip
of wine, cozy-up to your sweetie, and ...

Enjoy!

Tait Farm Foods

This place is as "going local" as you can get, and they totally fit my descriptor of "Unique Eats." The fact that they're not a restaurant, pub, or café doesn't matter. You can get some amazing food products here that are made in-house as well as fresh produce (planted, grown, and harvested there). Along with that, they offer local meats, cheeses, breads, and homemade goodies. I bet if you wanted to, owner Kim Tait wouldn't mind if you purchased a bunch of her foods, took your own table, chairs, and place settings, and set up somewhere on the farm and had a wonderful outdoor dinner right there. And you know what else? This is my book, and I can do whatever I want. Denying Tait Farm a prominent place here just because they don't have a kitchen or 25 beers on tap is just wrong. I love this place and so does most of central PA!

JUST A TASTE

Locally Owned By:
Kim Tait

Cuisine:
In-house and locally produced foods

Price Range:
$3.75 to $17.95

Hours:
Mon. - Fri. 9am to 6pm, Sat. 9am to 5pm, Sun. opens at 10am

Location:
Rt. 322 E. (2 miles east of Boalsburg)

Wi-Fi:
No

Contact Info:
(814) 466-3411 (800) 787-2716, www.taitfarmfoods.com

Vegetarian Offerings:
Yes

Supports Local Farmers:
Yes

Locally Owned Accommodations Nearby:
Aikins Cabins 814-466-9299; Earlystown Manor B&B 814-466-6481

Things To Do Nearby:
Tussey Mountain Resort, Hiking, Biking, Boalsburg Village, PA Military Museum, Boalsburg Heritage Museum, Boal Mansion Museum, Mount Nittany Winery

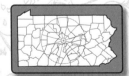

It all started when Marian and Elton Tait purchased their farm in 1950 to be "hobby" farmers of sheep, chickens, hogs, horses, basset hounds, and Christmas trees while working for Penn State. They also raised their three children Sandy, David, and John there.

Back in the late 1970s, the two sons left their day jobs to return to the family farm, deciding to make their living off the land. Perennial plantings of apples, raspberries, asparagus, and more Christmas trees followed, and by the mid '80s the farm was becoming State College's spot to pick-your-own fruits, vegetables, and Christmas trees. The food products business began after a bumper crop of raspberries in 1986 sat on the bushes because it was pouring rain and no one was coming out to pick them. The crop was harvested and frozen, but the problem was, what to do with all that frozen fruit?

After trying to sell frozen raspberries and failing, David remembered a recipe for something made during the Colonial era — a concoction made by preserving fresh fruit in vinegar, adding sugar, and creating a concentrate that was then enjoyed by mixing it with water. The first bottles of Tait's now famous Raspberry Shrub were hand-labeled and sold at the farm starting in 1987. Since that time, the farm and food product business has continued to grow. John Tait raises the Christmas trees and basset hounds while Kim K. Tait runs Tait Farm Foods.

Tait Farm Foods now manufactures over fifty food products, has a year-round Harvest Shop and Greenhouse (specializing in local foods, gift collections, seasonal produce, herbs, flowers, heirloom roses, and inspired gifts for the kitchen, garden, and home), and has a Community Supported Agriculture project known as Community Harvest. This is a fresh produce membership that provides over 175 families and several local restaurants with certified organic vegetables and fruits in half-year and full-year shares.

When it comes to locally owned, operated, and supported, Tait Farm Foods is a treasure. Kim has always been supportive of my endeavors, and now I want to support hers. She has a wonderful place! From pick-your-own veggies, locally produced foods, and products of their own and others, to basset hounds, Christmas trees, and all kinds of local stuff, Tait's is certainly "going local" with some very "unique eats." I love them! And so will you.

Enjoy!

LOCALLY OWNED GOODS & SERVICES

The following are just a few of our wonderful
independent businesses here in Boalsburg. There
are many more as well, and I encourage you to visit
and support them all. Because of space restrictions,
I've included only the name and basic information.
For my personal story on each place, please visit
my website and click on the link to read The Rest
of the Story.

Keene's Barber Shop

Just the Facts:
Locally Owned By: Rob Jackson
Goods or Service: Haircuts
Hours: Tue. - Fri. by Appointment
Location: 217 N. Church St.
Contact Info: 814-466-4868

Colonial Press

Just a Sample
Locally Owned By: Glenn "Butch" Dry
Service: Single, Multiple and Full Color Printing
Hours: Mon. - Fri. 8am to 5pm
Location: 500 Loop Road, Boalsburg
Contact Info: 814-466-3380 **www.colonialpress.net**

Boalsburg Apothecary

Just a Sample
Locally Owned By: Jean & Mark Doyle; Pharmacist/Manager:
Wayne Foster
Service: Pharmacy
Hours: Mon. - Fri. 9am to 6pm, Sat. 9am to 12pm
Location: 3901 S. Atherton St. (Boalsburg Medical Center)
Contact Info: 814-466-7936, **www.theboalsburgapothecary.com**

(For The Rest of the Story go to **www.goingLOCALpa.com/TRS**)

II.
HAPPY VALLEY,
MY NEIGHBOR

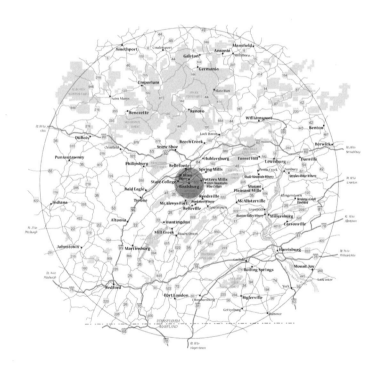

HAPPY VALLEY, MY NEIGHBOR

Truly, this is my home. Yeah, I wrote that it's Boalsburg, but Boalsburg is a part of Happy Valley. In fact, you might say that my family and I are founding residents here. My great-great-great-great-grandfather Evan Williams arrived here in 1793 with General Phillip Benner of Chester County, PA. He was the General's millwright, and built and ran both his saw and grist mills. They were located in the now famed and pristine Spring Creek Canyon, whose future is now under hot debate and I hope and pray cooler and wiser heads prevail.

Growing up in Happy Valley was awesome! I was born in Lemont and in those days, the train still ran through the village. My sisters and I would lay copper pennies on the train tracks so the train would smash them flat and elongated – this was a thrill. When we moved to Pine Grove Mills, I walked to school and spent the summers playing kickball and capture-the-flag when I wasn't exploring nature and fishing with my dad. When I was 10 years old we moved to the big city - State College Borough. It was then that mom and dad bought me my first mini bike, and my life has been influenced by motorcycles ever since.

Life then was almost utopian – tons of stuff to do, and people weren't so stinking uptight like they are today. Seriously, back then I could zip around the back of the Westerly Parkway Shopping Center on my mini bike like a moto-crosser, and my buddies and I would skateboard in the parking garage downtown (there was only one then) and nobody called the cops. When I was older and got my first trail bike, I would actually ride up Shingletown Gap without incident! If I tried that now in this day of insanity, I would either be wrestled to the ground by hikers or arrested by the DCNR.

Sorry. Yes, the good ol' days of Happy Valley were certainly good. Back then we never locked our house and we kids would roam free over a multi-neighborhood area without a care in the world. Our folks didn't have a care either, they were glad to have us out of the house. As long as we did our homework and were home for dinner, we pretty much did as we pleased. It was a great place to grow up and still is.

It's safe, still has tons of stuff to do (especially outdoor related), and most recently State College passed an ordinance to allow folks within the borough to have chickens in their backyards (some restrictions of course). CHICKENS IN THE BACKYARD! Even back in the day they didn't allow that – even my beloved/very open-minded Boalsburg doesn't allow that. Yes, we have the "Village Chickens," but they're rebels, loners, drifters, and not "domesticated." State College has now made it possible to walk out your backdoor and collect freshly laid eggs for breakfast. Right on! Maybe times are changing? Maybe like fashion, things will go back in time?

Happy Valley was truly happy back in the day. It still is, and despite the fact that it's plagued with, and over-run by, chains, it still has some amazing indie businesses that in my opinion kick the @$$es off the chain gang. The area is also growing by leaps and bounds. It seems every time I look around, a new development is being built. I personally don't like this, but I guess it's good for our local economy, and hopefully keeps bringing new folks in to buy local goods like my books and art. Not only that, but people need food and drink, and the more people you have, the better chance of having great places to enjoy both. So fortunately, between regular residents and PSU students, we have a population base that supports some amazing restaurants, pubs, and cafés. In the following pages, I want to point out a few of my favorites so the next time you're thinking of going to Lobster Trap, Olive Pit, Applefleas, or God forbid, McDiarrhea, you'll think again and go LOCAL!

Enjoy!

The Hotel State College
(3 IN 1) STATE COLLEGE, CENTRE COUNTY

Like Duffy's in book 1,
I guess the first stop in
Happy Valley should be a
Patriarch/Icon too. The
Hotel State College is more than the
name implies. Yes, one can stay there overnight,
but it is also three levels of eating and drinking
goodness. Standing beautifully and guarding the
corner of Allen Street and College Avenue, this
1855 hotel gleams from white paint and windows.
Grand pillars support a glassed-in second floor
porch where the hungry patrons of the Allen Street
Grill dine while watching students and townies
spring below like a fountain of youth.

Here at "The Grill" you'll experience fine dining in
a casual atmosphere. My friends and I like to go for
lunch, dinner, and late night drinks. The menu offers a variety of American cuisine selections prepared daily. They have time-tested favorites as well
as daily features. For an appetizer, try the Calamari Puttanesca: flash fried calamari served in putta-

JUST A TASTE

Locally Owned By:
Michael Desmond & John Cocolin

Cuisine:
New American to Pub Fare

Price Range:
$3.00 to $26.00

Hours:
Allen Street Grill: 11am to 1am;
Corner Room: 7am to 10pm;
Zeno's: 12pm to 2am (Sun. 1pm)

Location:
100 W. College Ave.

Wi-Fi:
Yes

Contact Info:
(814) 237-4350,
www.hotelstatecollege.com

Vegetarian Offerings:
Yes

Supports Local Farmers:
Yes

**Locally Owned
Accommodations Nearby:**
Hotel on Premise

Things To Do Nearby:
Lots

nesca sauce with capers and Kalamata olives. Soups include Maryland Crab Bisque, which is a combination of fresh crab meat, cream, and sherry, among others. How about a salad like Jack's Roadhouse Salad? Sweet and hot tips of filet mignon char-grilled then nestled on top of romaine lettuce with French fries, cheddar cheese, grape tomatoes, red onions and bleu cheese dressing. For dinner you can go for anything from Wild Mushroom Ravioli to Balsamic Maple Glazed Salmon. That, my friends, is a char-grilled Canadian salmon basted with a maple, balsamic vinegar and grapefruit reduction, then served with white rice and steamed vegetables. Mmm! They also offer yummy desserts and coffee too.

At street level you'll find an off-campus institution - The Corner Room. Heck, this place has probably seen more diners of various ages than anyplace you could imagine and is still very popular. On a foot-

ball Saturday or during Arts Fest, you can't even get in the place – don't be surprised if you encounter a line down the street. Don't let that stop you though, because it's definitely worth the wait. Breakfast, lunch, and dinner are served, as well as late night snacks to those who might need a break from "studying." One patron, Don Kepler, who has since passed away, ate breakfast there so many times and for so long that they dedicated a booth to him and it bears his name to this day. Grab a table by the window and people-watch while wait staff buzz around with everything from pancakes to roast beef sandwiches and, of course, coffee.

Speaking of coffee, they serve Rich Coast which is somewhat local, and man is it good! I don't know what it is about that brand, but the taste is great. Of all restaurant-grade coffees, this one is the one I prefer and "The Corner" serves up a great cup. They also offer wireless internet, so this place has become one of my faves for a place to work with a cup of joe. FYI, they also have beer on tap!

The Corner has the atmosphere of a diner but in a well equipped and quite large full-service restaurant. The décor here is really nice too, and so vintage and nostalgic. The woodwork, windows, classic high-backed booths, hidden tables, ceiling fans, and vibe are like out of an old Humphrey Bogart movie. I guess that's the advantages of a place built in 1855. There's even a hostess there from that era. Kidding, but Emma Gunsallus has been working there since the 50s! She keeps the customers moving through and is the go-to woman for all the newbie student wait staff. She's super nice, but I wouldn't want to mess up under her watch. You'll know her by her name badge because it notes 50+ years of service. How cool!

Both of these restaurants are overseen daily by the watchful eye of co-owner Mike Desmond. Mike is one of those guys that seems to have his hands on every working part of this trifecta of goodness, including the on-premise lodging in the actual hotel above it all. I swear I wouldn't be surprised if in the morning he was unloading a truck of beer, then cooking on the line during the lunch rush, then helping to get the rooms ready in the hotel for the evening's guests, and then after all that pinch-hitting as a bartender upstairs or at Zeno's below. Yet amid the chaos and running the extremely tight ship that is The Hotel State College, he seems to always have time for his customers.

I have never been to The Grill, The Corner Room, or Zeno's when Mike wouldn't at least come and say hi if he spotted me. Most often he takes the time to chat a bit and he always asks how my folks are doing. One day, while my web designer, Bien, and I were at The Corner Room, Mike interrupted a maintenance pow-wow to see how I was doing. Then, as he walked away, he grabbed our check and signed for it at the register. That's the kind of guy he is.

For many of us locals and about a billion post-21 students, the real treasure of The Hotel State College is buried underneath. Just around the Allen Street side of the building and down some very narrow stone steps below street level, and you'll find the treasure – Zeno's Pub. This place is, as they say, "Located directly above the center of the earth." For those of you who like a tavern setting similar to a pub in Ireland and you're a certifiable beer geek, this is the place.

Here is where quality beer drinking men and women are separated from the boys and girls of big batch and small taste beers. Dave Staab, the general manager of Zeno's, loves good handcrafted beer and it shows! He keeps over

30 on tap, and at least twice that in bottles. If you doubt me, get this - Zeno's offers an 80 Beers Around the World Passport! It's like the Jules Verne epic Around the World in Eighty Days, but hopefully you'll take more than 80 days (it's not about consumption, most students take their whole four years at Penn State to accomplish this daring feat). This is more like an ongoing adventure exploring 80 finely brewed beers from around the world. Oh, and BL Lime isn't one of them. Man or woman, young or old, one can set out like Verne's character Phileas Fogg. But instead of a balloon, you have a mug. You also get a little passport which the staff will stamp with each beer you visit. Very cool.

When you've traveled through all 80 beers, you get your name proudly displayed on a brass plaque, along with all your fellow explorers, which runs the length of the bar. Zeno's is one of my favorite spots in town, and offers you an adventure around the world with a balloon filled with the best beers this side of the center of the earth. And, with a full menu from upstairs and some of the best local and national live music, this will be the only place where being underground makes you feel like you're soaring next to heaven.

Yes, The Hotel State College is as stated, a true patriarch and icon of Happy Valley, as well as a trifecta of goodness - three amazing places in one. From the casual fine dining offered at the Allen Street Grill, to the very casual and classic dining at The Corner Room, and then the very cool, very "beer-geek friendly" pub Zeno's, this place has it all. It's no wonder "Meet me at the Corner" has become such a common phrase when folks are looking to meet up with friends or family at one of the most delicious and diverse places in town.

Enjoy!

Saint's Café
STATE COLLEGE, CENTRE COUNTY

For me, this place is kind of a blessing and curse at the same time. What I mean is, I love it; it's sweet, it's got a cool vibe, great coffee, good snacks, free Wi-Fi and it's very cozy. The problem is it's too cozy. What I mean by that is that the place is small and popular. That equates to not always getting a place to sit, which stinks because it's a very cool place to sit - hence the curse.

This Mecca of the bean started when the tsunami created by the coffee craze of the Pacific northwest hit lil' ol' central PA. Back then, Saint's was called Café Gourmet and was owned by a vivacious and hardworking woman named Kelly. She took a nondescript little corner space along Beaver Ave. and turned it into what we all thought had to be just like what they had out in Seattle. The place was done up with high top tables, a counter with barstools along big picture windows, cool lighting, warm colors, and a

JUST A TASTE

Locally Owned By:
Greg & Mary Kay Avedesian

Cuisine:
Coffees, Teas and light fare

Price Range:
$1.60 to $5.50

Hours:
Mon. 7 to 9 p.m., Tues. – Sat. 7 to 6, Sun. 8 to 4:30

Wi-Fi:
Yes

Location:
123 W. Beaver Ave. (between Fraser Street and Allen Street next to Kelly Alley)

Contact Info:
(814) 238-5707

Vegetarian Offerings:
Yes

Supports Local Producers:
Yes

Locally Owned Accommodations Nearby:
The Stevens Motel

Things To Do Nearby:
Lots

sofa with a coffee table. A sofa! This was definitely not your parents place to get a cup a joe. Back in my folk's day, you got your coffee at a diner or something and you didn't get comfy and hang around all day with just a 25 cent purchase. Granted, nowadays a fancy espresso drink can run you upwards to 3 or 4 bucks, but still, you can't make a living on just a dozen of those a day. Believe me, I tried. I had a little café in my art gallery in Boalsburg back in the day, and between my freeloader friends and the fact that I only had four tables, I was glad to sell a painting once in a while to stay alive.

Saint's has quite a few more tables than I did, and I wouldn't call the patrons there "freeloaders," but they do linger a bit longer than I would like when I'm looking for a spot to work. At least those at a bigger tables could be open to someone else sitting across from them – heck, everyone's glued to their computer screen anyway. So what's a nice guy who just wants to sit down and work on his book going to do?

Under the new ownership of Greg & Mary Kay Avedesian, the place is doing well and is a good place for the grad student, professional or just locals like me who want a place that's not too "coffee shopish." You know what I mean, those places where if you don't have dreadlocks, smell like patchouli, or have tattoos, you just don't fit in. Here it's more "genteel" and less "bohemian." I don't know why, it just is. They even have seating along the side of the building but instead of the standard plastic tables and chairs, these look like ones I've seen in France - metal with pretty designs painted on them and cool twisted wire backs.

So it seems Saint's is more a blessing than anything else. It is what it is - a little coffee shop with lots of spirit, coziness and great tasting coffees, teas and homemade goodies. The fact that it's full most of the time should not stop you from going - somebody's bound to leave at some point. And, if it wasn't such an awesome place it wouldn't be so popular. Come to think of it, Saints are all about blessings. This one sure is.

Enjoy!

The Enchanted Kitchen
STATE COLLEGE, CENTRE COUNTY

You know, sometimes things just
work out for the best. Sometimes,
even when things aren't going the
way you want, or you miss a big
deadline, it works out – it's
just meant to be. That's the
story here and was the case when
I came to terms with the fact

that this book wasn't going to debut in 2009 like I
planned. Even when I thought I could have it out by
spring of 2010 it didn't work out. But little did I
know that something was about to happen, and that
"something" needed to be included in this book – and
not just for content's sake (at that point I already
had too many places for the State College region),
but for your sake, and the sake of a young woman who
stepped out and took her gifts and talents to task
and made her dream come true.

I was only made aware of this one spring day at the
Boalsburg Farmers' Market. I saw a friend there who's
a big fan of my first book and asked me if I knew of
a place that just opened in State College that serves

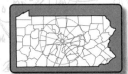

Locally Owned By:
April Myers

Cuisine:
Live, Raw, Vegan, Vegetarian

Price Range:
$5.00 to $15.00

Hours:
Call for hours

Location:
127 S. Pugh St.

Wi-Fi:
Yes

Contact Info:
(814) 231-0111,
www.theenchantedkitchen.net

Vegetarian Offerings:
Yes

Supports Local Farmers:
Yes

**Locally Owned
Accommodations Nearby:**
Hotel State College (814)
237-4350; The Autoport (800)
932-7678; The Stevens Motel
(814) 238-2438

Things To Do Nearby:
Lots

an all vegan/raw food menu AND has a yoga studio in-house. I told her no but was now curious myself. While we were talking about this, I saw a guy that I knew whom I thought was a vegetarian and might know something. As he passed by, I shouted out "Hey Peter, do you know of a new vegan/raw food restaurant downtown?" Before he could even respond, I heard a woman's voice shout "Hey, that's my place!"

There, with a big smile on her face, was yet another friend shopping at that market at the exact second I put that question out into the cosmos. April Myers was already known for her incredible vegetarian and vegan recipes served at Webster's Café, but that was just a sampling and only a part-time gig for her. So to hear her shout "That's my place!" I was really excited, and so was my friend who asked about it. April came right over, her face beaming, and told us about her Enchanted Kitchen.

I love to talk with people who are passionate and excited about what they do! Well, if April could have been any more passionate and excited, I think she would have burst. She told us that she had just opened her place the week before and when she talked about her menu creations and ideas for future features, it was all we could do not to ditch the market and make a beeline for her café.

April also told us that her café was subterranean, below the famed Gemelli bakery (which you'll read about in a few pages) and she shares the space with a mutual friend Karen Sapia, who is a well know yoga instructor and the wife of Tony Sapia – the baker at Gemelli's (gotta love community). The space was actually a former college student nightclub space, so I was eager to see and experience the transformation to a chill, peaceful and healthy café/yoga studio.

It was a couple weeks later when I had a chance to visit on a Wednesday. Because April had told us at that divine encounter that she focused mainly on lunch, I knew not to go too early or too late. I walked into a totally sweet place with a super cool vibe. April greeted me with that wonderful smile of hers and was so happy to see me and excited to tell me the day's special. She also told me some other yummy offerings but if I wanted the special I'd have to wait a bit before she finished making it. You see, April lives fresh, eats fresh, and creates fresh. So for her, a menu is like a paint-by-number kit to an artist or a cage to a bird. Every day is a new day at the Enchanted Kitchen and every day is a new canvas for this culinary artist. She paints with what's fresh, available, and what her muse tells her that morning.

That day had been blessed by a visit from a farmer friend, who presented April with a gift of freshly picked sugar snap peas. Taking that as her inspiration and base, she created the day's feature which she called Sunnie Snap Pea Salad. Well most guys may not consider an ordinary salad a lunch, but I'm not most guys and once she finished telling me what was going on with said salad, I realized there was nothing ordinary about it.

Here's the amazing combination of fresh ingredients April was able to put together to bring this masterpiece to the table: fresh baby spinach, arugula, and radishes from Jade Family Farm, sugar snaps from Howard's End, cucumbers, red bell peppers, avocado, and spiced roasted walnuts. All that goodness was finished with a scoop of sunflower seed pâté and served with spicy fig dressing. That is not ordinary, it's extraordinary, and it didn't stop there.

Since I was hungry and April needed time to prepare the salad, I ordered a Tropical Smoothie. Even that was nothing ordinary. April prepared it right before my eyes and with such loving care. In fact, when I commented how cool it was that she jams fresh mint into her water pitchers, she said without missing a beat, "We don't 'jam' anything in at the Enchanted Kitchen, we lovingly place it."

That one statement sums up the whole vibe of the place as well as the delicious food April creates. When my Sunnie Snap Pea Salad arrived I was blown away. I almost didn't want to eat it because it looked so good! Every ingredient was "lovingly placed" and carefully thought out. After drizzling on the dressing, I took a bite and knew right away that April was going to have her gifted hands full when the word gets out about her café. Every ingredient and every texture was fresh, flavorful, and crisp. I'm no food critic, but if I were, I would give April the highest accolades. What she has created at the Enchanted Kitchen is nothing less than ... enchanting.

Whether you're a confirmed carnivore or total veghead, you're going to love this place! It's a new idea and a brilliant one for the Centre Region. If you thought eating healthy meant eating tasteless and boring – my friends, you are sooo wrong. April offers way more than salads, and nothing is cooked over 120 degrees so as to keep all the nutritional value. She's just doing everything right.

Go with low expectations and you'll be blown away – go with high expectations and you'll be blown away. So just go! And think about taking a yoga class from Karen before or after – what a better way to bring mind, body, spirit, and belly together in perfect unity and pleasure. Let me tell you something, after eating at The Enchanted Kitchen, I was glad this book didn't come out on time. It was all meant to be.

Enjoy!

Gemelli Bakers (and Nola's Joint)
STATE COLLEGE, CENTRE COUNTY

Until this awesome bakery came to State College, the only place I had any hope of getting the type and quality of bread I've been spoiled by in Europe was – Europe.

Since this discovery, I've been enjoying "Europe" at home as well as in local restaurants. Any restaurant worth their reputation serves Gemelli's, and when you eat it, you know why. Take two of my faves for example: Ciabatta and Old Country French. They're very similar with only some difference in a few ingredients and shape. Ciabatta means slipper in Italian and I guess you can say its slipper shaped (if you know someone with feet that are like 18 inches long) which makes it ideal for sandwiches. The French is more oblong and much higher in profile.

Like their European counterparts they're crunchy on the outside and oh, so soft on the inside. Folks, if you think real French or Italian breads are supposed to be soft when you squeeze them, you might as well buy a loaf of Wonder Bread. In Italy, if the bread crust doesn't crack when squeezed, it's not even worth

---

JUST A TASTE

Locally Owned By:
Tony and Karen Sapia

Cuisine:
Artisan Breads and Baked Goodies

Price Range:
$0.50 to $6.00

Hours:
Wed. – Sat. 11am to 6pm,
Nola's 11am to 11pm

Location:
129 McAllister Alley

Wi-Fi:
No

Contact Info:
Gemelli's (814) 234-Twin (8946),
Nola's (814) 231-8828

Vegetarian Offerings:
Yes

Supports Local Farmers:
Yes

Locally Owned Accommodations Nearby:
Hotel State College (814) 237-4350; The Stevens Motel (814) 238-2438

Things To Do Nearby:
Lots

considering. It's the opposite of the American test for freshness. Hard and brittle on the outside means it's fresh. Soft and spongy means it's been around awhile and not nearly as good. I leaned this first hand from a baker in Italy on my first trip there.

Gemelli's breads crack when you tear them open and give way to an inside that looks more like wood that's been ravished by termites. Holes, pockets, and tunnels make an inside that has amazing texture and is just right for holding olive oil. I like to heat mine while preparing dinner and then tearing (never slicing) it during the meal – dipping it in olive oil laced with hand-grated parmesan. OMG, it is hard to say which is better, the main dish or the bread! And that's just two of their breads, my friends; I don't have space for the other styles or the other insanely delicious baked goods created there. But you do, and I suggest a complete sampling!

The man responsible for these creations is artisan baker, Anthony "Tony" Sapia. Tony is not someone I would have pegged as a baker. He's a local business-man, former bar owner, and is somewhat of an enter-tainer as well. If you've ever had the pleasure of meeting him you know what I mean. Funny, smart, engaging, talkative, generous and funny! But how did this former bar owner and funny guy become an accomplished baker?

According to Tony, it all started in 2001 with the birth of twin sons Giacomo and Fiorenzo, aka Jack and Enzo, and the dream to bake artisan breads. Gemelli means "twin" in Italian and a cool name for a bakery. At first it was wholesale only but now the place is open to the public. You can also buy these amazing breads and goodies at several locations besides the bakery itself – the one I like best is the Boalsburg Farmers' Market. Tony usually has a helper there, but every once in awhile he comes and the entire market is either laughing or other vendors are getting free samples – usually both! Other locations where you can pick up Gemelli breads are the Cheese Shoppe, Tait Farm, the Granary, Nature's Pantry, and Agostinelli's Deli among others.

Stop by first thing in the morning at the bakery and you can watch as Tony fills his gigantic oven with dough, and then watch as he takes out piping hot and beautiful loaves of bread. The place is very warm and the smell is amazing. Tony will be covered in flour dust and wearing his signature orange Crocs. He always has time for a chat, even if it's while he bakes. While I was there one day, Tony told me about his latest endeavor, yet another place to sample his creations, and even more!

Nola's Joint is a small very cozy café that he opened right next door to the bakery. Here's where you can sit down and enjoy not only his breads, but salads, antipasti, meats, cheeses, and pizza. It's also BYOB! So now you can come in with a bottle of your favorite wine or beer, order some local cheese from Stone Meadow Farms, slices of Prosciutto, a few antipasti items, fresh-baked bread from Gemelli, or in-house handmade pizza. It makes a great place for lunch, dinner, or an evening snack. Think of it as Italian tapas.

Tony Sapia is making breads and other baked goods in State College that were only previously dreamed about or acquired by an expensive plane trip to Europe. Even though I love traveling to Italy and France, it's hard to beat when something so special from there is found right here. Gemelli Bakers, along with Nola's Joint, makes living la vita here in Happy Valley a whole lot happier.

Enjoy!

The Deli
STATE COLLEGE, CENTRE COUNTY

In 1963, Andy Zangrilli came to State College from Altoona to attend Penn State. As a teenager, he worked in a pizza shop and eventually became the

manager. When arriving in Happy Valley, he talked his boss into forming a partnership with him and opened his own place called Hi-Way Pizza.

As a youngster, Hi-Way Pizza was my Mecca for all things good, and all things good were pizza, pizza, and pizza. I would stop on my way home from school just to inhale the sweet smell of this adolescent staple as it cooked in the immense, stainless steel Vulcan ovens. I have a way of warming up to people (so some say) and eventually I was able to wiggle my way behind the counter to try to learn the art of spinning pizzas. The guys took a liking to me and started me off spinning a damp round towel. I prac-ticed every day before going home and every day before I left I dropped a hint about wanting to work there.

JUST A TASTE

Locally Owned By:
Dante's Inc.; Andy Zangrilli, Founder

Cuisine:
A Bit of Everything

Price Range:
$3.99 to $24.99

Hours:
Mon. – Wed. 11am to 12am,
Th. – Sat. 11am till 2am,
Sun. 10am to 12am

Wi-Fi:
No

Location:
113 Hiester St.

Contact Info:
(814) 237-5701,
www.dantesinc.com/thedeli.htm

Vegetarian Offerings:
Yes

Supports Local Farmers:
Yes

**Locally Owned
Accommodations Nearby:**
The Autoport (800) 932-7678;
The Stevens Motel (814) 238-2438

Things To Do Nearby:
Lots

Well, one day I got the word and landed my first part-time job there. At fourteen years old, I was the youngest pizza maker at Hi-Way (Andy started when he was thirteen). I think I was actually underage, but the guys liked me, and so did everyone else, including Andy. I stayed on over the summer, but rock-and-roll and girls took over what extra time I had after school. And when Andy moved locations, I decided to move on as well.

With the success of Hi-Way Pizza, Andy went on to open other restaurants with more diverse menus, which catered to a more diverse palate. First up was The Deli, in 1973, at the corner of Heister Street and Calder Alley. Andy took his décor style of cool, vintage signs and mirrors (started at Hi-Way), added a bar area, created a room off the main room, put in skylights and one entire wall of glass. Then he filled it with plants and attached a giant hippopotamus head above it all. Whether he intended it or not, this room has been called the "hippo" room for as long as I can remember.

Andy, being pure Italian and an innovator/entrepreneur, was one of the first downtown restaurant owners to create an outdoor terrace for fair-weather dining. Hand-wrought iron work artistically fences you in and is a nice barrier between you and Calder Alley that is only inches away. Seeing that the outdoor scene was well received, Andy went total Euro and put a huge awning and seating along the Heister Street sidewalk. Now, two sides of The Deli are buzzing on nice days with a café crowd of young and old alike. Great meals, drinks, and desserts are consumed here in a sweet Euro/NYC vibe.

The menu at The Deli reads like a novel. They also support Buy Fresh, Buy Local - all of their produce is locally sourced when in season! They offer many healthy selections too, so whether you pack it in or pack it light, you'll have many delicious choices.

But save room for dessert – The Deli is one of the best places for dessert in State College. Everything from their Killer Cookie for Two to their famous cheesecake is all handmade and fresh. A lot of late-night guests come just for dessert.

One more thing that I must mention about The Deli is their choices and line-up of beers (go figure). I'm not sure, but I don't think Andy is a big beer guy, but his bar is a tribute to beer snobs and geeks alike. Plus, he has a least two cask-conditioned beers on the hand pump at all times – very often it's Victory Hop Devil (the only devil I hang with).

Andy didn't stop with Hi-Way Pizza and The Deli; he went on to form Dante's Inc. and opened The Saloon in 1976 patterned after a turn-of-the-century English Pub. The Saloon features only drinks and entertain-ment. In March 1990, after a lot of hard work and forethought, Andy opened Mario & Luigi's just a mile or so from downtown. This place offers an extensive menu serving authentic Italian dishes in a wonderful atmosphere. They do cool things there like wine tastings and pairings, and it's WAY better than the "Olive Pit." 2002 saw the opening of Bar Bleu & Bar Q – a combo bar & BBQ. The latest creation is called Inferno, a play off the Dante name, I imagine. This has got to be the hippest pizza shop anywhere, but they offer more than pizza. They have lots of starters and salads, paninis, and even a couple old world entrées. Nights are cool here as the lights are low, and comfy couches and chairs create a living room effect. Great place for a date!

As of summer 2010, Andy, along with his daughter Jennifer (Director of Operations) and her assistant J.P. Mills, completely redid the famous Hippo Room and greatly improved the beer selection at The Deli's bar area. There are beers there from all over the world and of almost every style, but J.P. is moving to feature more American craft brews. Here are some styles being offered: Pales, bocks, Belgians, cask conditioned, wheats, browns, stouts, herbed, spiced, fruits, heavy weights, session beers, ciders, and even a couple of the "yellow fizzy" stuff for you beginners.

All in all Andy Zangrilli has fed, and is feeding, the area quite well. Almost fifty years of serving everything from pizza to pasta and grilled reubens to cheesecakes, he has kept our bellies satisfied and our spirits happy. Now with his daughter Jennifer, who has taken over, I only hope for another fifty years of culinary goodness in central PA. Way to go, Andy!

Enjoy!

The Autoport
STATE COLLEGE, CENTRE COUNTY

This, my friends, is what happens when you take dreams, vision, desire, talent, a major capital investment, lots and lots of hard work, and let your hair down and try to breathe new life into an old but established local icon.

The Autoport was built in 1936 along what is now business Rt. 322, or Atherton St., a location that was then considered the outskirts of State College. Conceived and constructed by Marion B. Meyer, it quickly became a haven for travelers as well as town folk. At the time, for someone traveling east, it was the last oasis for gas, food, drinks, and lodging until Lewistown. The original design had a huge carport overhang along the road under which cars and small trucks could pull in, get gas, have the oil checked, and grab a hearty meal if they wanted.

The property is quite large and is dominated by the main structure which still houses the restaurant, bar, Blue Dog Diner, and reception area. Next to that is an outdoor seating area alongside a swimming

JUST A TASTE

Locally Owned By:
Greg and Linda Mussi & Kathy Punt

Cuisine:
New American

Price Range:
$5 to $26

Hours:
6:30am to 1:30am

Wi-Fi:
Yes

Location:
1405 S. Atherton St.

Contact Info:
(814) 237-7666, (800) 932-7678, www.theautoport.com

Vegetarian Offerings:
Yes

Supports Local Farmers:
Yes

Locally Owned Accommodations Nearby:
Lodging on Premises

Things To Do Nearby:
Lots

pool. Around all that is a combo of motel rooms and cute bungalow-style places where you can stay for the night or by the week or month. Pool, bungalows, and pretty much the whole place are under a canopy of old trees and pines that really set it all apart from anything else in town. They just don't build em' like they used to.

The fact is, you can have all that cool history and stuff, but if the place is crappy, it's crappy. I know of, and have been to many places, that are "historic," have "character," and offer food and drink in a "vintage" locale. But the atmosphere is crappy, the décor is crappy, and the food — let's just stick with crappy. But when you get a hold of a place that's already cool, and you're talented, have taste, vision, and a love for keeping the past alive while creating a new vibe that complements the old and embraces the new, you've got something.

When Greg and Linda Mussi and Kathy Punt bought The Autoport from the Meyer family early in 2008, they set out to preserve the past but also restore and improve it. They went for a complete restoration of the outside, new décor on the inside, new bar, and just a touch of class and coziness that makes it way better than before.

The dream of serving fresh, innovative, and quality food came from Greg and Linda back when they would host parties for friends and neighbors and do all the cooking. Their food was so good and they had so much fun doing it that the friends and neighbors would get them to cook for their parties, too. It was only a matter of time before they were able to stretch their culinary wings and do that for the public at large when they started a small catering business. Then one day, Greg overheard a conversation that would change everything.

He heard that The Autoport was going to be sold to a rabid developer (aren't most of them?) who was going to have the property leveled and a mega gas station complex built in its place. Greg then found himself talking to Meyer's son and pleading for its preservation. He joked about buying it himself just to save it and walked away. Well, some places are just not meant to be bulldozed for profit, and Greg got a call to see if his offer was serious. When the paperwork was signed, Greg and Linda said goodbye to catering and hello to the restaurant biz.

Kathy Punt had a successful career with the post office and was herself postmaster of Bellefonte, PA. Being a dear friend of the Mussis, Kathy was privy to all the hopes and dreams that this new enterprise was bringing forth. One day while she and her husband Bernie were having a beer with the Mussis on their front porch in Boalsburg, Kathy mentioned, "It's been a dream of mine to own and run a motel/hotel." Thus was born a partnership and the keeper of the inn. Kathy runs the lodging end of things, and is in charge of the 66-room operation. But her part doesn't stop there. Kathy and Bernie are master gardeners and help to supply the restaurant with fresh produce when in season. They have even started an herb garden on site.

As of this writing, some menu items at The Autoport include: chicken wings, chili, caramelized pear & mixed greens salad, pizza, deli sandwiches, burgers, filet mignon au poivre, grilled salmon, spaghetti, lasagna, shrimp fra diavolo, and some amazing home-made desserts. In fact, everything is homemade and they use as much local meat, produce, and dairy as possible. Their beer selection is quite nice, and they feature at least one selection from Otto's, the local State College brewery. The wines are amazing as well, with renowned expert Robert Denby as their "honorary" sommelier.

Greg, Linda, and Kathy have, in my humble opinion, saved The Autoport. Prior to them, the coffee shop was really the only thing cool about it. The restaurant and bar were more for a "mature" crowd with décor, food, and "entertainment" to match. What these guys did was make the whole place cool. Now young and "mature" can hang out, eat, drink, and enjoy music that is layered in vintageness (made that up) and style usually found only in trendy historic districts of big cities. They took an aging icon and landmark and turned it into a hip, cozy, cool, well-appointed, and delicious place for everyone from businessperson to biker. All their effort, time, and money have been well spent and worth it. Their dreams, vision, desire, and talent have become a reality.

Enjoy!

Harrison's Wine Grill
STATE COLLEGE, CENTRE COUNTY

Here's a world class place right in our own backyard that's innovative, creative, beautiful, relaxing, community minded, embraces local products, and offers food and drink that are among the best around. Locals eat here as well as travelers due to its placement at the Hilton Gardens Inn. I've even found the room frequently occupied by many international people, probably because they're used to this kind of quality food and dining. Not that Americans don't appreciate that too, but let's face it, we invented fast food along with the eat-and-get-out mentality. We've also traded quality for quantity (just look at the huge piles of food people are carrying away from all-you-can-eat places – heck, look at the size of the people!). We have also traded kitschy for tasteful. However, Harrison's has not given in or sold out.

The décor is super nice. Soft carpet and long drapes keep it from getting loud like a lot of places, and people as well as plants are totally bathed in

JUST A TASTE

Locally Owned By:
Harrison Schailey & Kit Henshaw

Cuisine:
Contemporary American/
California-style Fusion

Price Range:
$4.95 to $24.00

Hours:
Mon. – Fri. 11am to 9pm,
Sat & Sun open at 11:30am

Location:
1221 E. College Ave.

Wi-Fi:
Yes

Contact Info:
814) 237-4422,
www.harrisonsmenu.com

Vegetarian Offerings:
Yes

Supports Local Farmers:
Yes

**Locally Owned
Accomodations Nearby:**
The Hilton Gardens Inn
on premises

Things To Do Nearby:
Lots

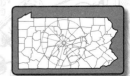

sunlight from huge wrap-around windows – as stated,
the place is beautiful. Even with upscale-grade menu
offerings they keep their prices very reasonable. And,
it's casual and relaxing – no need to dress up –
jeans, suits, leather, and lace are all welcome and
all are in for a great meal and dining experience.

Harrison's is named after Chef Harrison Schailey, the
co-owner along with his wife Kit Henshaw, who basically runs the place and is the in-house sommelier.
I first met Harrison at a WPSU-TV taping of the show
Lobby Talk. Along with host Patty Satalia, he and
other local food oracles spoke about the importance
and joys of buying and eating foods that are locally
grown and prepared. I had known of Harrison for years
because he and his wife Kit opened a little place
out on North Atherton in 2000. There they offered
quality foods for eat-in, carry-out, and catering.

A few years later he decided to move his business
and grow with a bigger place and the chance to have
a full-service bar. Now he and Kit run Harrison's
Wine Grill and Catering out of the Hilton Gardens
Inn. They offer contemporary American cuisine with

a bent towards California-style fusion foods, which are colorful dishes with many different layers of flavor from a variety of cultures and food influences. Harrison is also a master of the seasonal and regional use of ingredients. Their place offers breakfast, lunch, dinner, catering, and carry-out. They even do the banquet fare for the inn.

Speaking of seasonal and regional, I've got to hand it to Harrison. I see him quite often at regional farmers' markets buying produce in season and meats from local farmers. He's really into the Buy Fresh, Buy Local movement as I see him more at the markets than any other restaurant owner. Harrison not only shops at the market, he's a guest chef there too from time to time. If you ever want to taste his amazing creations using all fresh farmer-supplied ingredients, come to a market. Nothing smells better at a market than Harrison's grilled goodies.

Often while either shopping myself, or there as a guest vendor with my book, I've been completely intoxicated by smells of grilled foods coming through the marketplace. I'm like those old cartoon characters that are physically lifted up and carried by thin white wisps of smells. And sure enough, when I find the source, it's Harrison. I see him moving around a table and a fiery grill cooking up delights that look like they are to be on the cover of a cooking magazine. They're always abundant and always free to sample.

Why listen to me? Here's what Harrison's has to say about all this, right from their website: "*At our locally owned, award winning restaurant, we go out of our way to find and use the best products available for each seasonal menu and to encourage people to Dine Fresh, Dine Local. Whenever possible, we purchase ingredients from local growers and purveyors, in particular ones who arrive at the back door with freshly harvested offerings like elephant garlic, fresh green beans, or wild morel mushrooms. It inspires*

Chef Harrison to spontaneously make fresh, delicious culinary creations that delight our dining room guests every afternoon and evening. Seasonal is also important for both local items and for the fresh seafood features such as soft shell crabs, fresh day boat scallops, and other harvest from the sea.

Trust in the high standards that have become Harrison's long-standing reputation of cooking excellence. Menus change seasonally and never stay the same. Plan to check back and preview the delicious seasonal tastes reflected in each menu.

And as the name reads, Harrison's has a thing for wines. Here's another piece from their website: "Wine is in our name because the California Wine Country influence is obvious in Chef Harrison's cooking and it is the premise of pairing delicious food and wine to bring out the best of both. Because of this, we take great care in selecting diverse wines that represent a wide array of complements to each menu item. Time is spent each season choosing wines that will complement the tastes on the current seasonal menu and the specials presented each evening. Our staff is well trained in understanding these varieties and will be happy to make a recommendation."

All in all, Chef Harrison lives, breathes, and cooks local. He and Kit support our farmers and the community. They're a Buy Fresh, Buy Local Partner and their place is a utopia for all that is local and delicious. It's a world-class restaurant serving seasonal and regional foods in the heart of central PA.

Enjoy!

Café Lemont
LEMONT, CENTRE COUNTY

Here's a wonderful and super cozy café that just opened in my home town of Lemont in August 2010. It's located in The Lemont House, an historic building that stands at the corner of Pike Street and Boalsburg Road. Literally hours before my manuscript for this book was to leave my PC to head for production, I had the pleasure of running in for a quick look around. The place is awesome — the interior décor is lovely with warm colors, and the place has a great relaxing vibe. Out front they have a sweet little porch where you can sip your coffee, have a bite to eat, and watch the world go by. I can't wait to return and take it all in.

(For The Rest of the Story go to **www.goingLOCALpa.com/TRS**)

JUST A TASTE

Locally Owned By:
Jodi Hakes McWhirter and Michael Beck

Cuisine:
Eclectic mix of coffee pairings and light lunch fare

Price Range:
$1.00 to $6.00

Hours:
Mon. – Thr. 7am to 7pm, Fri. & Sat. 7am to 9pm, Sundays 9am to 5pm

Location:
921 Pike St. In The Lemont House (Parking behind)

Wi-Fi:
Yes

Contact Info:
(814) 321-4337
www.cafelemont.net

Vegetarian Offerings:
Yes

Supports Local Farmers:
Yes

Locally Owned Accommodations Nearby:
Rock Garden B&B (814) 466-6100

Things To Do Nearby:
Hike Mount Nittany, Art Alliance shows, Lemont Village Association Events

Olde New York
STATE COLLEGE, CENTRE COUNTY

Here's a place that has "risen like a phoenix" from the ashes, but not in the form it's in now. The look is new, the location has changed, and so has the menu. But the same hearts are beating, and the same souls are at work. And the only flame that remains is the flame of passion to bring you wonderful food and great drinks.

The story begins with Kenny and Susan Kempton, a very cool couple who opened a very cool German cuisine restaurant in 1988 called Schnitzel's in the basement of the Garman Opera House in historic Bellefonte, PA. The foundation of the Garman was laid of hand-cut limestone blocks, and the supports and beams were solid hardwood, so it was hard to beat the antique feel right from the start. They didn't cover up the limestone, and they exposed and restored all the wood.

Playing off that "olde world" look, they decorated the place in a way that was extremely cozy and comfortable. The food was great and the beer selection was all German and Überraschen! Kenny was maybe one of the first restaurateurs to serve quality imported

beers. Up to that point, the only thing that was considered "imported" in central PA was Molson.

With success comes more people, with more people comes expansion. Unfortunately, the basement of the opera house was not expandable, so a larger place was needed. The challenge would be to find a place that was as awesome as what they had. Fortunately they found it, and it was right down the street.

The Bush House was built in 1868 during the heyday of Victorian Bellefonte by Daniel G. Bush. Thomas Edison stayed there, which might explain why it was one of the first hotels in the country to have electric lights. Like the opera house, it had the same subterranean construction, so rather than going street level like most places, the Kemptons choose to go underground again. It made sense because it had the same look, feel, and vibe of their original place with the very nice addition of a streamside terrace. They took that space and turned it into a combination outdoor dining area and beer garden. I remember many an evening during the summer, sitting there enjoying a Franziskaner Hefe-Weizen with friends and thinking I was in Bavaria. It was an ideal place and with its success, expansion was in the works again. But as I alluded to at the beginning, fire would have the last say on the beauty and life of the Bush House.

On February 8, 2006, it burned completely to the ground. One of Bellefonte's most treasured landmarks was destroyed and so was Schnitzel's. Everything that Kenny and Susan had worked so hard for was gone. All their dreams had literally gone up in smoke. The community at large, as well as my friends and I, were saddened and our hearts went out to Kenny and Susan. We didn't know what would become of them and they went off the radar for awhile. I couldn't blame them.

Then one day I heard that a new restaurant was opening in State College and it was going to celebrate

the diverse tastes of New York City. I also heard
that the owners were none other than Kenny and
Susan! Awesome, I thought; two people so passionate
about food, beer, and bringing the best of the food
service industry to folks like me just can't be kept
down. I was so glad to hear the news and so happy
for them. So, in late 2007 they opened the doors of
their latest eatery endeavor, Olde New York.

The space is quite large and the bar is long and
well stocked. True to Kenny's original desire to
have authentic beers available to a very isolated
population, his tap selection is mostly German –
their food selection is not. Some say it's because
it's hard to top Herwig's downtown, but the real
reason is Kenny's roots in New York and the *"smor-
gasbord of cuisine available"* according to their
website. They also state that they liken their place
to *"the era when pockets of immigrants settled in
the boroughs of New York City and continued their
old world traditions of camaraderie with wonderful
food and warm hospitality."*

Menu items at ONY include that old world cuisine
with dishes like Mussels over Linguini; Wiener
Schnitzel; Italian Sausage; Smothered New York Strip
and Chicken Cordon Bleu. The menu also features Fat
Deli Sandwiches, Burgers, and Savory Salads. Yeah,
it's a great menu prepared nicely and in a big
open-air space, but the real proof that Kenny and
Susan have risen from the ashes to new heights is
the crowds that frequent their place.

What goes around comes around, I guess, and when you
try hard and don't give up, when you're down but not
out, and have a passion that burns, you will most
likely succeed. These guys sure did. Their flame of
passion is the only flame that remained from a tragic
fire. That flame has ignited a new fire at Olde New York,
and this kind of fire never looked or tasted so good.

Enjoy!

American Ale House & Grill
STATE COLLEGE, CENTRE COUNTY

I've been going to this location to eat and enjoy a beverage for a long time. I write "beverage," because I started going there long before I was 21, and that's a long time ago. I believe it was called "The Coffee Grinder" back then and was decorated like an old general store – dark wood, low light, and lots of "stuff" sitting around. I remember nothing about the food, but as a youngster, it was a cool place and I loved it. When my mom and dad said, "Let's go to The Coffee Grinder," I got excited! Even back then I had a love for local places.

Like I said, that was a long time ago and the place has gone through a few changes since then. The most recent has been the triad partnership of three hard-working and dedicated people to take a place that has been kinda the same for a long time, breathe new life into it, and make it an experience for all the senses. And, it's sexy and cozy! Yes, that's actually how they describe themselves. I like the sexy aspect and the cozy part is true too, but if you go there any given weekend, the place is jumpin'!

JUST A TASTE

Locally Owned By:
Scott Lucchesi, Linda Silveri, and Tommy Wareham

Cuisine:
Eclectic

Price Range:
$4 to $32

Hours:
11am to 1am

Wi-Fi:
Yes

Location:
821 Cricklewood Dr. Toftrees

Contact Info:
(814) 237-9701

Vegetarian Offerings:
Yes

Supports Local Farmers:
Yes

Locally Owned Accommodations Nearby:
Carnegie House (814) 234-2424; The Stevens Motel (814) 238-2438

Things To Do Nearby:
Golf, Tennis, Shopping, Museums, Sporting Events

One of the owners, Tommy Wareham, is an accomplished musician and performs as the "Original Piano Man" every Friday night. He's been giggin' in the State College area for 25 years or so, and has been voted the #1 entertainer by State College Magazine 5 years in a row.

Another owner is Scott Lucchesi. This guy is the guru of the north State College restaurant scene. He not only part owns and operates The Ale House, but owns a place called Champs. If you're keen enough, you can figure out Champs is a sports bar – and the biggest and best in the area. In 2008, I called Champs home as our Mighty Pittsburgh Penguins took the Stanley Cup championship. Scott made sure EVERY screen in the place (which is like 264) was tuned to the game! I, along with a ton of rabid Pens fans, were cheering, eating, drinking, and having an awesome time! It's *the* place for game time.

As stated Scott splits his time between Champs and The Ale House. I see him more at The Ale House, and he works like a dog. He's got a killer work ethic, but is always really cool with me when he has a moment — however, those moments are rare as he runs a tight ship. But it's not just Scott that cracks the whip — it's also the third owner, and the one that brings beauty, grace, and professionalism (laced with humor) to the establishment. Enter Linda Silveri.

Linda is one of those people (at least for me) that just makes you smile. And if you know her a little, be prepared for a monster hug and a sincere and excited greeting. She fills every role from hostess to server, prep cook to line cook, manager to therapist, and employee's best friend, until you mess up. Then you might hear (only if you're in the kitchen) "You better get that ____ing order out to that table or you'll be cleaning the kitchen with your ..." Seriously though, Linda is one of the sweetest people I know and adds a side to the Ale House that keeps me, at least, coming back time and time again. But if it were all about the owners, why would anyone come to eat? Well, I'm not done yet.

The food at The Ale House is awesome! Every plate I've had (and I've had many) has been nothing short of amazing – and that includes things as down-to-earth as a burger. Instead of offering a huge menu, Scott, Linda, and Tommy go for simple, sweet, and eclectic. They have the usual suspects like salads, soups, sandwiches, burgers, apps, and entrées. But it's what they do with "the usual" that sets them above the chains. A few of the salads include: Seared Scallop, Grilled Vegetable, Filet Mignon, and a Summer Salad, which has sultana raisins, Asian pears, Cabrales cheese, and champagne pear vinaigrette.

A few sandwiches are: 3 Cheese and Asparagus, Carolina Pulled Pork, and a Cowboy Steak Sandwich that's served medium, with gorgonzola, roasted red peppers, baby spinach, caramelized onion, and garlic aioli on sourdough, with fries. My favorite burger is the PittsBurger (go figure), which is a combo of beef, coffee BBQ sauce, Colby jack cheese, slaw, and fries piled on top!

Appetizers include: Baked Potato Soup, Stanley's Wonder Wings, and Kobe Sliders, which are served medium rare with country bacon, garlic aioli, gorgonzola-smoked cheddar blend, baby arugula, oven roasted tomatoes, and balsamic cipolline onions.

Entrées are all killer, but I'll just highlight a few: Australian Rack of Lamb, Pan Seared Chilean Sea Bass, Peppered Ostrich, Shrimp Basil Fettuccini, Dry Aged NY Strip, Blackened Chicken Penne, Braised Short Ribs, Sockeye Salmon, Grilled Wild Boar Chops, Pistachio Crusted Venison Chops, and Blue Grass Filet served withJack Daniel's onions, Yukon Gold mashed potatoes, and asparagus. OK, that was more than a few, but they're all sooo good I just couldn't stop.

If that's not enough for you, my foodie friends, I saved what might be the best for last. The Ale House features a seafood steamer bar that will transport you to New Orleans with one bite. Actually, just a peek at the menu is enough to take you there - check this out: Ale House Fish Chowder and Seafood Chowder, Steamed Shrimp and Clams, Bowl of Mussels, Jambalaya, Gumbo, Bouillabaisse, and more. How's that?!

Well maybe you're thinking "That's great Ken, but what do they offer to wash it all down with?" Good question, and here's an even better answer - 17 beers on tap! Not only that, but it's a very nice selection and most are hand-crafted and regional, if not local.

The American Ale House & Grill offers you great owners, awesome food, seasoned, professional, and friendly staff, live local music, amazing food and food specialties from chef Jami Steffen, great atmosphere, beer geek-approved beer selection, beautiful outdoor seating, AND if you're lucky, a big heart-felt hug from Linda! You see, it is sexy and cozy.

Enjoy!

The Way Café
STORMSTOWN, CENTRE COUNTY

I'm sitting here in what used to be an apple warehouse. Huge wooden crates were filled with every variety of the fruit from Delicious to Winesap and waiting to be bagged, sacked, or put in baskets. And not necessarily for widespread distribution mind you, but mostly just for local folks to enjoy. You see, Way Fruit Farm has been around since 1826, and everyone in the area knows this is where you go for apples, strawberries, peaches, cherries, blueberries, plums, apricots, and sweet corn.

Adjacent to the warehouse was a little retail shop were you could buy all the apple products, but also milk, eggs, a few baked goods, jellies, jams, bird seed, and even my book. Now the warehouse is a restaurant! That's right, the folks (the kids actually) at Way Fruit Farm opened The Way Café, a really nice little restaurant serving breakfast, lunch, and take-out dinners.

Saturday's full breakfast menu includes local meats, eggs, pancakes, French toast, and more, cooked to order. On the lighter side are muffins, slices of

JUST A TASTE

Locally Owned By:
Brooks & Sharon Way and
Jason & Megan Coopey

Cuisine:
Simple Country

Price Range:
$3 to $7.50

Hours:
Mon. – Fri. 8am to 7pm,
Sat. 8am to 5pm, Closed Sundays

Wi-Fi:
No

Location:
2355 Halfmoon Valley Road

Contact Info:
(814) 692-5211,
www.wayfruitfarm.com

Vegetarian Offerings:
Yes

Supports Local Farmers:
Yes

**Locally Owned
Accommodations Nearby:**
The Stevens Motel (814) 238-2438

Things To Do Nearby:
State College, Penn State

pie, sticky buns, fresh fruit cups, yogurt and granola parfaits, their own granola, cold cereal, bagels, apples, and peaches or pears (in season).

Weekly lunches and take-out dinners include soups, combos (soup and salad or ½ sandwich or side), fresh fruit cup, Way Café Apple Salad, Classic Grilled Chicken Salad, Chunk Tuna Salad, and Sweet Chicken Salad. Signature Sandwiches include the Oink and Crow, Cluck and Crow, Hogs Galore BBQ, Sweet Ham BBQ, Turkey Scampi, Little Italy, The Garden, Classic Club, Meat Lovers, Holy Guacamole Sammie, and made-to-order deli sandwiches and subs. They even have a kids menu. Drinks include a variety of things, but their own cold or hot apple cider is the best choice.

After I finished my yummy breakfast of eggs, bacon, pancakes (which they make from scratch and are super delicious), and the Way's signature side of apple slices, Megan Coopey (Way's daughter) sat down and joined me. I figured this was a golden opportunity to get the inside skinny on the place - its real history, workings, and the thinking behind the renovation and expansion project to allow for a café within a farm market.

She said, "The farm has been in my family for a long time. I'm the sixth generation to work here, my folks are the fifth generation, and my kids could be the seventh if they choose. It started out as a dairy farm like most farms in the valley, but in 1875 my great-grandparents received a wedding gift of 1000 apple trees. That's how the orchard started."

Megan's folks, Brooks and Sharon, took over the farm 25 years ago, and about two years ago Megan and her husband Jason moved back to become a part of the farm biz. All the expansion that I wrote about earlier, including the café, is really Megan and Jason's doing. She joked that her dad said, "It's the next generation's idea," but she went on to say that she and Jason had the blessing of her folks. "Dad and Mom had enough faith to say, 'Okay, we'll grow with you,' so we couldn't have done it without them." I love that. This is one of the great things about indie business - sometimes the whole family is involved, and you'll notice that any day you walk into Way's.

If you see a big guy with gentle eyes, skin permanently tanned by years in the sun, and hands that could crush steel, that's Brooks. If you see a woman with short hair, a friendly smile, and two adorable little girls trailing her all over the place, that's Sharon. If you see a young woman running after those adorable little girls, while trying to keep things going in the kitchen, that's Megan. If you see a young guy running after Megan and the two adorable little girls, while simultaneously mixing a batch of batter for most awesome pancakes around, that's Jason. Then, if you see a woman trying to keep all the apple crates full, the coolers stocked, and help the Ways in any way she can, that's Cindy. She's not family by blood, but she's one of the employees that treats you as if she were family.

Something else you'll notice is that Ways supports other local businesses. In the old apple cooler warehouse, among all the giant crates of apples, is a new and much-improved store. Here they have spices from Con Yaeger Spice Company; canned peaches, snack-size applesauce, fried apples, and sparkling apple juice from Knouse Foods; Raspberry and Lemon Shrub from Tait Farm; honey from Lost Hollow Farm; maple syrup from MacNeals; and Way's own dried apples, apple butter, and applesauce. From their bakery, they have breads, pies, muffins, cookies, sticky buns, apple cider donuts, whoopie pies, biscotti, and, when in season, shortcakes, pound cake, peach crisp and pudding, fruit cobblers, apple and peach dumplings, and more!

They also have huge banks of coolers with all kinds of locally produced meats and cheeses. Here's a rundown: pork products from Hogs Galore; cheeses from both Goot Essa and Clover Creek Cheese Cellar; goats' milk and cheese from Byler Goat Dairy; raw milk and fresh yogurt from Spring Bank Acres, free-range brown eggs from Marengo Hollow Farm and others; organic salad greens from Eden View Organics; potatoes, cabbage, and other vegetables in season from Ardry Farms as well as other local farmers; and Alaskan salmon from a local fishing couple at Wild for Salmon.

The original store was not much bigger than a roadside stand – this new one is huge and accommodates all the past products plus "way" more. While Brooks and Sharon go old school and keep the farm and farm market running like a well-oiled machine, Megan and Jason's café project is a wonderful addition. The Way Fruit farm has always been a great place for our community, now the community can enjoy all the "fruits," and foods, of this wonderful family enterprise.

Enjoy!

Mt. Nittany Inn
CENTRE HALL, CENTRE COUNTY

The Mt. Nittany Inn has also risen from the ashes – and more than once! This place has endured a lot. The first fire happened in 2003 in the kitchen and worked its way into the roof system. The damage was not total, but the place was totally rebuilt and expanded. Then only weeks before the grand reopening of the new place, fire struck again, but this time it was total destruction. Despite the gallant efforts of all the area's volunteer fire departments, the place that was a landmark for years again went up in smoke.

I sit here now trying to work on this book on a gorgeous evening with the valley below me lit in that orangey light that I've seen so many times during evenings in Italy. But as much as I want to write, I can't help but to look out over the deck and scan the beautiful farmlands and mountain ranges in the distance. However, my bacon cheeseburger and glass of Tröegs Pale Ale just arrived, so I've got

JUST A TASTE

Locally Owned By:
Doug Collins, Nancy Silvis

Cuisine:
Americana

Price Range:
$3.00 to $29.00

Hours:
Sun. – Th. 11am to 9pm,
Fri. & Sat. 10am to 10pm

Wi-Fi:
Yes

Location:
559 N. Pennsylvania Ave.

Contact Info:
(814) 364-9363,
www.mountnittanyinn.com

Vegetarian Offerings:
Yes

Supports Local Farmers:
Yes

**Locally Owned
Accommodations Nearby:**
Keller House B&B (814) 364-2225

Things To Do Nearby:
Penns Cave, Grange Fair in August

to stop writing and eat (I'm starving). I'll be back.
(1/2 hour later) Wow that was a good burger! I choose
the mashed potatoes as an accompaniment instead of
fries (watching the heart, you know).

Besides a tavern menu which has the basic fare of
appetizers, soups, salads, burgers, and sandwiches,
the Inn specializes in fine dining fare as well.
Here's a partial but tempting excerpt from the menu.
Appetizers include choices like Shrimp Cocktail, and
Bruschetta for Two with Portabella mushrooms, asparagus, tomatoes & roasted garlic sautéed with balsamic vinaigrette and dusted with parmesan. It's
served en croute (baked in a pastry crust). An "Our
Specialties" list includes Chicken Chesapeake, Honey
Almond Chicken, a variety of steaks like New York
strip steak, flatiron, and a slow roasted prime rib.
They also have veal, lamb, pork, venison, and seafood, such as crab cakes, sockeye salmon, tuna,
catfish, lobster, and a variety of pasta dishes.
Of course a dessert menu tops it all off and they
have a complete bar menu.

Sitting here, I start to wonder about the history
of the place. I know it's old, but how old? Hey, my
little internet indicator is on so they must have
wireless. Cool, I'll just jump on here and see if
Mt. Nittany has a website. They do! Ok, let's check
out a bit of history. Here it is: …the spectacularly
panoramic view has always been a part of the Mount
Nittany Inn experience, beginning in 1919 when M.E.
(Pete) Coldron opened a roadside stand so that view
seekers could enjoy a Nehi or a Coke, some peanuts
or pretzels and, if need be, get their car radiators
(which usually overheated because of the slow trip
up the mountain) refilled.

In 1928 Pete constructed the original building, primarily to keep his lumber from being thrown down the
mountain by his neighboring competitor. Since then,
in addition to a restaurant, it has been a coffee
shop, a grill, and a bar-complete with dancers and
plenty of brawls.

The first significant improvements were undertaken by
Bill and Betty Zang, who purchased the Inn in 1975,
and who worked long hours to rid it of its tawdry
reputation. Major renovations were begun in 1991,
and included relocating the kitchen, refurbishing
the bar, adding extensive decking and erecting a
large addition.

So, that's the history. Now, what can you expect
when you arrive? Like some other restaurants, this
place has different areas and is even multi-leveled;
it offers both casual and upscale dinning. The
upstairs bar area is big, wide open, nicely lit by
night and bathed in natural light by day. Windows
line the south wall and the other side is lofted
over the main entrance. The first floor is cool, too,
because it's kinda multi-leveled as well with open
areas and cozy ones. But what makes the Mt. Nittany
Inn unlike any other restaurant is the amazing
all-season deck (where I am now). If you like out-

door dining, love a nice view, and always wanted to know how the birds feel when they fly, then this is your place - it's mine for sure.

I've always loved the deck here, but for the owner it was a six-month-per-year waste of space - between October and April, you just couldn't depend on the weather. But that was the old deck. The new deck is all season! It's completely enclosed with glass, so even on the coldest, stinkiest days of a central PA winter, you can enjoy the amazing view and sky above. In good weather, the four center panels of glass slide back to expose almost 75% of the deck, connecting sky to earth and giving you an outdoor dining experience that's unequalled, as far as I know.

Just as I was finishing my last sip of Tröegs, Chef Jeremiah McClenahan stopped by to ask if all was well. I took the opportunity to thank him for my great meal and beer, but also put a bug in his ear about trying to put some local beers on tap. I was thrilled to hear he's moving in that direction. He told me he's a local and totally supports going local. He said I should see one, maybe two local beers soon! He also told me a cool story:

Jeremiah's first job was washing dishes at the Inn back when he was just 14. He did a little bit of everything, but when the head cook walked off the job one day, he pitched in until they found a replacement. After high school, he joined the military and then attended culinary school. Now he's back where he first started! Not washing your dishes, mind you, but creating great dishes for you.

What a wonderful day, and what a wonderful place to eat, drink, and write - the view was awesome and very inspiring. The Mt. Nittany Inn endured two fires but has truly risen from the ashes. It now stands high once again over Happy Valley, and I'm glad it's back.

Enjoy!

Cool Beans Coffee & Tea
BELLEFONTE, CENTRE COUNTY

This is one of those places that I wish were in Boalsburg. It's the kind of coffee shop you think of (at least I do) when you think coffee shop – comfy, cozy, cool vibe, unique in some way, friendly people, and good coffee. The latter is subjective, of course, but you know what I mean. Even if the coffee is so-so but the place is cool, it's a good spot. Fortunately Cool Beans has it all.

Back at the beginning it was owed by a dude named Mike Theuer, and he was pretty innovative. Prior to that, Bellefonte had nothing close to hip – let alone a hip café. Next, he was one of the first café owners I knew of that collected the spent coffee grounds for recycling in gardens – from puck to planting, nothing went to the trash ("puck" refers to the puck-like thing that you get after pulling a shot of espresso). Then, like a mad scientist, he actually developed the first potting container made from coffee grounds.

JUST A TASTE

Locally Owned By:
Wendy A. Fultz

Cuisine:
Café

Price Range:
$1.23 to $5.75

Hours:
Mon. - Fri. 7am to 7pm,
Sat. 9am to 5, Sun. till 4pm

Wi-Fi:
Yes

Location:
141 West High St.

Contact Info:
(814) 355-1178,
www.coolbeancoffeeandtea.com

Vegetarian Offerings:
Yes

Supports Local Farmers:
Yes

**Locally Owned
Accommodations Nearby:**
The Queen B&B, (814) 355-7946

Things To Do Nearby:
Shopping, American Philatelic Society, Talleyrand Park, Historic Bellefonte Railroad, Museums, Library, Victorian Home Touring

Mike figured out how to take the grounds, and then under a ridiculous about of pressure, form a little pot for starting seeds. Once the plant grew large enough for planting in the ground, you just put the pot in the ground and the biodegradable coffee acted as fertilizer and returned to where it once came. It was called "Grow Jo." Brilliant! Mike left Cool Beans awhile ago, but the new owner, Wendy Fultz, is now making her mark at this wonderful café in the heart of Bellefonte.

On a recent visit, I had the pleasure of meeting Wendy and asked her a few questions about her endeavors. The following is what we talked about:

Me: *What was your background and history with Cool Beans?*

Wendy: *I purchased Cool Beans September 1, 2008. Prior to that, I worked at Penn State for 19 years. I graduated from South Hills Business School in 1988 with a degree in Marketing/Business Management. Purchasing Cool Beans was like a dream finally coming to fruition – after a very long time. One of the best things about being at Cool Beans is that I have control of the end result – either making someone smile with a good cup of coffee, or just listening to someone who is having a bad day and they leave my shop just a little bit happier.*

Me: *Your aspirations?*

Wendy: *My future aspirations would be to continue to grow the shop's clientele and eventually break out into our own specialty bakery (along with the coffee shop). We bake all our own baked goods now and I would like to expand on them a bit and do some artisan breads, pastries, and cakes.*

Me: *What makes Cool Beans unique and a place people would want to come to?*

Wendy: *I think what sets us apart is that we have a very welcoming and "coming home" feeling when you walk in the door. We will remember your name, what* you drink, what your spouse, son, or daughter was doing last week, and we really care about what's going on with our customers. Our lounge resembles your own living room and is welcoming to high school students, college students, working professionals, retirees, or anything in between.

Me: *Tell me some of your specialties at Cool Beans.*

Wendy: *Our most famous baked item is our baked oatmeal, which some people call "highly addictive" because it's so good. If you are having a rough day, this, combined with our own house blend coffee, will surely make your world right! We are also highly known for our iced coffee which is served with our special coffee cubes. We brew and then quick chill our house medium coffee and serve it over our specialty coffee cubes. Our selection of candy bar lattes are very popular as well, such as Peanut Butter Cup, Peppermint Patty, Snickers Bar, and Milky Way, to name a few.*

Me: *What other foods do you offer?*

Wendy: *We serve breakfast and lunch. We always have a wide array of homemade (on the premise) baked goods including our baked oatmeal, scones, apple pie, pumpkin pie, a wide selection of cookies, apple dumplings, golden brownies, and we also always have a few selections of gluten-free items. We also always have at least one quiche to choose from, and usually two soups. We feature a daily specialty sandwich and have some staples such as our signature tuna salad and egg salad.*

Well, there you have it. Oh, I must add that they have a little outdoor seating area tucked neatly just below street level with windows behind that which bathe the inside with natural light, and that "lounge" that Wendy mentioned is super cozy and very chill. Yes, Cool Beans is truly cool.

Enjoy!

The Gamble Mill Restaurant
And an Ode to Artist Rob Fisher
BELLEFONTE, CENTRE COUNTY

I've been here many times, but one memorable visit was on the night of an exhibition of fellow artists. "Food for Thought" was an exhibition of food-related artwork in varying mediums and subject matter from paintings of garlic cloves to photographs of bread loaves. Throughout the year, the Gamble Mill opens its doors to artists and lovers of art alike. This particular night, my good friends and fellow painters Susan Nicholas-Gephart and Holly Fritchman were exhibiting, along with other very talented artists.

While patrons were busy ogling their work, the three of us snuck away to the tavern/bar below (my favorite). This was a great place to soak in the cool historic and cozy vibe while talking art, life, and love. We were hungry, so I ordered up the Vegetable Lasagna accompanied by an Otto's Mt. Nittany Pale Ale. Holly got the BBQ Chicken Sandwich, and Susan, being the

JUST A TASTE

Locally Owned By:
Dave Fonash & Paul Kendeffy

Cuisine:
Contemporary American

Price Range:
$4 to $32

Hours:
Mon. – Th. 11:30am to 9pm,
Fri. & Sat. till 10
(Restaurant seating varies)

Wi-Fi:
Yes

Location:
160 Dunlap St.

Contact Info:
(814) 355-7764,
www.gamblemill.com/main.html

Vegetarian Offerings:
Yes

Supports Local Farmers:
Yes

**Locally Owned
Accommodations Nearby:**
The Maid's Quarters B&B,
(814) 355-7946

Things To Do Nearby:
Shopping, American Philatelic Society, Talleyrand Park, Historic Bellefonte Railroad, Museums, Library, Victorian Home Touring

flamboyant painter she is, went for Pappardelle Pasta
finished with champagne sauce. The place was abuzz
with artists, art aficionados, and just plain folks
enjoying themselves in the warm and casual atmosphere
within the great walls of the historic grist mill in
the heart of Bellefonte.

Gamble Mill was built in 1786 as a water-operated
flour and feed mill, drawing its power from the
famous Spring Creek, which is enriched by a beautiful fresh-water spring that bursts to the surface
only a short distance from the mill. The original
waterway still runs underneath, but the waterwheel
was replaced in the 1890s with a turbine that today
pumps water to various sections of Bellefonte.

Believe it or not, this mag-
nificent structure of brick,
stone, and wood became so
dilapidated that it was
condemned and scheduled for
demolition. Thankfully, a
group of visionaries from the
town stepped in, and in 1975,
Mr. Ted Conklin purchased the

mill and by the next year, it was the first building
in Bellefonte to receive the great honor of being
placed on the National Register of Historic Places.
Jeanne Murphy and Courtney Confer opened the restaurant in 1986, and in 2008, the team of Dave Fonash
and Paul Kendeffy took over the helm.

I have to confess that when I heard that Dave and
Paul who also own Zola New World Bistro in State
College were taking over the place, I was a little
scared. Not that food would be bad – on the contrary,
Paul's creative and culinary genius stands high in
the realm of the fine dining crowd – I guess what
scared me was that they would change things somehow.
Yeah, I'm getting older, but I'm not nearly at the
age bracket where change is considered evil. Zola is
super nice for sure - very haute cuisine. And if I

want to go all out and have a really top-notch dining experience, it's a great choice. But for me, and especially in this economy, I can't go "all out" all the time. So when I found out the Zola guys were taking over The Mill, I thought it would become only an "all out" place too. Fortunately it did not, and they didn't change the awesome layout or décor either.

The Mill has two dining options. On the ground level, to the right as you enter, is the tavern/bar where we were sitting that night. Surrounded by 20+ inch thick locally-quarried limestone, soft light greets you by night and huge sash windows bathe you in the light by day. Here, they serve the Tavern Menu which includes Soups, Salads, Sandwiches, Specialties, and the "Build Your Own Mill Burger." The bar there is cool, as it wraps around on three sides allowing patrons to converse with each other as the bartender in the middle keeps it all together. Libations, food, and banter flow like the water underneath the floor.

The fine dining restaurant above is just that – fine! Old brick, hand-hewn beams of wood, grand windows fitted with antique glass, tables of linen, and of course, really, really good food. Sous Chef Scott Witmer prepares wonderful offerings, like appetizers of Butternut Squash Ravioli and Yellowfin Tuna; salads include Goat Cheese, Caesar, and Spinach; entrées go from a Flat Iron Steak to Venison Stew, and Susan's dish of Pappardella Pasta to Salmon Bordelaise. Between the menu, the setting, and service, you are in for a special treat that will satisfy the casual diner, as well as the gourmet.

As Holly, Susan, and I were chatting away and drinking our wine and beer, we were joined by another great artist and his lovely wife, True. The late Rob Fisher was a world-renowned sculptor from Bellefonte. Rob is now recognized a pioneer in the application of the computer to art. His work in this genre includes "Olympos" for the 1996 Centennial Olympics in Atlanta, and "Osaka Skyharp" in Japan. In 2000, Rob was awarded a major public art commission for the Philadelphia International Airport Arrivals Hall. His winning artwork, "American Dream," is one of the largest ever granted in the Philadelphia region. Other sculptures of his are here at our own Penn State Applied Research Lab and the Penn Stater Conference Center. More recently, one of Rob's suspended works was hung in the Horizon Suite Hotel in Hong Kong.

Although internationally known, Rob was so down to earth. That night he and True generously ordered a couple of bottles of The Mill's finest wine for us all to enjoy. I figured at that point, we weren't going to make it back to the exhibition upstairs anytime soon. "Don't you want to know if anyone is buying your work?" I said to Holly. She sat back and said, "Yeah, but this is too much fun, and that's too much like work." "Spoken like a true artist," Rob said, and just shook his head. He put his arms around True, gave her a kiss, and said, "Honey, remember those days?" True looked at him with a loving smile, and replied, "Rob, it's still those days and always will be."

So as we sat there drinking wine, eating great food, laughing, and telling stories – works of art were being swooned over and sold right above our heads. However, Susan, Holly, Rob, True, and I were creating art of our own right there in the little tavern of a grand restaurant in the stories we told, the ideas we shared, and the canvas of food, drink, vibe, and friendship that bound us together. We shared an amazing evening at The Gamble Mill on that night of "Food for Thought." How fitting. How delicious.

Enjoy!

Update: *If this place weren't awesome enough, they now brew their own beer! Head brewer Mike Smith, a native of State College, started out as a home brewer, went to* *brewing school, apprenticed and worked at Dogfish Head in Delaware, went from there to Ithaca Beer Co. in New York, and then returned home to bring all that experience and natural talent to The Gamble Mill. Co-owner Dave Fonash always recognized the beauty of local craft beers — he even had Otto's brew beers exclusively for The Gamble Mill and Zola. Now, he's brought in Mike to brew on-premise. A few of Mike's amazing new beers are:*

Lame Devil Farmhouse Ale: I love Farmhouse Ales, and this one is named after Charles Maurice de Talleyrand-Périgord, the guy who supposedly named Bellefonte and whose nickname was Lame Devil.

HB-48 Session Ale: A Golden Ale named for the HB-48 bill that had to get passed to allow The Gamble Mill to get their PA Brew Pub license.

J. Rose Pale Ale: This mild but very tasty Ale is named after Jeremy Rose, a horse jockey native to Bellefonte.

Upcoming beers include a Brown Ale and a India Pale Ale.

Bonfatto's

BELLEFONTE, CENTRE COUNTY

I confess that most of what is written here is from the Bonfatto's website. When I come across such a wonderfully written history, I figure why reinvent the wheel? I tweaked it a bit, but at least I'm honest. I also confess that this piece focuses more on the history because it's very rare to have this kind of legacy behind your business. As far as the wonderful menu and delicious food, you'll just have to stop in.

The story of Bonfatto's started in Raccuia, a small village in the north of Sicily. Guy Bonfatto was born there in 1894, and emigrated to America in 1910. His future bride, Pauline, was born in the same town in 1899, and immigrated to America in 1916. The two landed "conveniently" in northern PA – Pauline to Renovo and Guy to South Renovo.

Two years later, Guy opened a confectionery and grocery store. Unfortunately, he closed it in 1917 to serve in the army during WWI. After coming home he married Pauline. The two moved to Bellefonte in

1919, and opened a grocery and produce store in the Bush Arcade building downtown. Besides retail and wholesale sales, Guy also made door-to-door deliveries of produce to Bellefonte residences, which marked the beginning of the Bonfatto quality and service.

Guy was an entrepreneur before "entrepreneur" was cool. He was also an industrious hard worker who was determined to offer customers the best products available. To do so, he handpicked merchandise to offer his customers. Driving his own truck, he traveled to Pittsburgh and Baltimore to personally inspect the goods to bring back to Bellefonte. The Bonfattos soon became well known, and their business grew and prospered.

Pauline worked in the store serving customers, keeping records, and doing the billing. She was warm-hearted and thoroughly enjoyed serving the public. People often commented on what a joy she was with her smiling face and cheery, friendly manner (honestly, I can't imagine being cheery after moving from Italy to central PA, but hey). Guy and Pauline had nine children but sadly, three of them died at birth. The six surviving children were Mary, Josephine, John, Francis, Annette, and Rose, who all helped in the family business. The couple faithfully operated the business together until Guy's untimely and sudden death in January 1960. Pauline kept going long after she "retired," and was in the store daily until an illness forced her to stop working in May of 1987 and sadly, she passed away that November.

It seemed like things might end there, but fortunately back in 1958, brother John created the Bonanza Sub Sandwich while working at the store. It was so popular that he trademarked the name "Bonanza," and it was that creation that would keep the Bonfatto biz going. Back then there was only one variety of the Bonanza, what today would be called an Italian. It came in two sizes, 8" and 16". The 8" sold for 35 cents and the 16″ for 65 cents. As popularity of the Bonanza Sub grew, other varieties were added. In later years, the sizes were changed to 6″, 12″, and 18″. The Bonanza made Bonfatto's famous for quality food and quick service at a reasonable price.

The store began to evolve from grocery and produce to prepared foods. In 1965, John remolded a building at the rear of the store for selling pizza, and later added cheese steak sandwiches, hamburgers, fries, spaghetti, and a host of other sandwiches and meals to go. In 1970, further expansion occurred when the family acquired a bar called The Bellefonte Grille. In 1974, a full-scale restaurant was opened in the same building as the Grille, which was next to the store – a whole new level of service began.

On January 1, 1990, David Letterman, grandson of Guy and Pauline (Rose's son) became the third generation to join the family business, and in 1999, took over complete ownership. He also expanded the business to include Bonfatto's Complete Catering Services, which specializes in business meetings, picnics, theme parties, wedding receptions, and all other occasions. Then, in 2000, Dave and his wife Sherri made a big move in the Bonfatto's legacy by closing the original location on High Street, and opening Bonfatto's Restaurant and Lounge on Bishop Street.

With a seating capacity of 173, full bar, lounge for meetings and small gatherings, expanded menu, great food and atmosphere, and drive-up window, this more modern facility quickly became a local favorite. I've been there on many occasions, and once for a high school reunion of which Dave was a class member. He totally pulled out all the stops for us and we had a wonderful time! It's a really local place with real local history. The atmosphere is great, the menu complete, the price fair, and I think it's so cool that Dave's mom Rose still greets you at the door.

Today, Dave continues to expand on the success of the Bonfatto tradition with his latest creation — Bonfatto's Wing Sauce & Marinade. After the restaurant closes, he sometimes works until 3am, blending, bottling, and labeling his signature sauces. As Dave says, "Taste the flavors - then feel the flavors. This sauce is great on everything from wings to cream cheese, baked beans, and ice cream." What? "Your imagination is your only limitation," he says. You can check out all the flavors and even input your own recipe at www.feeltheflavors.com.

Now, with a new product in the Bonfatto's line of quality creations, I bet they'll be going strong and continue on for more generations to come. I hope so! Guy and Pauline would be proud of you, Dave.

Enjoy!

LOCALLY OWNED GOODS & SERVICES

The following are just a few of our wonderful independent businesses here in Happy Valley. There are many more as well, and I encourage you to visit and support them all. Because of space restrictions, I've included only the name and basic information. For my personal story on each place, please visit my website and click on the link to read The Rest of the Story.

Appalachian Outdoors
DOWNTOWN STATE COLLEGE, CENTRE COUNTY

Locally Owned By: Geoff Brugler
Goods or Service: Outdoor Apparel & Equipment
Hours: Mon. – Th. 9:30am to 8:30pm, Fri. till 9pm, Sat. 9am to 8pm, Sun. 10am to 6pm
Location: 123 S. Allen St.
Contact Info: (814) 234-3000 or (800) 690-5220, **www.appoutdoors.com**

Supports Local Manufactures or Suppliers: Yes

Hull's Floor Covering
STATE COLLEGE, CENTRE COUNTY

Locally Owned By: Merle "Hap" & Pat Hull
Goods or Service: Floor Coverings, Installation, and Floor Care Products
Hours: Mon. – Fri. 8am to 4:30pm, Sat. 9am to 12pm
Location: 240 E. Hamilton Ave.
(Hamilton Avenue Shopping Center)
Contact Info: (814) 238-7187 **www.HullsFlooring.com**

Supports Local Manufactures or Suppliers: No

Nature's Pantry
STATE COLLEGE, PA

Locally Owned By: Michele Briggs
Goods or Service: Natural Foods & Local and Regional Products
Hours: Mon., Wed., Fri. 10am to 6pm, Tue. & Th. 10am to 8pm, Sat. 10am to 4pm
Location: 2331 Commercial Boulevard (near College Gardens Nursery and Celebration Hall)
Contact Info: (814) 861-5200, **www.naturespantrypa.com**

Supports Local Manufactures or Suppliers: Yes

Ace Hardware

STATE COLLEGE, CENTRE CO.

Locally Owned By: Grant H Rosenberger & James L Rosenberger
Goods or Service: Hardware & More
Hours: Mon. – Fri. 7 to 8, Sat. 8 to 8, Sun. 10 to 5
Location: 150 Rolling Ridge Drive, State College, PA 16801
(Hills Plaza next to Weis Market)
Contact Info: (814) 237-3333,
acehardwareofstatecollege@gmail.com

Supports Local Manufactures or Suppliers: Yes

The Stevens Motel

STATE COLLEGE, CENTRE CO.

Locally Owned By: Jeff & Randa Harman
Goods or Service: Accommodations
Hours: 24/7
Location: 1275 N. Atherton St.
Contact Info: (814) 238-2438, **www.thestevensmotel.com**
Supports Local Manufactures or Suppliers: Yes

(For The Rest of the Story go to **www.goingLOCALpa.com/TRS**)

CHAPTER 1
1 O'CLOCK

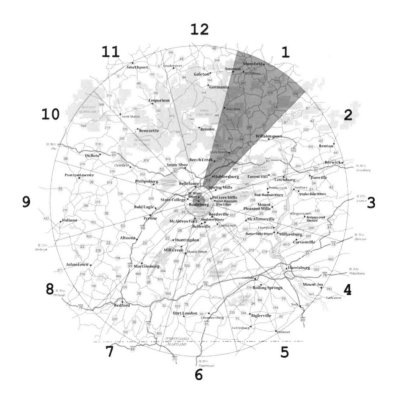

Hublersburg Inn
HUBLERSBURG, CENTRE COUNTY

I've known about this place forever, but it wasn't until recently
that it became a frequent stop on
rides through Nittany Valley, as
well as a dinner destination when
I wanted great atmosphere, great
beer, great food, and a kindred
spirit all in one. You see, this
place is more than just a great
place to eat and have a cold adult

beverage — it represents what happens when your
destiny catches you in mid-life, in the midst of not
knowing what's next. You hope and pray for something,
anything, to let you be what you've been created to
be. When it presents itself, "You don't think about
it too much, you don't debate it too much, you just
accept that it was meant to be and that there is
a reason it fell into your lap and happened the way
it did." That was a quote from the owner of the
Hublersburg Inn, but I wrote it as much from my
own experience going from artist to author as I did
from her experience in becoming the new proprietor
of this wonderful country inn.

JUST A TASTE

Locally Owned By:
Andi Heidt

Cuisine:
American

Price Range:
$4.95 to $20.00

Hours:
Mon. – Wed. 4pm to 10pm,
Th. – Sat. 11:30am to 11pm

Location:
449 Hublersburg Rd.

Wi-Fi:
Yes

Contact Info:
(814) 383-2616,
www.hublersburginn.com

Vegetarian Offerings:
Yes

Supports Local Farmers:
Yes

**Locally Owned
Accommodations Nearby:**
6 guest rooms on location

Things To Do Nearby:
"Watch the corn grow." —Andi

Andi Heidt was born and created to be a restaurateur
— she has really known nothing else. But when faced
with a decision to pursue her passion or turn and
go a different direction in teaching (her college
degree), she struggled. In the end though, she chose
wisely; she chose to follow her heart's passion,
which is being in the food biz, and where she's been
in some capacity since the age of 14. The passion
was born at a fine dining restaurant in New Hope,
PA, cultivated over 18 years at The Gamble Mill, in
Bellefonte, PA, and eventually burst forth to blossom at her very own place, where she can experience
my mantra, "It's a hell of a way to make a living,
but it's a great life."

That day, over my anticipated burger and beer, I had
the wonderful opportunity to meet this entrepreneur,
restaurateur, mom, caretaker, and super cool woman.
As we sat in the bar area together, she told me her
story, and what a story it was. We laughed and joked,
and I felt like I knew her forever – which I did, in
a way, because we come from the same place – the
place of wanting to be a free spirit and not working
for "the man," but working for ourselves and experiencing the adventures of life as they unfold before
us. She told me of a life-long passion for fine dining,
and the twists and turns on her journey that allowed
her to tell me those words of wisdom I quoted previously. It warms my heart when I meet people like
her, and I feel compelled to support her and encourage folks like you to support her, too, because she
needs you, you need her; she needs our community,
and our community needs her.

Hublersburg may be a tiny rural village, but there's
nothing tiny or rural about the sense of community
there or the diversity of the customers who frequent
the inn. Locals know the place by its former name,
the Hublersburg Hotel (not Inn) and still refer to
it as just the "Hotel." Andi and her bartender Darren
(who, by the way, is a super cool guy, a fellow beer

geek, and a serious foodie – Andi is fortunate to have him), joke about this. An indication of this community support is found in what Andi told me. She said, "It's sometimes hard to get people to their seats, because they all have to stop at different tables to chat with their neighbors or friends from down the road — everybody knows everybody!"

That's a mixed blessing though, Andi explained. Because it's been such a popular gathering spot over the years, folks come to like certain things, and they don't want to see changes with new ownership. When Andi took the place over, the rumblings of change were felt throughout the valley, and if she hoped to keep the locals, she better keep some of the favorites. This was a challenge because of her fine dining passion, but she came to appreciate compromise, and realized the beauty of giving people what they expect with her own splash of creativity at the same time — both are happy and both get what they want.

So it was this compromise that led to one of the Hublersburg Inn's most popular offerings — the Hubie Burger. This is a hamburger combined with wing sauce, fried onions, French fries, and cheese. Paired with a draught of Victory Hop Devil, it was most delicious!

As I chatted with Andi, she told me that more change were in the works, including outdoor seating. She went on to tell me so much more about her place and her philosophy that I could have just quoted Andi in this entire piece. She's got to be the most quotable restaurant owner I've ever encountered.

She told me where she's been, where she's at, and where she's going, and it's something I want you to hear and experience for yourself, because you won't ever find it at a chain place. It's a passion for pleasure — your pleasure — that has found its way through the twists and turns of a journey to open a country inn that offers heart and soul, along with the Hubie Burger and many other amazing offerings. So, to end this piece I'll let one of Andi's quotable quotes do it for me. She said, "I want my place to be a local, well-respected restaurant, the kind of place that people are willing to drive out of their way to come to. A place where people from State College or anywhere are going to come to and say, 'Oh my gosh, we found a great place,' and come back with four or five of their friends. A place that offers everything from simple to fine dining fare, but in a strictly casual setting, and a place where you don't have to spend a lot to get a lot."

Enjoy!

Furst Corner Restaurant
BEECH CREEK, CLINTON COUNTY

Walking into The Furst (as the locals call it) today must be similar to the way it was at the turn of the nineteenth century when Mr. and Mrs. George Hess owned it. The couple ran a general store there, and sold everything from clothing to grain. It was very successful, and when they retired they passed it to their son – the grandson of the original owner, George Furst. This young George Furst Hess, as well as the other males in the Hess family, became magistrates in the area and the building served as a courthouse. Eventually, it also served as the main telephone exchange for the area.

After changing hands a few times, it was slated to become an antique shop, but that didn't work out (that's interesting, because now the restaurant has many antiques all around). In the winter of 1986, Charles and Donna Bittner bought the old empire-style building, and after a ton of renovations opened the restaurant that stands today. With the success of that, they moved forward to open a B&B next door.

JUST A TASTE

Locally Owned By:
Charles and Donna Bittner

Cuisine:
American Home Cooking

Price Range:
$1.50 to $16.95

Hours:
Mon. – Sat. 5:30am to 9pm,
Sun. 7am to 9pm

Location:
39 Main St.

Wi-Fi:
No

Contact Info:
(570) 962-3371

Vegetarian Offerings:
Yes

Supports Local Farmers:
Yes

**Locally Owned
Accommodations Nearby:**
5 B&B rooms on site

Things To Do Nearby:
Bald Eagle State Park

The two places connect by a little hallway, and walking through to the other building you'll find a lovely dining room with a beautiful wooden staircase leading up to the rooms.

I asked about the dining room, and it's not just for the B&B customers, but mostly for the restaurant customers. So, if you want a bit more of an upscale setting while you enjoy your dinner, this is the place! The day I was there, I was with a date, but we sat in the cafe side. My "date" was actually my dad, and I took him to The Furst as part of a Father's Day outing. We were there for lunch and he loved it! The menu offers Breakfast, Sides, Sandwiches, Salads, Meals, Drinks, Desserts, Hershey's Ice Cream, Ice Cream Sodas, and Sundaes. Co-owner Donna Bittner makes all the pies, and said that whenever she tries to slip in a store-bought pie, nobody eats it. The prices are very reasonable, and the food is well prepared.

Dad and I hung out for awhile, and he even ordered one of Donna's pies for us to share. We continued to sit and talk over coffee. After dessert, we took a walk around the place. Like I mentioned, it has all kinds of antiques around, and if you like Mr. Peanut from the Planters Peanut Co., you'll love the collection they have there. Big ones, little ones, and a even couple that went through a fire at The Furst in 1992. Those guys are really funny, as they're kind of bent over and crooked from the heat (kinda like me on a wicked hot summer day). The fire was almost devastating, but prior work to upgrade the old building and sheer blessings kept it from reaching the restaurant.

Adding to the collection of curios and the family-owned aspect of it all was lots of stuff, like a hand-built little train that's to scale, signs, a glass jar of little sugar cubes from around the world, and even something that the co-owner Donna Bittner did herself. On the counter, by the cash register, was a milk carton with her co-owner-husband Charles' photo. Just like on those milk cartons to alert the public about missing children, was this: *"Charles Bittner. Age 68 (in dog years). Identifying marks and features – short, appears as of Mexican descent, dentures, and rolls his own. Gets violent when he can't locate his papers. Has one candled nut [I have no idea what that means and probably don't want to]. Give*

him a home and you'll get a month's free meals at The Furst. If found, take directly to the nearest mental institute for processing. If not admitted take to Furst Corner, they often accept strays. 'Chink' as he is known by his Damn Few friends was last seen driving the alleys in Beech Creek, mumbling dis-gruntled sounds about his check and the damn mail. PIN NUMBER 'br549.'" That right there is proof this little family run place is just that – family (and with a sense of humor!).

I usually try and come up with a great ending that's somewhat of a recap and encourages you to visit the place I'm writing about. Well, when the place itself has a great ending already written on their menu, why reinvent the wheel? So here's what they write: *"Today The Furst Corner Restaurant is known for 'extremely large home-cooked meals at way-below average prices!' (Some customers have even complained about their over-sized meal portions!) This unusual combination has made the historic 'old-time' restaurant a favo-rite to thousands of people all over the state, from Beech Creek natives to traveling Penn State football fans. From all of us here at 'The Furst,' THANK YOU for sharing with us 'A Taste Of The Past.'"*

Enjoy!

Night and Day Coffee Café
MANSFIELD, TIOGA COUNTY

"Enriching our neighbor-
hood one latte at a
time." That's the motto
of this very cool little
coffee shop at the very fringe of my 1 o'clock
region. And if the motto alone doesn't draw you in,
the great décor, coffee, food, and super sweet vibe
will. Even before you walk in – actually even from
across the street – you can tell this is no chain
place. And unless you're opposed to warm, cozy,
cool, and funky décor, art, good music, free internet (a very rare thing in Tioga Co.), yummy food,
great coffee, and happy, chatting locals, you are
going to absolutely love this place!

I first stumbled into the N&D a few years back and
was instantly taken by the place. I was on my way to
Corning NY, and pulled off of Rt. 15 at the Mansfield
exit hoping to find a coffee shop. Since Mansfield is
a college town, I figured the chances were pretty
good. I was right. As I sat at the red light at Rt.
6 and Main Street, I looked across the intersection
and spotted an old building on the corner. On street
level was a place with huge bay windows divided by a
glass door and the words "Night and Day Coffee Café"

JUST A TASTE

Locally Owned By:
Jes Ricker

Cuisine:
Café

Price Range:
$1.50 to $6.00

Hours:
Mon. – Fri. 7am to 8pm,
Sat. 8am to 5pm, Sun. 9am to 5pm

Location:
2 N. Main St.

Wi-Fi:
Yes

Contact Info:
(570) 662-1143,
www.nightanddaycoffee.com,
Facebook page

Vegetarian Offerings:
Yes

Supports Local Farmers:
Yes

**Locally Owned
Accommodations Nearby:**
Crossroads Bed & Breakfast
(570) 662-7008 or (800) 661-3581

Things To Do Nearby:
Shopping, Outdoor Activities,
Festivals, PA Grand Canyon

written across the bottom of the bay windows. Above
that was painted a radiant sun-and-moon graphic,
along with a steaming coffee cup. Behind that on the
inside was a couch and little coffee table on one
side, and high back chairs and a little coffee table
on the other. Café tables stood on the sidewalk, and
market umbrellas shaded folks enjoying the day with
food and drink. No need to look any farther – I found
exactly what I was looking for.

After parking on the street (which is FREE in Mansfield – take that, State College!), I walked in and
was instantly in love with the place. It was full of
folks eating, drinking, and chatting, and the vibe
was so sweet. Dark blues, violets, and greens filled
the walls while old, narrow, blank hardwood floors
were beneath. A tin ceiling painted deep cobalt blue
hung overhead, with fans swirling the air that was
thick with the smell of fresh ground coffee beans.
Art hung from every wall and by the looks of it, it
was local art and very cool.

Very distracted by my surroundings, I somehow made
it up to the counter to place my order. A young woman
named Jes was very friendly and while she got me my
coffee, I soaked in as much as I could. However, she
was fast and I was back on the road without much
"soaking in." I knew I needed to return someday. So
it was on a very cold, snowy day in mid-October that
I was within striking distance again of this wonderful café of my memory.

I was in the neiborhood because of an invitation
from an indie bookstore called From My Self Books in
beautiful downtown Wellsboro. They were hosting a
first annual BookFest, and I was invited as a parti-
cipating author. I arrived around noon the day
before the event, and needed lunch and a hot coffee.
Wellsboro may be an amazing town, but one thing they
lack is an authentic coffee shop. For that you must
drive 12 miles to Mansfield, which for this part of
the state is like going around the corner.

I arrived at the same intersection as before, and across the street, on the same corner, was the café. Of course, no one was outside, but the window seats were full and it appeared the rest was, too. I parked again for FREE (take that again, State College) and went on in. It was just like I remembered, but with different art on the walls. The place was buzzing, and I was lucky to get a table where I could watch the goings-on and soak up what vibe I missed from my quick visit before.

This time, wanting more than coffee to go, I took a serious look at the giant chalkboard menu above the counter. I saw many coffee combos and many different sandwiches, including a Breakfast Sandwich selection. The coffee menu board listed espresso drinks, hot and iced. They don't do American-brewed coffee, but offer an Americano, which is better and more flavorful. Lots of other drinks, like lattes, mochas, chai, smoothies, hot chocolate, steamers, teas, Italian sodas, iced tea, and lemonade, rounded things out.

The food menu board listed grilled and cold sand-wiches, wraps, and bagel offerings. A sample of the cold sandwiches includes Tuna, Egg, and Chicken Salad, Hummus, Fruity Turkey, TMR (tomato, mozzarella, and roasted red pepper and basil), TTMR (TMR with turkey), and Greek Chicken. A few of the hot sandwiches available include Tuna Melt, TMR, TTMR, Grilled Cheese, Chicken Cheesesteak, Turkey Reuben, Veggie Burger, and The Jackie (mozzarella, tomato, sun dried tomato, and basil). All sandwiches can be on sourdough ciabatta, wheat, or marble rye. They offer tomato, wheat, or spinach wraps. Bagels are served plain, toasted, or as a sandwich (plain or toasted, too). Plain, Wheat, Everything, and Cinnamon Raisin are used for Egg & Cheese, Sausage Egg & Cheese, Guacamole Egg & Cheese, Hummus, Cream Cheese & Tomato, P/B & Banana, and Cream Cheese Guacamole & Cheddar. Yum! I ordered a Greek Chicken Wrap on a tomato wrap with a Night & Day Mocha, and took my lunch to a picnic table with benches and a side wall.

From my table, I was able to check out the scene and the clientele gathered inside this sweet place. It was clear that 99.9% were locals, and I was the .1% non-local. At a table across the large open room, sat an older cat, dressed like the quintessential professor – long, full, gray hair, tweed blazer with the classic suede elbow patches, and a thick book opened next to his sandwich. He was obviously a professor from Mansfield University, just up the street behind the café. He was also a very popular cat, because just about everybody stopped to chat with him. Turned out he was not only a professor, but also a poet who would be joining me the next day at the BookFest.

Since I had internet access, I decided to check the web and see what I could find out about N&D. I found a Facebook page and a simple, not-so-complete website. What the website did yield was that the barista who served me my first coffee way back when, was the owner herself. Jes Ricker considers herself a true Aquarius — someone that is genuinely interested in community. She lives "life to the fullest" and is "only interested in something if she believes it will make the world a better place."

Well, one visit to Night and Day Coffee Café and you'll be experiencing what Jes means by living life to the fullest and making the world a better place. I'm convinced that if everyone in the world could meet up at N&D, soak in the sweet vibe, décor, art, drink a marvelously prepared coffee, enjoy a delicious meal, and hang with the cool community that supports this place, there would be no meanness, no fighting, and certainly no wars. This is a place worth spending some time in. It has certainly enriched my life every time I've been there, and I'm sure it will for you, too – even if it's only "one latte at a time."

Enjoy!

Ansonia Valley Inn
& Burnin' Barrel Bar
ANSONIA, TIOGA COUNTY

Pennsylvania's northern tier holds some of the most pictures-que scenery in the state. Histo-ric Rt. 6, the Grand Army of the Republic Highway, carries you through from the Delaware River at New Jersey to the Ohio border. Up here, good food is plentiful, but good beer is not. So when I was on an epic ride across Rt. 6 with my pals, parched and delirious from the heat of summer and miles and miles of places displaying Coors Light signs, I considered pulling a "Thelma and Louise" and riding us right over the west rim of the PA Grand Canyon. Fortunately, we came upon a lonesome old building standing by the side of the road in the "town" of Ansonia.

Like many places in the hither-most regions of PA, a signpost for a town is not necessarily an indica-tion that an actual town exists. So it was with Ansonia. The only things there were the old building and a combo mini-mart store, ice cream parlor, and gas station next door. But it wasn't the store, ice

JUST A TASTE

Locally Owned By:
Chris & Amy Middleton

Cuisine:
American

Price Range:
$3.50 to $24.00

Hours:
Tue. – Sun. 10am to 2am

Location:
5440 Rt. 6

Wi-Fi:
Yes

Contact Info:
(570) 724-1333, Facebook page

Vegetarian Offerings:
Yes

Supports Local Farmers:
Yes

Locally Owned Accommodations Nearby:
Colton Point Motel (570) 724-2155

Things To Do Nearby:
PA Grand Canyon, Outdoor Activities, Wellsboro

cream, or gas that saved me and my friends that day from ending up in the Pine Creek Gorge – it was the old lonesome building.

Standing outside said building was the hottest red-head I had ever laid eyes on. Kidding, but that's how delirious I was. Actually, it was just a sign out front with a banner that read "18 Beers On Tap." If I hadn't been riding lead with three other bikes on my tail doing 60+ mph, I would have locked up the brakes right there. Instead, we slowed down, turned around up the road, and made a bee-line back.

As we pulled into the gravel parking lot, I could read the entire sign to see that we were at the Ansonia Valley Inn & Burnin' Barrel Bar, offering Victuals, Fine Spirits, and Lodging. Well we didn't need lodging, we don't drink fine or not-so-fine spirits when we ride, and we had no idea what "Victuals" were. We just knew we wanted good, cold, QUALITY beer, and if "Victuals" meant food, we were all in!

OK, this place is a bit deceiving from the outside, but hey, we're a gang (if you can call four guys "a gang") of bikers, and a deceiving facade means nothing to us. In fact, some of the best places to eat and drink in the world hide behind a deceiving facade. The AVI (Ansonia Valley Inn) is not scary or seedy by any means, it's just not spit-shined like the chain places - but if that's your thing, you wouldn't be reading this book. It's an old building, and old buildings can worry some folks. But like many things, real beauty is on the inside.

Four road-dirt covered, sun-burnt, thirsty guys walked in, and were stopped in our dusty tracks. Before us was a beautiful, open room with polished wood all around, lots of tables, a shuffle board, a nice big U-shaped bar, dollar bills pinned to the beams above the bar, and the most mouth-watering line up of 18 taps of brewing goodness at the bar. Granted, a few of the taps were brands I wouldn't serve a dying dog, but most were beauties, and such a welcome sight. Some of them were take-out beers from Sly Fox, Tröegs, Great Lakes, Long Trail, and Magic Hat. We went straight to the bar to get our refreshments.

I chose the Commodore Perry IPA from Great Lakes, McC (aka David) went for Hop Back from Tröegs, Mike chose a pale ale from Sly Fox, and Jeff had the Magic Hat #9. We went to a table, held our fine adult beverages high, looked each other in the eye, and toasted to life, love, travels, and adventure. Let me just say here and now, those beers went down wonderfully, and tasted oh, so good. Ahh, finally – great beers for a great journey. Thank you AVI & BB!

As we talked about the beers and reminisced about the miles we'd traveled that day, our stomachs were reminding us that it's not all about beer. We needed to eat, too. As though scripted, our server came over with menus. I must admit, she was a very good-looking woman – total hippie chick, with long, curly blond hair and cool glasses. She was also super sweet (I was enamored). She handed us a menu of all kinds of choices from apps to entrées.

Since this would be an epic trip, I wanted an epic dinner. I don't usually order steak unless I know where the meat comes from. And because a lot of places (especially chains) use western feed-lot beef, shot full of toxic waste and left to stand and feed in their own filth (sorry), I shy away. But I asked our server about the source of their filet mignon, and what she told me saved the day. She said their place uses beef from right down the road, and it's all grass fed and free range. Awesome! Thank you AVI & BB once again! I ordered the filet, Mike went for fish and chips, McC got a T-bone, and Jeff ordered a salad (of course) and a big ol' burger. We sat back, enjoyed our beers, and plotted the next leg of our adventure.

My filet was so ____ing GOOD! I don't remember what
the boys thought about their dinners, but I still
lie awake some nights thinking about mine (truth be
known, I think about the hippie chick server, too).

That was a wonderful trip across Rt. 6, and this stop
was one of the most memorable. If you're ever up
that way to visit our amazing PA Grand Canyon, and
you go to the west rim (the best, in my opinion),
you have to drive right past this place – it's at
the corner of Rt. 6 and the road back to the west
rim. The Ansonia Valley Inn and Burnin' Barrel Bar
with their "18 Beers On Tap" is an awesome oasis
along the Grand Army of the Republic Highway. A
highway to heaven, if you ask me.

Enjoy!

CHAPTER 2
2 O'CLOCK

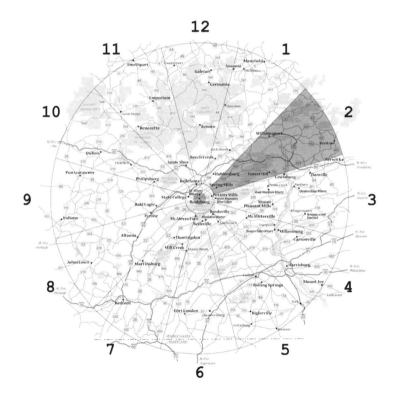

The Frosty Hook
SPRING MILLS, CENTRE COUNTY

This story is a little dated, as you will read, but this place is time-less. And whether a few years ago, many years

ago, or when you visit, it pretty much stays the same. It's just one of those places - one you're likely not to forget. I didn't.

It had been a year or so since I stopped at The Hook (as the locals call it). When I walked in this time, nothing had changed except for a sign on the door which read "No Smoking Permitted Inside" and a dozen "NO SMOKING" signs scattered throughout the bar and dining room (funny thing was that they still have one of those old-school cigarette machines with the pull handles to release packs of smokes right beside the dining room). This was great for me (the No Smoking thing) because the main reason I didn't go there much was the smoke. On any given night it was like a smoker's paradise, and even the 15 mile ride home wasn't enough to air out my clothes. It was a fun place, but the smoke ruined it for me. Now, thanks

Locally Owned By:
Bob Musser

Cuisine:
Country Pub Fare

Price Range:
$1.50 to $17.95

Hours:
Mon. - Sat. 10 to 2am,
Sun. 11am to 2am

Location:
113 Firehall Rd.

Wi-Fi:
No

Contact Info:
(814) 422-8881

Vegetarian Offerings:
No

Supports Local Farmers:
Yes

Locally Owned Accommodations Nearby:
Lead Horse B&B (814) 422-8783

Things To Do Nearby:
Penn's Cave & Wildlife Park,
Fishing, Camping

to a new PA law, smoking is banned in many taverns, but even an act of Congress couldn't change some things.

There's still all kinds of NASCAR stuff all over the place, and Bud and Bud Light neon signs casting their alluring (alluring?) glow over the bar area. The tap selection sure hadn't changed either, and the only thing I could even consider ordering was Yuengling (if only my beer snob friends could see me now). I was hoping that by this time (well into the twenty-first century) they would have something from Elk Creek (just down the road) or Otto's. I would think the regulars would take to something different, especially if it came from a neighbor. I know these folks value both their neighbors and community. Heck, I bet they would love Tim's Winkleblink Ale from Elk Creek! It would make a great beer for their dart league.

These are Penns Valley folks, and like I've written about in my first book, they are the salt of the earth and good people. They aren't caught up in the trappings of the world, like some State College folks, or have the need to be or act like something they're not. No, they're the real thing and they make no bones about it. And if you try to pull any shenanigans, you'll get the stink eye, at the very least. So I felt it very prudent to check that no Obama '08 buttons or stickers were anywhere near my person. Why? Well, you decide.

The Hook is never short on passionate conversation. So when a news commentator on TV mentioned the previous evening's first address to Congress by newly elected president Obama, a quite rowdy and funny exchange took place at the other end of the bar about the president's attempt to stimulate the economy. When one old cat said, "Nancy Pelosi looked like a ____ing jack-in-the-box the way she kept popping up to clap," I thought I was going to spew my beer all over the bar! Actually, I was impressed they even watched it.

Anyway, The Frosty Hook is just one of those places
you just gotta visit and soak in the local color,
drink a plain ol' beer, and eat some good ol' food.
The menu is simple, but they offer a lot. With
headings like Dinners, Soups, Pizza, Sandwiches, Club
Sandwiches, Salads, and Wings, you can get most of
what you might want. The dinners feature cuts from
an 8 oz. filet mignon to a whopping 24 oz. Porterhouse.
They're big on steaks, and their steaks are big!
Not only that, but all the steaks are from Penns
Valley Meats in Millheim, so the cattle are locals,
too! The soups are homemade and there's a ton of
different sandwiches.

If you are coming for more than a beer, as I am today,
you'll find a very spacious dining room with another
room off to the front and to the left of the dart
board with a couple really nice old-style wooden
booths. Across from that, there's another big room
with a pool table and more tables. They must be big
on pool, because there's another table right when
you walk in the front door.

All in all, The Hook is just a neighborhood pub in a
small rural town. The people are down to earth, and
tell it the way it is. That's just how they roll.
Non-locals as well as travelers are always welcomed
and treated with hometown hospitality. But if you're
a Democrat, or a beer or food snob like me, it's
just best to eat, drink, listen, laugh, mind your
own business, and ...

Enjoy!

Forest House Hotel
FOREST HILL, UNION COUNTY

This is a place I've ridden by a ton of times, but for some reason never stopped. With each pass though, my curiosity grew and I knew it was just a matter of time before I would find myself there. Then one day it happened, and more out of necessity and sanctuary than a planned visit. I wasn't alone either; three of my most excellent pals and riding companions were with me. But no matter the reason or the company, I'm sure glad it happened just the way it did – sometimes (many times) you need to "Just Do It" or you never will. And when you do, you're glad you did. That was certainly the case here at the Forest House Hotel, and now that I've tasted and experienced it, I'll be back more often.

The story begins when my friends and I were out for a ride on one of our favorite roads, Rt. 192. From the time we left home, we kept getting hit by summertime cloudbursts – one right after another but we pressed on. Then, like an apparition or oasis in the mist, we saw a bright glowing neon beer sign. There it was, the Forest House Hotel – the place I passed many times before, and now it was there to save us

from the rain. We pulled in and made haste for cover, which just happened to be the bar.

As soon as we sat down, we got "the look" from the locals. I'm not sure if it was because we were soaked, or just that we were newcomers. No matter, it was out of the rain and seemed like a nice and friendly place. The bartender asked what we were having and it wasn't a hard choice – apparently only beers sanctioned by NASCAR are allowed there. We all chose the only PA brand available on draught, clinked our mugs and sat back to dry and take it all in.

The place was really cool and very authentic in the old time hotel and tavern motif. The bar was in a U shape, so it's great for talking and bantering with friends and locals. It was also surrounded by tons of NASCAR stuff and what seemed like hundreds of photos of a young woman with all the big name drivers. And while my amigos stayed put there, I did what I always do, and took a look around the rest of the place.

Beyond the bar were two rooms. One seemed to be a kinda spill-over for the bar and a dance floor when a band is in the house. The other was the dining room with some artifacts and cool old photos from the hotel's early days – there's even a picture showing a large group of cavalry dudes mounted on horses and lined up out front. This place really goes back!

I headed back to the bar, and the consensus was that the rain was going to stick around a little while longer and we should have a bite to eat. I was all for it. The place was full of folks eating, drinking, talking, and laughing, and it seemed like a great place and time to wait out the storm. I told the barkeep we would be staying awhile and asked what they offered. He handed us menus and also pointed to a glowing menu sign behind him. I asked his name and if he was the owner. He said "Nope, I'm Randy, the owner's nephew."

I don't remember what the other guys got that day, but I do remember what I got (and the price was something to remember too). What's better on a chilly, rainy day? Chili and a grilled cheese sandwich are right up there for me. I went for  both and a bag of chips, and Randy yelled my order across the bar to an older guy who was in the middle of what must have been a funny story with some friends because they were all laughing-up a storm. This guy got up right away and headed for the kitchen. A short while later he returned with my food and went right back to his bar stool to continue where he left off.

With one bite of chili and a bite of grilled cheese, I knew I was in a place where they make good, honest food that tastes like what my mom would make. The grilled cheese was golden brown, and nice and crispy on the outside, and oh so soft and gooey on the inside. The chili was obviously homemade and absolutely delicious! When I asked Randy who made it he pointed to the older guy who had gone to the kitchen and said, "My Uncle Merle made it – he's been making that chili for long time." No doubt Uncle Merle knows what he's doing. And with that comment I found out who the owner was. Merle seemed like a good dude, and it was cool that he hung out with the customers.

Afterwards, I asked what they had for dessert. Randy pointed to a selection of candy bars and chewing tobacco under the counter. I asked for a 2 pack of Reese's Cups and a pouch of Red Man (kidding about the Red Man). Seriously though, this place serves real food made by real people at bargain prices. Like most out-of-the-way places, the meals are usually homemade with love and tradition as the main ingredient. The Forest House Hotel offers this, and way more than chili and grilled cheese, in a setting that's certainly a throw-back to bygone times. Some other offerings are Steaks (from a local butcher), Home Baked Ham, Honey Dipped Chicken, Haddock, Home Made Crab Cakes, Salads, and a variety of Seafood. Plus the great pub fare that you can read from the old 7UP sign behind the bar.

After an hour or so, the boys and I were almost dry and the sun was shining brightly outside. The food hit the spot, and the road was calling. We mounted the bikes and for a moment I imagined myself in that old photo inside. Where once a cavalry troop lined up with their horses back in the 1800s, now a troop of friends were lined up on their bikes 200 years later. How cool.

So whether you go by bike, car, or horse – and whether you arrive wet or dry, Just Do It! Please say hi to Merle for me, and try his chili. Maybe have a grilled cheese too, and then a Reese's Cup for dessert. Or heck, go all out and have a real meal. Wash it all down with a PA brewed beer, and pay with little more than pocket change.

As we rode off I remembered that credit card ad where they priced a bunch of stuff out then priced the experience itself. Here's my version.

Bowl of Chili: $2.50
Grilled Cheese Sandwich: $1.30
Mug of Yuengling: $1.25
Reese's Cups: 85¢
Chips: 25¢
Hanging out with friends, locals, Randy and Uncle Merle at the Forest House Hotel: *Priceless.*

Enjoy!

Note: On a recent visit I learned that Randy passed away from a heart attack at the young age of 49. He was a big part of the Forest House, and staff as well as customers loved him.

Bavarian Barbarian
WILLIAMSPORT, LYCOMING COUNTY

I first heard of the Bavarian Barbarian while selling my first book at the Selinsgrove Hops, Vines & Wines Festival back in the summer of 2008. Honestly, I don't remember the beers as much as I remember the barely-barbarian-dressed and tattooed young woman who was pouring that day. If only I were Conan, I would have grabbed her with all her beer, jumped on my mighty battle horse, and ridden away with my sword held high in victory. However, alongside this young barbarianess was a guy who looked way more like Conan than me, and would have proceeded to cleave me in half with his battle axe.

The following summer I had another chance to sample the BB's beers (averting my eyes) and found them quite tasty! One was called Weldspatter IPA, a "not your typical" India Pale Ale. It wasn't as hopped-up as many other American versions, and it was a little darker. Another was the Hammerin' Ale, and was Mike's first beer. He brewed it to be a "well-balanced,

JUST A TASTE

Locally Owned By:
Mike Hiller

Cuisine:
Beer

Price Range:
Only tastings

Hours:
Tasting Room: Th. 5pm to 8pm,
Fri. 2pm to 8pm, Sat. 11am to 8pm

Location:
429 W. 3rd Street

Wi-Fi:
No

Contact Info:
(570) 322-5050,
www.bavarianbarbarian.com

Vegetarian Offerings:
Yes

Supports Local Farmers:
No

Locally Owned Accommodations Nearby:
Wood Cliff Cabin: www.vrbo.com/306623#ownerprofile

Things To Do Nearby:
Drink Mike's beer at the places listed in the following story

easy-going beer." This is a year-round beer that goes very well with summer grilling. Mike recommends Hammerin' Ale as an excellent choice for "Barbarians" who are new to craft beers.

Recently, I made the journey to Mike's brewing facility in Williamsport, and you know the old saying, "It's not what's on the outside, but what's on the inside that counts"? Well, not that Mike's place is bad on the outside – it's just that you would never know a cool brewery was on the inside. If it weren't for the address, Google Maps image, and Mike's written description from the BB web page, I would have never guessed where it is. The only real sign was above a glass door. But inside, and down a florescent-lit hallway, was where the barbarian brews for his "Horde" and plots his invasion of PA!

I walked into a HUGE warehouse and was greeted by the one and only employee and owner, Mike. Turns out he was the Conan-looking guy at the beer fest, but without the long hair and the barbarianess. Darn! Most of the warehouse is the brewery, and the smaller area you walk into first is the tasting room. There you'll find a couple vintage couches and chairs, some cool signage, and of course, a tasting bar with a small lineup of tap handles in the shape of hands gripping battle axes. That day, he had three beers available: Headbangerz Brown Ale, which is based on English brown ales, Steel Drivin' Stout, a roasted, dark oatmeal stout with hints of dark chocolate and toasty caramel, and his new 2x4 IPA (my favorite)! This beer boasts Columbus, Nugget, and Amarillo hops. Golden pale malts and flaked rye are also added to the mix, yielding a noticeably robust hoppiness with just the right touch of bitterness.

While I was nursing my little six-ounce sampler of 2x4, he told me how he got started, and what's going on now and into the future. Mike's a native of South Williamsport, and first started in the craft brewing biz in 1997. After nearly a year at a beer distri-

butor, an opportunity came up for him to work as a
brewer for Legend Brewing Company. He did all kinds
of stuff there including brewing, cellar work, cleaning,
and maintenance. After four years there, he moved to
Boston so his wife, Kira, could attend grad school.

Tired of listening to Mike whine about how much he
missed brewing, Kira gave him a home brewing kit as
an anniversary gift. He began brewing whenever he
could find the time and developed the recipes for his
Hammerin' Ale, Headbangerz Brown Ale, Square Feet
Wheat, and Weldspatter IPA, as well as several other
beers in five-gallon batches out on his apartment
balcony (If I had been a neighbor, I'd be climbing
a latter every night).

After Mike read the
book "Brewing Up a
Business: Adventures
in Entrepreneurship"
by Sam Calagione of
Dogfish Head Brewery
fame, he was inspired
to start his own bre-
wery. He spent almost
two years researching,
writing a business
plan, and gathering
support. Thanks to
family, friends, and
other area businessmen
who believed in Mike,
his dream came true to
have his own brewery
in July 2007.

Now Mike's operation
is in full swing, and
his beers are "inva-
ding" (as Mike likes
to say) a big portion
of eastern PA. Here

are a few of the places within my radius where you can enjoy them by the glass. In Williamsport: 4th Street Grille and Ale House (Genetti Hotel), The Bridge Tavern, Crippled Bear Inn, Franco's Lounge, and the Old Corner Hotel. In State College, it's The Deli and Zeno's Pub. In Pleasant Gap, you can find BB at the Red Horse Tavern. In Danville, go to BJ's Steak and Rib House. In Lewisburg, it's the Lewisburg Hotel. In Selinsgrove, try BJ's Steak and Rib House. These are only a few of the places. Check out the website's "BEERFINDER" tab for a complete list by city or zip code.

But don't forget, you can purchase BB beer on location at the Williamsport facility in 22 oz. bottles, 64 oz. growlers, and 5 gallon kegs. I had mentioned earlier about the "Horde" – this is Mike's version of a pub or mug club. You can pay $100.00 to belong to the Barbarian Horde, which, among other things, gives you privileges like buying four growlers and getting the fifth free.

The Bavarian Barbarian Brewing Co. has invaded my realm, and I hope he'll invade yours too. Mike's currently planning to "conquer" the Philadelphia region, and I bet he'll take it by storm. This little one-man operation is gaining ground, and the Horde is growing. However, this barbarian doesn't conquer and divide, he conquers and unites. He brings the best of craft brewing to folks who love it, and even those who just don't realize they love it yet. Join the Horde that rises a glass, not a sword.

Enjoy!

The Old Filling Station Restaurant
BENTON, COLUMBIA COUNTY

Up until this place came along to rock my world, my only knowledge of Benton, PA, was that it's the home of some old friends and fishing buddies, Barry and

Cathy Beck, a Bluegrass Festival in July, and Rickett's Glen State Park nearby. That was it. So when my friend, Otto, from the Columbia/Montour Visitors Bureau, told me there was an American restaurant in Benton also serving Thai food, I said, "Yeah, Otto, whatever." He insisted it was true, and not only did they have a culinary school-trained chef doing wonderful American cuisine, they also have a cook from Thailand making authentic and amazing Thai food! Benton? Thai? Authentic? Amazing? "I doubt it," I thought, but in my Thai-loving mind, I was already planning my quest to find out the answers.

Otto had said he wasn't sure of their hours, and advised me to call before I traveled there. I called, and sure enough they were open for lunch, but Otto neglected to tell me something I wasn't to know about until I got there and ordered (and something that would have been good to know before the almost

JUST A TASTE

Locally Owned By:
Chris Dawson

Cuisine:
American & Thai Home Cooking

BYOB:
Yes

Price Range:
$4.99 to $25.00

Hours:
Tue. – Fri. 8am to 9pm, Sat. 7am to 9pm, Sun. 7am to 2pm (No Thai on Sunday or Weekday Lunch)

Location:
140 Main St.

Wi-Fi:
No

Contact Info:
(570) 925-6556

Vegetarian Offerings:
Yes

Supports Local Farmers:
Yes

Locally Owned Accommodations Nearby:
The Mattress & Muffin B&B
(570) 925-5466

Things To Do Nearby:
Antiques, Fly Fishing

two-hour ride). I jumped on The Steed, laid a course northeast, and asked myself again, "Benton? Thai? Authentic? Amazing?" It just couldn't be.

I rolled into town to find The Old Filling Station right where Otto said it was, but it looked to me like a residential home and not the renovated gas station or hidden Thai gem I was expecting. I was starting to have serious doubts. But, in front of the house was a big sign with an image of an old classic car alongside an old style gas pump, and an oil drum with the words "The Old Filling Station. Let Us Fill You Up!" and "Open" in lights below that. No mention of Thai food, or even a hint of anything ethnic.

I turned back the driveway to the rear parking lot to see an incredible sight that instantly began to change my feelings about this place (and Otto). There, on the backside of the two-story house, was an amazing outdoor patio filled with the most beautiful hanging baskets of flowers I'd ever seen. Two or three levels of wooden deck held not only big market umbrellas with tables and chairs under them, but also a lovely fish pond surrounded by more flowers and exotic plants. This space was beautiful, and I had to go inside and see what this was really all about.

I walked in and instantly knew that somehow, some way, TOFS was linked to a gas station at some point, or at least they were obsessed with gas station memorabilia. Apart from the typical, they must have had license plates from all 50 states hanging on the walls. This décor was cool and not cheesy in any way, and they also had a more refined dining room at the front of the house without the memorabilia. I chose the back half amongst the license plates and a table underneath an original concert poster for Hank Williams Sr. The events that occurred next are a testimony to why I so emphatically encourage you to support your indie-owned places vs. the chains, who

can't see beyond corporate protocol and have no
desire to do so.

As I settled in under Hank and looked over the menu,
I saw many wonderful dishes just as Otto said, but
no Thai. I quickly asked my server about the Thai
food that I had heard about and was told that yes,
they do serve Thai, but they don't offer it at lunch
except Saturdays. "Disappointed" is not a strong
enough word for how I felt. In desperation, I tried
the only thing I knew to do given the situation - I
informed my server that I had traveled ALL THE WAY
from near State College just to try their Thai - and
I did it with my most sad little kid face.

The woman behind the register overheard my comment
and immediately came to my table. Again I expressed
my disappointment, and how I travelled sooo far to
enjoy what I heard was amazing Thai. She was so
sweet, and said she would call the Thai cook to ask
if she would come in early and make something for
me. "Oh, no!" I thought, I just got myself in a fix
- I didn't want her to have to do that! Now I was
going to have to back-pedal to keep her from calling
in the cook early, but at the same time I was thinking
I was about to ruin exactly what I came for.

Fortunately for my selfish taste buds, no back-pedaling or persuading could change her mind. She told me that the Thai cook needed to come in to prepare for the evening's menu later anyway, she only lived down the street, and she knew she was home because they had talked earlier. "Plus," she said, "we serve authentic Thai, not American Thai. And if you like Thai, you will be blown away – it's amazing." There were those words again! What could I do now? I accepted her generous offer to make the call and have a custom-made, authentic, amazing Thai lunch prepared exclusively for me. Sweet!

This was obviously the owner I encountered, and I started to wonder if she secretly knew of my true reason for being there (this book) but how could she? No, she's just one of our many wonderful indie business people who don't have to worry about corporate protocol – they just do what they want or need to do for their customers (even for those customers who are whiny babies like me). She handed me the Thai menu and said that if I wanted anything other than what was offered, to let her know.

As I was looking over the featured selections, a tiny Asian woman approached my table and asked what I would like her to make. I don't know what happened during that phone call, but apparently I was mistaken for some sort of Thai food critic. I asked her name and she told me "Noi." I asked what she thought was one of her favorites. She suggested I try her special that week, a dish from Laos called Laap (pronounced "Larb"). Here's how the menu describes it: *"Fresh ground chicken breast sautéed and mixed with Thai herbs such as coriander, spring onion, ground roasted rice, and seasoned with spices and lime juice. Served with raw vegetables and Jasmine rice."* Laap is the national dish of Laos, and its popularity has spread to northeastern Thailand. This makes sense, because that's where Noi is from. As I found out later, she learned to cook from her mom, who still lives there, and has never left the village her whole life. OK, "authentic" has been answered.

Since it was going to take a little while for Noi to get everything ready and cook my meal from scratch, and I was really hungry, I asked for an order of spring rolls. Because they're so popular, Noi makes up a batch of them three times a week so they're always fresh and on hand. She also makes her own dipping sauce. Both the rolls and the sauce were really, really good! Best I've had.

After I walked around and took some photos of the place, my Laap arrived. Wow, it looked and smelled wonderful, and had a slice of lime and a sprig of mint on top. It was surrounded by lettuce, vegetables, and the bowl of rice. I took my time and savored every bite. It wasn't just really, really good - it was, as both Otto and the owner claimed, amazing! I sat back, closed my eyes, and went into a state of Thai bliss. "Amazing" had now been answered.

Having finished, but still in my state of bliss, the owner returned to join me at my table and noticed me making notes. At this point, I had to tell her what I was up to. She was thrilled. She introduced her-self as Chris, and called Noi back out. The two of us then went out onto the beautiful back deck and chatted about food, travel, and life. I asked how a little mountain town like Benton became known for Thai, and Chris told me the story.

Noi arrived on the scene when she and her American husband were walking across the restaurant's back parking lot. Chris was on the deck when Noi's husband (who had eaten at TOFS many times) asked her if she would like to serve Thai food (until then, TOFS was straight-up American cuisine). Chris said she might, and Noi said with a very shy and polite voice, "I bring you sample tomorrow." The next day, she arrived with so much wonderful stuff that Chris asked her lunch customers to try it. They were all "blown away!" That sealed the deal – The Old Filling Station would also be serving authentic Thai.

Their main menu is still American and awesome. Chef Corey Hess does a vodka sauce that Chris said "is to die for." Some of Corey's other offerings include steaks, chicken, pasta, and seafood along with weekly and weekend specials.

It was time for me to hit the road and head back home. I paid my bill and thanked Chris and Noi profusely. I especially thanked them both for breaking protocol and having Noi come in just for me. As I rode out of town, I asked myself the same questions as when set out – Benton? Thai? Authentic? Amazing? I certainly knew all the answers now.

Enjoy!

Note: Chris asked me to add that TOFS is BYOB! She loves to see folks bringing in their own beer or wine. And remember, the Thai menu is only available for dinners and Saturday lunch only (unless you whine like me, maybe).

CHAPTER 3
3 O'CLOCK

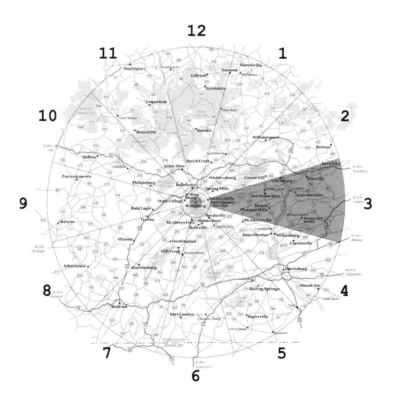

Seven Mountains Wine Cellars
POTTERS MILLS, CENTRE COUNTY

What a wonderful place to spend an afternoon. A winery, you ask? Well, not if it's just any winery. But when it's a winery that's more like a wine spa? Yes!

Whether you're alone, with a friend, with a group of women on a girls' day out, or even guys doing a guys' day out, this is an awesome place to visit, and an even better place for a needed reprieve from the hustle and bustle of life - especially when said life includes those never-ending gray days of winter here in central PA.

Just imagine yourself on a cold, cloudy day sampling a wonderful selection of hand-crafted wines, then buying a glass or bottle of your favorite, cozying up to a fireplace on a big comfy couch, or sitting with your friends at a large wooden table. Spread out in front of you is an array of local cheeses, fruit, hummus, artisan bread (from Gemelli), olive oil, and a few thick chunks of dark chocolate that you brought from home. If it's a group, you might have even brought a whole basket of goodies or perhaps

JUST A TASTE

Locally Owned By:
Scott and Mary Ann Bubb

Cuisine:
Wine

BYOF (Bring Your Own Food):
Yes

Price Range:
$10 to $28

Hours:
Mon. & Tue. By Appt., Wed. & Th. 11:00am to 5:00pm, Fri. & Sat. till 7:00 pm, Sun. till 5:00 pm

Location:
107 Mountain Springs Rd.
(Decker Valley Road)

Wi-Fi:
Yes

Contact Info:
(814) 364-1000,
www.sevenmountainswinecellars.com

Vegetarian Offerings:
N/A

Supports Local Farmers:
Yes

Locally Owned Accommodations Nearby:
Aikens Cabins, (814) 466-9299

Things To Do Nearby:
Penns Cave, Grange Fair

a prepared meal from a local restaurant. All you need are the table settings. See, what makes this place so cool is that they encourage customers to hang out, bring your own food (BYOF), and enjoy! And enjoy I did with a couple friends on a Saturday afternoon.

It all started when I remembered hearing that Seven Mountains Wine Cellars was like an oasis of sorts (wine spa, perhaps) no matter what the season or weather. I had also heard that Seven Mountains had a fireplace and was BYOF. Not being sure about the BYOF part, we decided to call and check. The woman on the other end said yes, and actually sounded excited that we would be bringing snacks. How cool!

After a short drive back into the mountains we were first greeted by a large, beautiful, lodge-type structure among the trees. We must not have been the only ones needing a wine spa respite, because the parking lot was packed. But with a few spaces left, we were able to find one and gathered our goodies and place settings and walked in. Wow, what a beautiful place! We looked at each other, and knew right then and there we wouldn't be going anywhere for a while.

It was better than I had imagined from the descriptions I heard – the staff friendlier, the space larger, the couch bigger and cushier, the vibe sweeter, and there was even a big outdoor deck! But best of all, as we were to find out, all the wines were pretty much excellent. Having a place to hang with your good friends and favorite cheeses and breads is one thing, but if the wine's crappy, it really doesn't make sense to go there – you might as well stay home with a bottle of store-bought wine. However, no worries here.

So after we tasted the full complement of Seven Mountains' wines, we bought a bottle (glasses provided) and settled into the big comfy couch with a blazing fire in front of us. The sun was now out and streaming in though the huge windows, and our BYOF gourmet picnic was on the coffee table in front of us. I poured us each a glass and we raised them to life, love, and the blessings of God. I took a sip and was blown away. The wine was sooo delicious, and at least for me, I was experiencing and tasting something really special – and my friends agreed. We were also experiencing Scott Bubb's passion for winemaking, which he's been doing for 35 years, starting in his basement.

They've come a long way in a relatively short amount of time. Growing from a basement to an amazingly beautiful wine making facility and tasting room is impressive and great for all those who want to visit, taste, and buy...and buy you will, when you taste what they offer. Here's the rundown, as of summer 2010.

Dry Red Wines: Merlot, Cabernet Sauvignon, Ten Point (a Bordeaux blend), Cab Franc Private Reserve, and Redtail

Dry White Wines: Chardonnay, Dry Riesling, Whippoor-will White (a French hybrid blend), Vidal Blanc, and Black Tie (a sparkling wine)

Semi Dry Wines: Traminette, Riesling, We are Cayuga White, and Rattlehead Red

Sweet Wines: Vignoles, Afternoon Delight, Tickled Pink, All RAZZED Up, Blue Diamonds, and True Ice Wine

Fruit Wines: We are Blue-berry, Black Bear-y, Red Raspberry, Rhubarb, Black Raspberry, Strawberry, Yellow Jacket, Spiced Apple, and Cranberry

Port Style Wine: General Potter's Fort

The popularity of these wines, and medals earned, have allowed them to grow a little more. Recently, Scott and Mary Ann extended their "spa" by spreading out beyond the large wooden deck. The forest that surrounds the property provides a wonderful backdrop for Adirondack chairs, benches, picnic tables, and fire pits. Beyond that is a huge, level grassy area where they set up a massive tent for weddings and other functions – they even have an outdoor movie night there! Check the website often as they do all kinds of cool stuff, including live music.

On any given day, whatever the weather, whatever the occasion, alone, with a friend or friends, Seven Mountains Wine Cellars is an wonderful place to spend an enchanting afternoon or evening. The wines are exceptional, and the space is very hang-out-&-chill-out friendly. The staff is super friendly, down-home, and best of all – you can buy just a glass of wine if you want, or a whole bottle (which is a better deal). Either way, with your own BYOF snack or meal, you can enjoy it inside the winery, out on the deck, or under the trees on nice days or evenings.

Even on the sunniest days of summer, Seven Mountains Wine Cellars will make the day even brighter and better. And what about those gray days of winter? Well, when you go, I think you'll agree – Scott and Mary Ann should rename the place Seven Mountains Wine Spa. Take a deep breath, sip, and ...

Enjoy!

Country Cupboard
LEWISBURG, SNYDER COUNTY

It seems there is a common misconception that the Country Cupboard only caters to the elderly, and I must admit I was guilty of thinking that, too. Yes, this place is a mecca for seniors, but after a few visits and seeing all that goes on there - the flagship restaurant, the diversity of shops, how it all got started, finding out about the family who owns it, and finding out some amazing statistics, I realized some things, want to set the record straight, and confess my change of heart.

First of all, as I get older I've come to understand and agree with the saying "With age comes wisdom." You see, older folks have been around - they know crap us young upstarts don't. They don't mess around with all the high prices and fancy trappings of upscale restaurants - they go for good ol' fashioned country comfort food and a good value that they can enjoy whenever they want. Who do you think "Early Bird Specials" were invented for?

JUST A TASTE

Locally Owned By:
The Baylor Family

Cuisine:
Country Cooking

Price Range:
$3 to $16

Hours:
Sun. – Th. 7am to 8pm,
Fri. & Sat. 7am to 9pm

Location:
Rt. 15, 101 Hafer Rd.

Wi-Fi:
Yes

Contact Info:
(570) 523-3211,
www.countrycupboardinc.com

Vegetarian Offerings:
No

Supports Local Farmers:
Yes

**Locally Owned
Accommodations Nearby:**
Their own Best Western and
Country Inn & Suites next door;
Wood Cliff Cabin: www.vrbo.
com/306623#ownerprofile

Things To Do Nearby:
Shopping, Visitors Center, Downtown Lewisburg, The Campus
Theater, Bucknell University,
Antiques, River

Getting older and wiser is one thing, but another is that 2,500 to 3,000 customers a day can't be wrong. And if you think that's a lot, on Mother's Day they make approximately 5,500 meals! I exaggerate and make stuff up sometimes, but not those figures – they're from the Cupboard itself. Go there on any given day of the week and the parking lot is packed! And if you ever wondered where all those tour buses you see on the interstate go for breakfast, lunch, or dinner, it's probably the Country Cupboard. People love this place! Kids, teens, singles, young couples, 20 and 30 somethings, middle agers, and so on. My friend Nichole is in her 30s, very hip, and she would eat there every day if she could. Her husband and two girls love it too!

Yes, people of all ages, appetites, tastes, and interests come here. Why? Well, something else I realized was that it's not just a restaurant – it's an entire complex of interesting stuff. The area on which the restaurant sits actually contains two different restaurants, two accommodation options, a little picturesque lake, and the Susquehanna River Valley Visitors Bureau. Inside the Country Cupboard itself are many wonderful shops and even a bakery.

Check this out. There's a place called the Greenhouse (no explanation needed). The Flower Shop is a combination flower, gift, and card shop. The Specialty Foods shop has things like Asher's and Purity chocolates, homemade fudge, old fashioned candy, the Cupboard's own salad dressings, jellies, and jams. Celebrate the Seasons has candles, jewelry, bath stuff, scrapbooking stuff, craft supplies, Christmas doodads, plush animals, clothes, and accessories. The Country Home and Interiors shop features furniture, lighting, decorating accessories, kitchen linens, curtains, a Williraye Studio, and Boyd's Bears. I personally would steer clear of a few of those places, but a lot of the older gentlemen are there with their wives, because with age comes wisdom. Guys, if you don't understand now, you will.

For me, the best shop is called Country Delights Deli & Bakery. Here you'll find a fully stocked bakery with all kinds of goodies, from breads to pies to their self-proclaimed "World Famous Sticky Buns." I've had them and I would be hard pressed to find any other as good. There's also a deli where you can choose from a bunch of different meats and cheeses. Not only that, but you can get a deli sandwich to go or eat by the lake!

So, what about the food at the Country Cupboard? It's simply country cooking and folks love it. Rather than give my take, I'm going to let the Country Cupboard's own, very nice website tell you. "*Enjoy a hearty, country-cooked meal served from our sumptuous break-fast, lunch, or dinner buffet. Or order our original recipe roasted chicken - a favorite crowd pleaser in these parts since 1973! Perhaps you'll be tempted by our real country ham platter with the giant slice that will cascade over the edge of your plate. Or try one of our tasty Pennsylvania Dutch Pot Pie or Chicken & Waffles specials. Whatever you choose, don't forget to leave room for one of our made-from-scratch desserts...delicious!*" Now how could you not love that?

As they wrote, Country Cupboard has been around since 1973, and is truly a family owned and run business. It was started by Dan Baylor, who originally just wanted to open a farmers' market on his property. After a lot of hard work and listening to the wants and needs of his customers, Dan and his grandchildren (who have now taken over the business) have created more than a place for food, shopping, and accommodations; they've created an icon and a real point of interest.

I confess that I had a misconception of the Country Cupboard. It offers so many nice things, including good ol' fashioned county comfort food for all ages, and I think it's a wonderful place. The seniors had this place figured out right from the start. With age comes wisdom!

Enjoy!

Cherry Alley Café
LEWISBURG, UNION COUNTY

I've been here many times over several years because I love the place. I love the vibe, décor, food, and coffee. I also love the town. It's a university town (Bucknell) which means a great mix of young and old, students and teachers, professionals and good ol' workin' folks, tourists, and "townies." The architecture and downtown is absolutely beautiful. It's clear the community cares about things like preserving architecture and history, or making sure the little shops and services survive.

Lewisburg's Market Street (Rt. 45) is lined with nice shops, restaurants, galleries, an art supply store, the post office (which is a classic and beautiful), a wine and spirits store, cafés, and the coup de grâce, the Campus Theater. This movie house is a classic from the Art Deco era with couches, wing-back chairs, and coffee tables. They even allow BYOB! Think of it; you can take your sweetie to the theater and enjoy a movie on an authentic big screen while sipping a glass of wine. Very cool.

Something else that's very cool here is Cherry Alley Café. This is a wonderful place to go for coffee

JUST A TASTE

Locally Owned By:
Chris Wheeler & Jessie Yamas

Cuisine:
Café

Price Range:
$3 to $15

Hours:
Mon.-Wed. 7am to 6pm, Th.-Fri. 7am to 9pm, Sat. 8am to 9pm, Sun. 8am to 5pm

Location:
21 N. 3rd St.

Wi-Fi:
Yes

Contact Info:
(570) 524-1234, www.cherryalleycafe.com, Facebook page

Vegetarian Offerings:
Yes

Supports Local Farmers:
Yes

Locally Owned Accommodations Nearby:
Tawsty Flower B&B, Copperbeech B&B, Wood Cliff Cabin www.vrbo.com/306623#ownerprofile

Things To Do Nearby:
Shopping, Museums, Campus Theater (cool Art Deco-era movie house)

before a movie, before, after, or while shopping, after dinner or anytime. You can even go here for dinner, lunch, or breakfast. And that's just what I'm doing right now on a beautiful Friday morning – having breakfast, soaking in the sweet vibe, and writing this piece.

I'm sitting way in the back on an old sofa with an oriental rug under my feet and a big, funky coffee table on top of that. Large oil paintings are hanging to my left and right, and cool singer-songwriter style music is streaming in via satellite. Ahead of me is a long room filled with tables, and chatting folks fill most of them. At the far end, a big picture window provides a view of the neighborhood across the street. Free Wi-Fi is a given with all the laptops open, and there's even a grandma-aged woman having a Smoked Salmon Bagel and pecking away on what looks like Facebook from here. Funny.

Me, I'm just snuggled into my sofa and typing away, enjoying the cool music and the smells of espresso and home-cooked food in the air. It's a great vibe. I'm also enjoying the Tofu Scramble, which is tofu sautéed with onions, peppers, and spices. It's served with home fries and a choice of toast or mixed greens. Really good! Some other breakfast offerings at Cherry Alley Café are the aforementioned Smoked Salmon Bagel, Granola, Fruit & Yogurt, Eggs, French Toast and Pancakes, Crepes, and Omelets. Lunch and dinner offerings include: Build Your Own Deli Sandwiches, Marinated Steak, Grilled Chicken Pesto, Grilled Vegetable Panini, Grilled Tofu and Tempeh Wraps, Homemade Soups, Salads, sides, and even a kids' menu.

Now that I finished my delicious breakfast, I flipped over the menu to read something that made this place hit an even higher level of coolness. Here it is: "Cherry Alley Supports Local Foods. Here at Cherry Alley Café we offer tasty, healthful foods and drinks served in a friendly, stylish atmosphere. We operate with both the local and global communities in mind.

*We are active participants in the Pennsylvania Buy
Fresh, Buy Local program and support these local farms
and businesses.*

Tewksbury Grace Farms, Muncy
Folds Farm, Montandon
Dreamcatcher Farm, Lewisburg
Fisher's Meat Market, Lewisburg
Landis Poultry Farm, Watsontown
Catherman's Bakery, Lewisburg
Beaver Run Farms, Turboville
Martin Brothers Produce, Hummels Wharf
Golden Harvest Acres, Mifflinburg
Pocono Produce Co., Stroudsburg

*There is great music featuring various local musicians.
Local artists feature their work on our walls."*

Their Facebook page has this: *"Freshly Roasted Coffees!
Breakfast Everyday Until 3pm! Dinners Around the
World! Live Music! Local Artwork! All Farm Fresh Eggs!
Vegetarian/Vegan Friendly! Wi-Fi!"*

This is a wonderfully cool place in a wonderful town.
Please pay a visit to both. Not only will the town
welcome you, but Cherry Alley Café will embrace you
and send you home with a happy belly and warm heart.

Enjoy!

Cruiser's Café

MOUNT PLEASANT MILLS, SNYDER COUNTY

I found Cruiser's Café when I was looking for another place. Once I found it, I was delighted and disappointed at the same time – delighted because it's a really sweet little place with a really sweet atmosphere inside and out – disappointed because I had already eaten at the other place (which wasn't that great). Actually I wasn't too disappointed because I figured it would only be a matter of time before I'd return. On that trip, I planned to bring a posse of biking buddies with me because Cruiser's is a perfect destination for bikers, classic car owners, or anyone looking for an authentic retro-style '50s café. Well, as life goes sometimes, it was almost a year before I was able to return, and when I did it was without the posse. No worries, I was just glad to be there, and this time I was HUNGRY.

I pulled into the parking next to a Harley Road King, just as a guy was walking up to it. He asked if I was there for the fries, too. I said I didn't understand what he meant and he explained that Cruiser's had the best fresh-cut fries ever –

JUST A TASTE

Locally Owned By:
Joel Snyder

Cuisine:
American Diner

Price Range:
$1.90 to $6.45

Hours:
Mon. – Th. 11am to 8pm,
Fri. – Sun. 11am to 9pm

Location:
Intersection of 104 & 35

Wi-Fi:
No (But I picked it up from a place across the street)

Contact Info:
(570) 539-0043,
http://cruiserscafe.blogspot.com/

Vegetarian Offerings:
Yes

Supports Local Famers:
No

Locally Owned Accommodations Nearby:
Wood Cliff Cabin: www.vrbo.com/306623#ownerprofile

Things To Do Nearby:
Millersburg Ferry Boat
(717) 692-2442

so good that he rides two to three hours from Bethlehem, PA, for them. Impressive, I thought, but he didn't realize my French fry expertise – I could almost write a book about fries. Wait, I kinda did and kinda am. Looked like a French Fry Smack-Down was about to happen in Mount Pleasant Mills.

I asked this cat his name, and he told me Bob. I then asked Bob what else he recommended. To my surprise, he only had one other thing. Seems he comes all the way from Bethlehem for two things – fries and a milkshake. Now I was impressed! The cat rides up to three hours for fries and a shake – my kind of guy. He mounted his bike and was off. I wish I would have gotten his contact info because I would like to have let him know how much I enjoyed the place and how their fries held up to my "expert" standards.

Even though I'd been to Cruiser's that one other time, I had to walk around the outside again because it's just such a cool place. You know how some places try to pull off the '50s thing and it just ends up being cheesy? Well, Cruiser's is not cheesy by any means. What they did there is take an old-school corner gas station and convert it into a restaurant. It's got the carport deal sticking out the front, and the gas pumps are still in place! All around the outside are those cool tin signs advertising every-thing from oil to Coca-Cola. In fact the overall theme is Coca-Cola-ish. The inside is pretty much red and white – the colors of Coke.

The inside is small, which I feel adds to the sweet-ness of the place – you feel like you're a part of the whole scene. Two little café tables-for-two in the middle, six ice-cream-parlor-type stools at the counter, then only four small booths along the wall. I took a seat at the last booth so I could take it all in. It was a super nice day outside and Cruiser's does have a bunch of tables outside with umbrellas, but if I want to get the true vibe of a place, it's usually good to sit inside.

When my waitress arri-
ved, which only took two
seconds, and asked what
I wanted, I had no idea.
Like I usually do, I
asked her what they did
best. She said the
cheesesteaks were really
good and very popular.
That sounded great, and
I ordered the six-inch
version. When she asked
if I wanted anything

else, I was quick to ask for the fries that Bob
recommended. The error here was going for the small
order. I realized my mistake when my meal came –
not that the small was too small, but they were
sooo GOOD, that I wish I had the large size. Bob
was totally justified in a nearly three-hour ride
to eat these delicious fries! And my cheesesteak?
It was deelicious, and with the added fried peppers
and onions, it was as good as my waitress claimed.

As I sat there, I enjoyed the flow of locals and
travelers coming in and out for lunch or something
as simple as a shake or ice cream cone. That's right,
what's a '50s place if they don't serve ice cream?
They do here, and it's 16 flavors of Hershey's! Other
Cruiser's offerings are Burgers & Sandwiches, Salads,
Soup, Side Orders, Kiddie Kar Meals, Baskets, and Pies.

So what about the French Fry Smack-Down? Well, you're
gonna have to go and order a big ol' plate for yourself. Whether you drive three minutes or three hours,
it's worth it! Bob thought so, and hopefully you
will, too. Go check it out – it's very cool, the
staff is great, the vibe is sweet, and the décor
is old-school and authentic. Just like Coca-Cola,
Cruiser's Café is The Real Thing!

Enjoy!

Old Forge Brewing Co.
DANVILLE, MONTOUR COUNTY

I really think Danville should be called Manwhatanawesomeplace-toliveville. Why, you ask? Let's just start here with the Old Forge Brewing Company. This little brew pub in the historic downtown district is about as close to the subtitle for going LOCAL! as you can get – they have Unique Eats, it's a Cool Pub, and it's pretty Cozy. It also fits what the book is about – locally owned, and community supportive and supported. It also serves something close to my heart – locally minded and healthy food, and really great handcrafted beers.

The first time I visited, I walked in and immediately noticed a dude perched high on a ladder with his head down inside a brewing tank. I suspected he was the brewer, and from what I heard was also the owner. Since he was obviously busy, I asked a young woman who was busy taking care of customers if I could talk to someone about the place. She said, "That would be me." I just figured she was the manager, but when she said with a smile "I'm the boss, HE works for me,"

JUST A TASTE

Locally Owned By:
Damien & Maria Malfara

Cuisine:
Unique Fresh Pub Cuisine

Price Range:
$3.00 to $10.00

Hours:
Tue. – Th. 11am to 10pm,
Fri. – Sat. 11am to 12am,
Sun. 11am to 8pm

Location:
282 Mill St.

Wi-Fi:
Yes

Contact Info:
(570) 275-8151,
www.oldforgebrewingcompany.com

Vegetarian Offerings:
Yes

Supports Local Farmers:
Yes

Locally Owned Accommodations Nearby:
Doctors Inn B&B

Things To Do Nearby:
Knoebels Grove Amusement Park

and pointed to the guy in the tank, I figured she must have been his wife and co-owner. She politely asked if she could join me at the bar later. I said I wasn't going anywhere and took a seat at the bar and ordered up a pint of their Underbite IPA.

As I sat enjoying my IPA, I took an opportunity to go on the Old Forge website to get a little info beforehand. As it sometimes happens, they had a very nice About Us page on their site. So good, that I just had to include it.

"Old Forge Brewing Company is a fun, casual, comfortable brewpub, specializing in healthy pub fare and fresh brewed beer. Our country was built on the skills and labor of old-world artisanal craftsmen. Woodworkers, carpenters, stonemasons, ironworkers, blacksmiths, tile workers, and many others came here and employed the knowledge and skills of their craft in building their farms, homes, and towns.

Nowadays, it is so easy and convenient to purchase generic products from big-box stores, that we sometimes neglect to appreciate the uniqueness and quality of a hand-crafted product. At Old Forge Brewing Company, we strive to honor personal craftsmanship. Our hand-crafted beer is made in small batches to ensure quality and peak freshness, while the healthy and delicious menu has ingredients sourced from local farms and markets wherever possible. Take the time to notice our bar, furniture, and fixtures which were all handcrafted by local wood and metal worker Keith Kocher (Lightstreet Custom Woodworking). Check out our unique tap handles carved and forged by local artist/sculptor J. Mark Irwin (Irwin Sculpture Studio), and our plates, bowls, and beer mugs, all hand-made by local potter Mike Hart (M. Hart Pottery).

We welcome you to stop by and visit us on Mill Street in downtown Danville. Have a bite to eat, sip a fresh pint of beer, and enjoy the friendly and comfortable atmosphere. Leave your troubles on the doorstep and let us take care of the rest."

See what I mean?

Once the young woman who greeted me finished up her tasks, she came and sat down next to me at the bar. She introduced herself as Maria and called over to her husband, Damien, who emerged from the tank and joined us. The three of us had a great talk, and I asked them was how it was for them being married and working together. Maria said right away, "Really good! We really like each other!"

She said they have only been in business together for a couple years now but were so excited that things are going so well – the community is supporting them, and they're trying to support the community. I agreed and told her that I loved what was written on their website. I also told her and Damien that the word is definitely getting out beyond Danville, because of how many folks suggested I visit, and how many of my friends travel there for great food and beer. Speaking of great beer, here are just a few of Damien's handcrafted brews:

Classic Kolsch: A light-bodied, slightly dry, straw colored ale, with low hops.

T-Rail Pale Ale: An amber colored medium-bodied American pale ale.

Bellows Brown Ale: Medium-bodied, full-flavored, with a subtle roasted-chocolate malt flavor.

Underbite IPA: Traditional well-hopped English IPA.

Paradise Pilsner: Traditional Bavarian Pilsner – crisp, clean, mildly hoppy.

All Day Lager: A true session beer at 3.6% ABV – a great beer for hanging out all day!

These are just a sampling - Damien does many other
beers, as well as seasonal styles. With limited taps
and brewing capacity, all his beers rotate so they're
not always available. Don't be sad, this is the beauty
of small-batch handcrafted brews - they may be limited,
but they're always fresh!

Beside great handcrafted brews, Old Forge offers a
menu that's handcrafted and fresh as well...plus
good for you! Main menu items include Appetizers,
Salads, Soups, Cold Sandwiches, Hot Sandwiches, a
Kids' Menu, and a Sunday Brunch Menu. A few menu
items include: Soft Pretzels, Field Greens Salad,
Beer Chili, OFBC Ham and Cheese, Colossal Club Wrap,
The Big Jerk, and Grilled Spinach & Roasted Peppers.
The Sunday Brunch menu Offers things like Quiche
Du Jour, Frittata Du Jour, French Toast Sandwich,
Wrangler Wrap, Cajun Breakfast Burger, and the
Piggly Wrap, and more

I ordered what was on special that day, which was a
wonderful sandwich featuring grilled morel mushrooms
picked fresh that morning, and a delicious cup of
chicken soup. Maria, Damien, and I continued to talk,
and I spent a really nice afternoon with them. They
were so kind, and are so passionate about what they
do! They're running a wonderful business doing what
they love. And I, as well as their ever-expanding
family of customers, love what they do, too! This
place not only embraces so much of what this book
has in its subtitle, but what it's all about - going
local. Please stop by. You might even see Damien in
the brewing tank, and you will most likely see "his
boss" Maria taking care of business. But whether or
not you meet them, know that they are there somewhere
taking care of you.

With Old Forge Brewing Company in the 'hood, Danville
is definitely Manwhatanawesomeplacetoliveville!

Enjoy!

La Maison Blanche Bakery

DANVILLE, MONTOUR COUNTY

One of the sweetest memories from my childhood is going to the local bakery with my mom on Saturday mornings. Oh, the ecstasy my little self would experience as we approached and I got a whiff of the day's delights waiting for me inside! It wasn't until I was old enough to travel to Europe (France mostly) did I rediscover my childhood ecstasy for bakeries and the treats I enjoyed. Then one day I landed in Danville PA, and all those memories and trips abroad came together at a wonderful mom-and-pop bakery just next to the famed Geisinger Hospital.

I use the term "mom and pop" often for describing independently owned businesses. Most of the time it's neither a mom nor a pop at the helm, it's just a man or woman and usually they're not what I'd call mom-ish or pop-ish. However, this place is the real thing and very much like the bakery of my youth. Plus it's a bona fide mom and pop, and the closest thing

JUST A TASTE

Locally Owned By:
Jim & Pat Diehl

Cuisine:
Baked Goods

Price Range:
$.50 to $15.00

Hours:
"The door is always open."
Ring Bell & Self Serve

Location:
17 Poplar Street

Wi-Fi:
No

Contact Info:
(570) 275-2033

Vegetarian Offerings:
Yes

Supports Local Farmers:
Yes

Locally Owned Accommodations Nearby:
Doctors Inn B&B

Things To Do Nearby:
Knoebels Grove Amusement Park

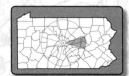

you'll get to the Boulangerie of my beloved France. Even its name, La Maison Blanche, means "The White House" in French.

That not only tells of its cultural influence and a hint to the baker's "other life," but of the building itself. It's actually a sweet little white house at the top of a street with an even sweeter little bakery in the basement. Mom and pop, Pat and Jim Diehl, live in the house above, and do business below. They've been doing this since 1996 after retiring as school teachers (Jim taught French for 30 years). The two make a lovely couple and a great partnership. Jim's the baker and Pat is his assistant, the greeter, sample giver-outer, and runs the register. He wears the classic all white pants, shirt, apron, and that tall baker's hat. Pat wears white too, but dons a red and white candy-stripe apron that couldn't be any cuter on her. They're classics, and of the school (like my mom and dad) that works hard and takes pride in their work.

So how did Jim go from French teacher to French baker? Did HE go to school? Well, if you ask him, which apparently a lot of people do, he's quick to say "Yeah, the school of Hard Knocks. I'm from a family of 15 and I was [baking] since I was eight years old." Jim went on to tell me what he could do at that age, but it was how he had to do it that he seemed most excited about. You see, he's got it pretty easy these days - back in those days he didn't have pro-fessional gas-heated ovens, he had an old wood stove. He had to load it full of wood, fire it up, and then once it reached proper temperature, he had to keep it there for the duration of the baking. Not an easy task for an adult, let alone an eight year old.

By the time he was a French teacher, he had become a master, and would use his baking skills to hone language skills in his students. He would bring his baked goods into class and have the kids identify each by their French names. He would also bring in a loaf of fresh baked bread and then assign the class 100 vocabulary words, and the first one who got all the words right would win the bread. "Oh, they'd go through their dictionaries like crazy trying to win that bread," he said. So it wasn't too difficult for Jim to transition out of teaching - he had a wonderful skill all ready to make a business out of.

Pat's history and contribution to the biz is that she was also a teacher in the area, and La Maison (the house) belonged to her parents. They purchased it in 1940, and Pat had lived there all her life. The two met in ninth grade, and were married in 1960. Pat's house was their house and would serve as the bakery too, as a "Home Occupation." It's a clean and well organized space, and is regularly inspected. The couple have three sons and 10 grandkids who love to help when visiting.

The day I was there, Pat kept giving me samples to try. They can't help themselves. If you ask about something, Jim can't just tell you about it, you have to try a piece. I made the mistake of having breakfast before I went there, and every time I asked him about his creations, I had to take a bite. And if that wasn't enough, the coup de grace came when Pat snuck away to the bread Jim had just taken out of the oven. A few seconds later she returned with a thick slice smeared with fresh butter and handed it to me to try. Well, how could anyone resist an adorable grandma-type dressed in a candy cane striped apron holding out a steaming piece of buttered bread? I couldn't. Talk about good! It melted in my mouth and was like eating a buttery cloud from heaven. I was hooked. Before I left I bought several loaves and many other treats! The Diehl's plan worked, and I felt like I was in Europe again.

This place is sweeeeeet – the house is sweet, the property is sweet (Jim and Pat spend hours making their yard like a show piece), Jim's baking is sweet, Pat is a total sweetie, and together the Diehls are a sweet couple. They love their customers so much that even if they're closed, they'll open up as long as they're at home. Jim told a reporter once, "If our car's here, you may come in." That's awesome, and yet another testimony to the business practices of the mom-and-pops. However, I imagine by how good their stuff is, if you don't get it while they're open (while it's hot), you're not getting it at all.

This is a wonderful place! It's a true mom-and-pop, and the closest thing you'll find to a Boulangerie de France. It has also renewed my childhood memories and love for baked goods. Best of all though, I no longer have to rely on those memories or travel to Europe – La Maison Blanche Bakery is local and I love it!

Enjoy!

Berwick Brewing Co.
BERWICK, COLUMBIA COUNTY

This amazing brewery/brewpub started out as One Guy Brewing. That's because the owner, operator, sole employee, and brewmaster were all one guy, AND his name was Guy! I loved that. It also started out only serving hot dogs, so it could be an officially state-sanctioned brewpub (barely). I loved that too! Now, only a few years later, it's got a partner, a staff of employees, has ditched the hot dogs in favor of handmade pizzas and other German beer garden fare, and is sporting a new name. So how did all this come about? And why are the beers at BBC the most authentic and deelicious beers this side of Germany? Read on, my friends.

In the summer of 2010, I enlisted the help of a friend and fellow beer geek to join me on a journey there. My friend Sam was not just great company, but actually got me an audience with Guy himself and his new partner, Tom Clark. We all hung out on a beautiful Saturday afternoon talking beer, drinking their amazing beers, and enjoying some great eats in the outdoor beer garden that overlooks the Susquehanna River. This afforded me a wonderful opportunity to get the inside scoop on all I mentioned earlier.

JUST A TASTE

Locally Owned By:
Guy Hagner & Tom Clark

Cuisine:
Pizza/Kielbasa

Price Range:
$1.00 to $10.00

Hours:
Tue. – Fri. 3pm to 11pm, Sat. 1pm to 11pm, Sun. 1pm to 7pm

Location:
328 W. Front St.

Wi-Fi:
Yes

Contact Info:
(570) 752-4313,
www.berwickbrewing.com,
Facebook

Vegetarian Offerings:
Yes

Supports Local Farmers:
Yes

Locally Owned Accommodations Nearby:
The White Birch Inn B&B
(570) 759-8251

Things To Do Nearby:
Here – Okoberfest in Fall, Rickett's Glen and Worlds End State Parks, Historic Society, Fly Fishing

Like many brewers, Guy Hagner started out his career in the biz as a home brewer – and as he puts it "with only marginal success." It wasn't until he traveled to Germany in 1980, during college, that his knowledge and desires started to expand. There in the German countryside of Franconia (northern Bavaria), he learned to really appreciate the beer-making process and the love the German people had for their local brews. Every town had a brewery, and the people supported it. The beer was wonderful and the community was happy.

Guy returned to the states with a whole new appreciation of brewing, beer quality, community support, and the brewing business itself. He thought to himself, "This is what I want to do... I'd love to create a small local brewery where people come, hang out, and enjoy a pleasant day in a beer garden."

After he graduated, he took jobs in various breweries which gave him an inside look at the beer making process and biz. After that, he sent himself to brewing school at the Siebel Institute in Chicago, did his apprenticeship, and was then hired at The Lion Brewery in Wilkes-Barre. After that Guy started a brewery in the Poconos called Franconia Brewing Company. Unfortunately Franconia didn't make it – a few other circumstances caused that, but it certainly wasn't because of the beer quality.

My friend Sam Komlenic is not just a beer geek, he's like a Jedi Master of the beer world! Here's what he said about Guy's beer-making skills back in the day. "To this day, other than the beers we're drinking here, the most German tasting domestically brewed beer I ever had came from Franconia Brewing Co. You could drink their Bamberger Pils and have no idea you were not drinking something that was brewed in Germany. It tasted like a German beer. And it's the only German tasting beer I ever had that came in a bottle from the United States." Guy very humbly said, "Thank you."

So with great authentic German beers on his resume,
and a better understanding of the biz, Guy tried again
and opened One Guy Brewing Co. in Berwick. Where
Franconia was strictly a production brewery and therefore only able to sell beer by the case or keg, this
new place would be a brewpub and allow Guy to be
able to share his gift by the glass. This was made
possible back around the '90s by the PLCB so that
breweries could sell by the glass as long as they
served food as well. This was a huge break but also
created a hurdle in that the breweries that wanted
to do that now had to be a restaurant too. Or did they?

Guy Hagner is no dummy. What he offered at One Guy
was hot dogs - just hot dogs, and that was pretty
much only in theory. He had them, but only enough
to adhere to the PLCB law, which required enough to
supply the average number of customers. Guy would
actually discourage his customers from ordering hot
dogs because they weren't that good and he didn't
want to be bothered - he wanted to brew beer.

What he did encouraged though was for customers to BYOF (Bring Your Own Food). This was brilliant, and freed Guy to concentrate on what he did best – make the best tasting beer this side of Bavaria, and sell it by the glass.

This worked out great for awhile, but now Guy was making beers that were as good as or better than in his Franconia years. Well, in the beer geek world, once this kind of news hits the streets, you can pretty much forget about trying to own, operate, and be the brewmaster all-in-one. Guy had already taken on help in the pub to try to keep up, but what he really needed was an all-around expert in the brewing biz, a fellow brewer, a fix-it man, and somebody to help take the brewpub to where it is now and will go into the future. Enter Tom Clark.

If I thought Sam was a Jedi Master, Tom is that and Renaissance man combined. The dude knows his beer, plus, he knows brewing equipment (I bet he could assemble and repair an entire brew house blindfolded). He brews, manages, does the marketing and advertising, builds stuff, and maintains the entire facility (which was an old abandoned bakery, and probably a nightmare).

Now with Tom on board, a dedicated staff, and all working together, it was no longer just one guy – it was time for a name change. One Guy is now Berwick Brewing Co. With a new name came a new and improved menu – it doesn't take much to improve on hot dogs.

BBC acquired a pizza oven, and is now making killer pizza! They also offer Landjäger, which is a German-style smoked and cured hard sausage, and Hungarian Kielbasa. Hot dogs are great beer food, but that lineup is WAY better! And what's great beer food without a great line-up of beers?

Here's the line-up at BBC the day we were there:

Berwick Lager: A straight-up local lager

Front Street Wheat: A German style wheat, or "Hefe-Weizen"

Grumpy Bill's Porter: A Porter created for Tom's dad, who loves dark beer

Hondo: A German Keller Bier brewed with Tettnang hops and German malt

Atomic Punk IPA: A very hoppy beer made with American, Simcoe, Cascade, and Amarillo hops

Vaughn's Cream Ale: A very nice and smooth ale named for the bread made in the old bakery

BBC also brews seasonal and specialty beers.

That wonderful summer afternoon, Guy and Tom treated Sam and me to an equally wonderful time. Their time and generosity was the perfect match to their amazing beers and excellent food. Guy has come a long way from his solo days, but what he wanted to achieve after his travels to Germany has been realized. "This is what I want to do... I'd love to create a small local brewery where people come, hang out, and enjoy a pleasant day in a beer garden." We sure did, and you can too.

Prost!

CHAPTER 4
4 O'CLOCK

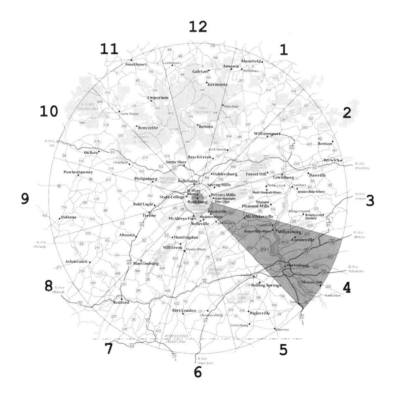

The Bread of Life Restaurant
MCALISTERVILLE, JUNIATA COUNTY

I had heard about The Bread of Life from a fan of my first book. He said it was off in the countryside of Juniata County, and a great place to eat. So, on a sunny Saturday morning after a week of gray skies, and feeling a bit stressed and overwhelmed, I hopped on the bike to clear my head and soul. I was also hungry and needed to get a good breakfast, and hopefully find a great place for my new book. After a beautiful ride out Rt. 35, I pulled into the parking lot, shut down the bike, and walked into a packed house. I found a seat at the counter and was quickly greeted by a friendly young woman who handed me a menu.

While I looked it over, I noticed how many of the features had biblical references (this made sense because their sign bears a cross, and the guy who told me about the place mentioned the owner was a Christian). For example some of the menu items were: Heavenly Manna Mushrooms, Red Sea Fries, and 12 Tribes of Israel (onion rings). Most of the salads are named after noted women of the Bible, like Esther, Hannah, and Lydia. Specialty Sandwiches include the

JUST A TASTE

Locally Owned By:
Greg Spece & sons Nick and Gabe

Cuisine:
American

Price Range:
$.50 to $18.99

Hours:
Tue. – Th. 6am to 8pm,
Fri. & Sat. 6am to 9pm

Location:
30644 Rt. 35 N.

Wi-Fi:
No

Contact Info:
(717) 463-2838,
bolrestaurant@yahoo.com

Vegetarian Offerings:
Yes (By Request)

Supports Local Farmers:
No

Locally Owned Accommodations Nearby:
General Evans House,
(717) 535-4398

Things To Do Nearby:
Scenic Drives, Amish Stores, Golf

Samson Burger, Paul's Panini, and Jeremiah's Hot Roast Beef. This next is classic but a bit confusing – the Clubs are named Shadrach, Meshach and Gideon. Gideon? I thought it was Shadrach, Meshach & Abednego. Oh well, Gideon was a great guy, and that club involved a cheeseburger and bacon. (John the Baptist Bacon, perhaps?)

Main course dinners are all lumped under the heading of "Manna" where they offer Steak, Chicken, Ham, Liver & Onions (gulp), Fish, and Shrimp. "Lighter Manna" has most of the previous, but in smaller portions. In the dessert selections, they return to the creative descriptors like Footprints in the Sand (vanilla ice cream smothered in hot fudge and marshmallow, then dusted with graham cracker crumbs and topped with whipped cream), Heavenly Cheesecake, and Garden of Eden (vanilla ice cream rolled in cinnamon-roasted pecans and surrounded by apples, then smothered in hot caramel and topped with whipped cream). Yum! They also offer a selection called Martha's Frozen Creme 'n Sugar which is a locally-made ice cream by Hall's.

By this time, I was getting really hungry, and thank goodness it wasn't biblical times, because dried fish and unleavened bread just wouldn't have cut it. But there before my eyes was exactly what would – the Daily Special – a big ol' Belgian waffle with a side of scrambled eggs and bacon! They offer many other breakfast items including baked oatmeal, which is one of my favorites. But the waffle won, and I placed my order accompanied by a cup of 50¢ coffee. To my delight, they served Rich Coast, which in my humble opinion is the best restaurant-grade coffee there is.

While I waited for my breakfast, a sweet older lady strolled in and went right behind the counter. My waitress said, "Hey Gram! How are you today?" I thought this must be the owner and the girl was her granddaughter. Turns out she's the mom of the real owner, and everyone calls her "Gram," whether or not they're related.

Gram was cool, and I had a chance to speak with her. She told me her son, Greg, had dreamed of opening a restaurant for 20 years. He and his best friend were going to open it together, and planned for it while Greg cooked at a truck stop down the road. Greg's friend Cliff Geesaman worked in construction at this time, and one day while on the roof of a house, bumped the main electrical wires and was killed. In honor of his friend, Greg didn't give up. He pursued their dream of opening their own place alone, and with Cliff's wife there for the event, Greg opened The Bread of Life Restaurant and dedicated it to his friend and now eternal partner.

Gram said being in the restaurant biz was in Greg's blood, because his grandfather and great grandfather were restauranteurs. Greg keeps the place spotless and the service and atmosphere are friendly and welcoming. There's a very nice vibe there - one of caring and concern, which made sense when Gram told me that Greg travels to India on mission trips annually to help the poor and underprivileged. Restaurant life is busy enough as is - this guy sets apart time, money, and management, to help others in a land very far away and very much in need.

When my breakfast arrived, I saw the biggest, most delicious looking Belgian waffle in front of me, and I tore into that sucker like a wild dog that hadn't eaten for days. Let me just say here and now that was *the* best waffle I ever had!

After a wonderful breakfast and chat with Gram, I got a refill of coffee and sat back to take it all in. I thought to myself that this place was a keeper for sure. The Bread of Life Restaurant provided me with more than great food for my stomach - it provided me with food for my soul. The prior week had me stressed and overwhelmed, but this place had me well on my way to a whole new attitude. The guy who told me about it was right - this is a great place to eat. For me, it was a blessing as well, and one I can't wait to return to.

Enjoy!

My Little Big Adventure across the Mighty Susquehanna

This is not a place to eat or drink—well, I imagine you could eat or drink here if you BYOB and BYOF, and actually they do offer a Beer and Pizza Party in August, but it's not a restaurant, pub, or café. But this is my book and I can include whatever I want—especially if it's AWESOME, and something you just don't see much or experience these days so you've got to check it out.

I travel a lot, and I meet a lot of people. So I don't always remember cool places that I'm told about. But after looking at my map one evening and plotting a course for a ride which required crossing the Susquehanna River, I noticed a tiny dashed line with the letters FY. Seeing that, I remembered someone telling me about a ferry boat that makes daily trips across the river between a campground on the west bank and Millersburg on the east bank. How cool and how convenient, because as the map shows, the only bridges across the river in that region are about 35 miles apart. The idea of crossing the river there made sense, and crossing a river by ferry boat seemed like an adventure that I couldn't pass up.

The next day I asked my friend David, aka McC (McCormick), to join me. With him on his Yamaha Road Star, and me on The Steed, I led the way and set a course that would take us through some beautiful country to end up just south of Liverpool at a campground along Rts. 11 & 15 called Ferryboat Campsites. Warning, it's not directly accessible from the north or via Rt. 34 that ends there at 11 & 15 from the west. You actually have to go south a little, exit off and re-enter 11 & 15 to the north. It's no big twig, just a little confusing.

Ferryboat Campsites is really nice! They offer a wonderful variety of outdoor activities, community recreation, weekly events (spring through fall), a mile of picturesque views of the river, 285 wooded and semi-wooded campsites, satellite TV, Wi-Fi, comfort stations with hot showers, game room, boating, fishing and other water activities, Sunday worship service, 18 hole mini-golf, laundromat, cabins, and a really cool store called the Paddlewheel Store.

We rolled in to the dock area and the first thing I noticed was an old white door hinged to a big oak tree next to the dock. Written with black paint on it were the words "Swing Out To Call Ferry." Just as I swung it out, McC said he could see the ferry boat coming into view. Wow, it was a real paddlewheel ferry boat! It was painted red and had a low profile with a main cabin for the wheelworks, engine, captain's bridge, and a little open (but covered) seating area for passengers. Alongside that was a long wooden-planked deck for the vehicles to come aboard and disembark. We then watched as the captain skillfully and gently glided the ferry in to the dock. Two boys who looked like they were working a summer job on high school vacation helped to get the ramp to line-up, and jumped off to tie it off and secure it before the two cars aboard pulled off.

As we rolled on to the deck, I felt like I was rolling back in time. This ferry boat was sooo cool! Once our bikes and an SUV behind us were aboard, the boys untied the boat and pushed it back out into the water.

MAP

Our captain engaged the sternwheel in reverse, spun the boat around, re-engaged forward, and off we went. If it wasn't for the bikes and SUV, I would have sworn it was the 1800s. What an awesome way to cross a river! McC and I just stood still and took it all in. After we were offshore a little way, our captain, whose name was Tom Mallonee, called all of us together for a little safety presentation. After that, he told us about our boat, The Roaring Bull, along with a great bit of history. For $3.00 I not only got passage across the mighty Susquehanna River, but felt like Lewis and Clark, learned some history, and had the time of my life.

As we approached the east bank at Millersburg far to the upstream side of the dock, Captain Tom cut the engine back to idle speed but engaged the paddlewheel in reverse. The boys went forward, and with super long wooden poles stuck down in the water to the bottom, gently pushed the bow around. Captain Tom then allowed the current, combined with slow reverse of the paddles to continue to turn the ferry completely around and right into the dock—sweet! We rolled off one at a time with Captain Tom waving goodbye.

McC was to ride home from there and take the bridge across at Sunbury, leaving me to continue my journey east. But he, like me, enjoyed the ferry so much that he decided to take it back. However by that time the ferry was already reloaded and had cast-off. I immediately called for a debriefing of the river crossing adventure over a cold beer at a nice place in Millersburg. I took him to Wayne's, a very cool place right next to the railroad tracks and the historic Millersburg Train Station. We each had a Tröegs from right down the river in Harrisburg in frosty mugs and talked about how awesome our little big adventure had been.

Folks, no matter your age or gender, you've got to take a trip across the Susquehanna aboard the Millersburg Ferry. It's been added to the prestigious National Register of Historic Sites, and is something you should do – at least once. Stay at Ferryboat Campsites and ride as a passenger for $2.00 and walk to Wayne's (two short blocks) for a beer, lunch or dinner – I say all three! Or take your bike or car and a picnic – there's a really nice little park on the east shore at Millersburg overlooking the dock and river. The Paddlewheel Store has stuff to eat and you can picnic there, which is a beautiful spot (with bathrooms only a few steps away). Have fun and...

Enjoy your Little Big Adventure!

Opens seasonally May through October as water conditions allow.

The ferry connects the town of Millersburg with an adjacent landing in Perry County on Route 15 about 2 miles south of Liverpool at Ferryboat Campsites.

Ferryboat Campsites offers the finest in fun-filled family camping blended with a variety of outdoor activities and community recreation. There are 285 completely modern campsites nestled amid lush shade trees overlooking the beautiful Susquehanna River at one of its widest points. Endless hours of excellent fishing, boating, and water activity are but a few steps from every site.

Historic Millersburg is a quaint town with unique shops, fine dining, bed and breakfast accommodations, art galleries, heritage museum, and golf resort. Ferry souvenirs are available at the Millersburg Information Center located in the Old Train Station on Center Street.

Each ferry accommodates 4 vehicles and 50 passengers. Private charters available for reunions, birthdays, anniversaries, school groups, receptions, etc. Catering services offered.

Daily Schedule: Saturday and Sunday from 1st weekend in May through October, 9:00 a.m. until dusk. Weekdays from June 2nd to and including Labor Day, 11:00 a.m. until 5:00 p.m.

Fares: One-way "walk on passenger," $2.00; Autos, $6.00 (includes driver's fee); Motorcycle and rider, $3.00

For pricing information, brochures, reservations and/or charter bookings can be obtained by phoning the business office.

Millersburg Ferry Boat Association
P.O. Box 93
Millersburg, PA 17061
Phone: (717) 692-2442

Millersburg launch:
From Harrisburg, 22-322 W to 147 North to Millersburg
From Sunbury, Rt. 147 South to Millersburg

Ferryboat Campsites Campground launch:
From Harrisburg, 11&15 N – approx. 8 miles from Amity Hall
From Selinsgrove, 11&15 S – approx. 2 miles south of Liverpool

Carsonville Hotel
CARSONVILLE, DAUPHIN COUNTY

You've heard it said "It's not about the destination, but the journey." I say, give me both! The journey (detailed in the previous story) here was not that long, but certainly one I would call epic. It had all the elements, including this great destination, which made for a wonderful and needed end to a wonderful and needed journey. Life can get so stressful and overwhelming sometimes, so it's good to bust out and see where the road can take you. This day I was taken to the Carsonville Hotel.

(For The Rest of the Story go to **www.goingLOCALpa.com/TRS**)

Appalachian Brewing Company
HARRISBURG, DAUPHIN COUNTY

I've been visiting Appalachian Brewing Company (ABC) for a number of years and am still blown away every time I go. This wonderful place - its building, huge interior, décor, layout, different levels, and overall sweetness, is what I think of when I think of a great city brewpub. Well, I also think of brewing great beer and serving great food too, of course, and fortunately ABC does both, and does them well!

Let's start with the building itself. The huge old structure sits on Cameron Street and is a stone's throw from the PA State Farm Show complex. It's a three-story brick place built around 1915. The original purpose isn't clear, but in the 1920s and '30s the Auchenbach Printing Co. occupied the building. However, the ABC's lagering room dates back to 1890, when it was owned by the Harrisburg Passenger Railway Co. In the '30s the building was almost completely destroyed by fire, and in 1993 another fire rendered the building useless.

JUST A TASTE

Locally Owned By:
Artie Tafoya, Jack Sproch, Shawn Gallagher

Cuisine:
Innovative Pub Cuisine

Price Range:
$4.00 (beer) to $18.00

Hours:
Sun. – Th. 11am to 11pm,
Fri. & Sat. 11am to 12pm;
Abbey Bar 5pm to 1:30am daily

Location:
50 North Cameron Street

Wi-Fi:
Yes

Contact Info:
(717) 221-1080,
www.abcbrew.com/harrisburg

Vegetarian Offerings:
Yes

Supports Local Farmers:
Yes

Locally Owned Accommodations Nearby:
Milestone Inn, (717) 233-2775

Things To Do Nearby:
Brewery tour on premise
Saturdays at 1pm

In July of 1995, a restoration project began, and in 1997, ABC opened its doors. It's beautiful now. Part of the beauty (for me at least) is the size of the interior space and the elements that make it up. Huge windows, massive wood

beams and joists, giant support columns, ultra high ceilings, and behind the long bar and part of the seating area are the enormous brewing tanks. Don't get me wrong, I love cozy, but there's just something beautiful about a huge old structure that's been made into a brewpub.

Upstairs is the Abbey Bar, and again, it's beautiful. Honestly, I'm not sure which I like more, the first floor or second. The Abbey bar has a really nice bar, three pool tables, a performance stage, a banquet room off to the end (which is very nice for private gatherings), and access to a sweet rooftop patio open to the sky above and surrounding city below. BUT, what makes the Abbey Bar extra wonderful is a cooler behind the bar that contains the mother-lode of Belgian beers! At last count, I estimated over 50! Everything from Abbey style to Witbier, to one of my most faves, La Chouffe Belgian Golden Ale. But this is a true microbrewery and they brew amazing beers in-house for year-round enjoyment at the pub or wherever quality beers are served and sold. They also brew their own Root Beer, Ginger Ale, and an amazing lineup of seasonal specialty beers by the month. Here are just a few of their flagship beers offered year round:

Purist Pale Ale: A light copper version of a classic English pale ale style beer, with a delicate malt attribute balanced by an aggressive hop flavor and aroma.

Water Gap Wheat: An unfiltered wheat beer or Witbier style ale, traditionally served with a lemon slice.

Mountain Lager: This is a Dortmunder-Export style (whatever that means) of beer developed in Westfalen, Germany, and is a classic light lager with great character that's rich yet mellow.

Susquehanna Stout: Named for the mighty Susquehanna River nearby, this classic Irish Dry Stout has a smooth roasty flavor due to the use of specially roasted barley and is so dark it's almost opaque.

Hoppy Trails India Pale Ale: A very hoppy IPA loaded with extra hops, giving it wonderful hop flavor and floral aroma.

The food here is great, too. Every meal I've had (and I've had a bunch) has been great – their menu is four pages and includes headings like Fun Appetizers, Homemade Soups, Brew A Salad, Homemade Handhelds, Black Angus Burgers, Brewery Entrées, Hand-Tossed Pizza and Bolis, ABC Originals, and Desserts.

Overall, food included, this place is really great! Appalachian Brewing Company is a beer geek's haven and a place food lovers will enjoy, too. Truth be known, I'm sitting here right now enjoying a lovely Peregrine Pilsner with Artie Tafoya, Director or Operations and Brewmaster at ABC. He just got done guiding me and a bunch of folks on a brewery tour and, wow, what a great tour! Having the brewmaster do the tour is the way to go. He really knows his stuff and is totally passionate about the beer making process, which makes all the difference.

During our talk together he informed me of something I wasn't aware of. I knew that ABC had two satellite locations, but I assumed they didn't brew there – I thought the main brewery here in Harrisburg did all the brewing. Artie told me that's partly true, as they brew all the flagship beers here, but the Camp Hill location as well as the Gettysburg location do all their own specialty brews. In fact, ABC Camp Hill hosts a home brewers competition every year, in which home brewers from all over the country compete. Judges pick the top three beers, and the winner gets his or her beer brewed by ABC to be bottled and distributed throughout their region!

ABC is, as I stated, a wonderful place housed in a huge old historic building. But what's even more huge is what's at the heart of this brick and wood microbrewery and brewpub - a true revitalization of not only an old city building, but the dedication to brewing great beer, offering great Belgian beers, serving great food, and providing a great gathering place for the surrounding community and visitors like me.

Enjoy!

HARRISBURG

Pennsylvania's capital since 1812. As Harris' Ferry, was settled a century before by John Harris Sr. Laid out as a town in 1785 by John Harris Jr. For over 200 years a center of travel, trade, and historic events.

PENNSYLVANIA HISTORICAL AND MUSEUM COMMISSION

BUBE'S BREWERY
MOUNT JOY, LANCASTER COUNTY

OK, this is one of the coolest places I've ever been! Seriously, I've been to a lot of cool places, including many places in Europe, and this one is among

the best of them all. I almost don't know where to start. Why? Because it's more than a brewpub; it's a tavern, fine dining restaurant, banquet facility, dinner theater, art gallery, inn, museum, souvenir shop, and just an amazing and awesome place! Between all that, and the different layers and levels, you could easily get lost here. But believe me, you'll never enjoy getting lost so much - especially if you hook-up with a wench like I did recently.

I first discovered this place for myself back in the '90s when a group of friends and I headed to Bube's for a Medieval Feast. When we got there, we were escorted down a steep narrow stone stairway by a wench - seriously, it was a woman dressed like a middle-ages prostitute. Not only was she in period garb, but had a colloquial British accent. She was a bit crass (hey, she's a wench) but delightful and

JUST A TASTE

Locally Owned By:
Sam and Jan Allen

Cuisine:
Eclectic

Price Range:
$3.50 to $39

Hours:
Lunch Mon. – Sat. 11am to 5pm,
Sun. 12pm to 5pm
Dinner Mon. – Th. 5pm to 10pm,
Fri. – Sun. 5pm to 11pm
Bar Mon. – Sat. 11am to 2pm,
Sun. 12pm to 2am

Location:
102 North Market Street

Wi-Fi:
No

Contact Info:
(717) 653-2056

Vegetarian Offerings:
Yes

Supports Local Farmers:
Yes

**Locally Owned
Accommodations Nearby:**
The Olde Square Inn,
(717) 653-4525

Things To Do Nearby:
Touring Amish Country, Antiquing

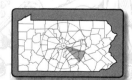

fun, and set the tone for a most memorable evening. Speaking of wenches, on a more recent visit I got up-close and personal with another one.

It was after an all-day killer hot ride that I ended up in Mt. Joy at Bube's Brewery for a beer and dinner. Since it had been so long, I was kinda lost about where to go in. I finally decided to go in through a door at the top of a small set of stairs, which turned out to be exactly the right door to choose because that's when I met the wench. Actually she wasn't a wench (at the time) but she was only an hour away from becoming a Victorian lady of high society involved in a murder plot that was going to take place in the old hotel above our heads. So why was this "exactly the right door to chose?" Please read on.

I love moments like this. I walked in the door hot, sweaty, and grimy from a 125+ mile ride and thoroughly confused about where I was going or what I was doing –

all I wanted was a cold beer. The Victorian lady-to-be introduced herself as Lori, and by her charm, and welcoming and fun personality, I thought for sure she was the owner. She politely informed me that this was the upstairs dining entrance and asked if I was there for the murder. Eyes big, I said "Uh, no, I just need a cold beer for now, thanks." She laughed and said, "Follow me!"

I don't know how this stuff happens to me. Some may say it's luck, others karma, and yet others say it's just being in the right place at the right time. I say it's the blessings of God first, and then just doing what I do (and encourage you to do) - letting go, being open, and embracing all that comes along. Lori proceeded to take me on a private tour of Bube's that must be similar to what visiting dignitaries get.

First she escorted me upstairs to the old hotel part of the building which is now called the Alois Restaurant - named for Alois Bube (great name), a young German immigrant who bought the brewery in 1876. He died in 1908 at the age of 57, and the brewery closed just before the start of prohibition in 1920. This level of the building is sooo beautiful, and was left totally intact. Everything from the wallpaper, ceilings, woodwork, trim, furnishings, and mirrors, to the awesome bar were amazing (there's even a hidden room where the women had to gather while the men hung out in the bar)! The Alois was where Lori performed later along with the Bube's acting troupe for a Murder Mystery Dinner Theater.

Next she took me down some steps, through some hallways and back down to street level to show me the Bottling Works - a restaurant and tavern in the original bottling plant of the brewery. Lori told me this was where the beer was bottled and the water for making the beer was drawn from limestone caverns below (my mouth was watering at this point and if she wasn't so sweet to be taking me on this tour, I would have ditched her right there and then and headed to the wonderful line-up of taps calling out to my parched throat). This part of the place is _____ing awesome! You just can't recreate or build something like this.

Lori then showed me to the outdoor Biergarten. Wow, it was like a combo Garden of Eden and drinking garden from Bube's Bavarian homeland! In the middle of it was a huge original boiler and smokestack used to create the steam power necessary to run the brewery back in the day.

Next, she took me to the in-house microbrewery itself (key part of that word being micro). The brewery is tiny - I mean like the size of my kitchen. Actually this was cool because the brewer can brew in small batches and therefore keep a nice selection rotating often. Here are the "usual suspects" brewed for The Bottling Works:

Kolsch: Clean, crisp, easy drinking, Colonge, Germany style ale.

Red Ale: Slightly sweet malt flavor balanced with East Kent Golding hops.

Stout: Full-bodied stout is perfect with a meal or as a meal.

Brown Ale: Pleasantly malty with nutty, toffee-like undertones.

Heffweizen: Traditional German-style wheat beer

India Pale Ale: Classic IPA style made with fine 2-row malted barley and west coast hops.

From there, we went down about a story below the street to a place with huge wooden tanks where Alois would ferment the beer before sending it to be lagered several more stories below. But along the way, through what appeared to be a tunnel carved by hand, we came to an open area (also seemingly carved out) that acts as their gallery, where they feature the works of fine artists.

Winding our way beyond the gallery, and now totally surrounded by carved-out limestone, we came to the top of an unlit stairway going down into total darkness. Lori reached for an old antiquated light switch, flicked it, and the stairway lit up with a beautiful glow. Before me was like a stairway to heaven but going down, not up. If I were a kid (or an older cat with a bladder control problem) I would have wet myself with excitement. Now, all the memories of the Medieval Feast came flooding back, because we were heading down to where it all took place - the famed Bube's Catacombs! This place is sooo cool!

Cool indeed, as we descend 43 feet into the stone-lined vaults where Alois lagered his beer. Here is where the Feasts take place. A few steps up into another catacomb you will find a unique fine dining exper-ience, with a menu that includes a variety of traditional and gourmet dishes. A costumed guide will greet you and lead you on a tour of the brewery on your way to dinner. Here you can sit among giant fermenting tanks under low lighting, and in probably one of the most unique dining areas I've ever experienced. Here are just a few of what you can order in the catacombs: Stuffed Mushroom Caps with Crabmeat, Crabmeat Stuffed Lobster Tail, Roast Duckling with Raspberry Citrus Sauce, Chicken Costello, Mediterranean Veal with Lemon, Steaks, and many more fine dining entrées.

Lori and I then climbed the long stone stairway back to the Bottling Works and the main entrance. From there, we climbed a set of wooden steps to a level somewhere between all the rest where they have a retail shop. Again, like everything else in this grand old building, it looked like nothing had changed in over 100 years - sooo cool. Lori then had to bid me good-bye and prepare for her performance at the Mystery

Dinner Theater. I must have thanked her ten times for the wonderful personal tour and asked if she was the owner. She laughed and said, "No, but I'll be your wench any day." We both laughed, and she disappeared through another passageway.

I headed straight for the Bottling Works, ordered a cold glass of Kolsch at the bar from Bill, picked a table along the wall, and just took it all in. This is truly one of the most awesome places around – maybe in the state, maybe in the country – I could write 100 times more than what I did. I can't emphasize enough how cool it is here, and how much I encourage you to visit. Whether you go for a handcrafted beer, pub food, a fine dining evening in the catacombs, a Medieval Feast, Dinner Theater, or just to get lost, you will not regret it. And if you are fortunate enough to get a personal tour from Lori, aka "Kitty, the Wench," you will not forget it.

Bube's is a one of a kind place – one of the coolest places I've ever been.

Enjoy!

CHAPTER 5
5 O'CLOCK

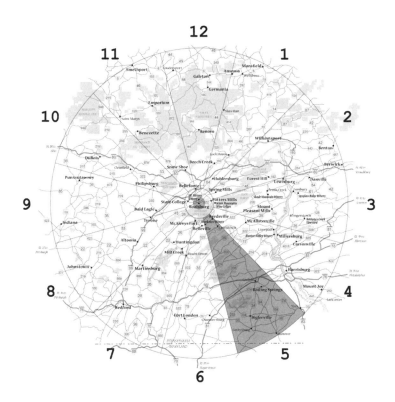

Reedsville Seafood Co.
REEDSVILLE, MIFFLIN COUNTY

It's no secret that PA is landlocked. Therefore, it makes sense that there's no direct access to the sea and the bounty of food it provi-  des - until now. No, New Jersey didn't suddenly fall off the continent (too bad) making the Delaware Water Gap become the Delaware Beach. No, but a wonderful little seafood shop and bistro has washed ashore in the little country town of Reedsville.

I first found out about this pearl of the sea from a good friend, fellow writer, mentor, and foodie - Jack Williams. Back in 2009, he sent me this email:

"Ken, you have to check this place out: Reedsville Seafood Company. Though they've been selling fresh fish from Baltimore and Boston for 7 years, their restaurant opened up just two weeks ago. We just had lunch there and it is fantastic. Great sandwiches, best seafood chowder this side of Boston, home-made potato chips, and great folks. Haven't tried it for breakfast yet, but we will be doing so soon. Nice ambiance too."
Jack & Nan

The next week, I got another email from a couple who bought a copy of my first book, asking if I had been to the Reedsville Seafood Company. They confirmed

JUST A TASTE

Locally Owned By:
Bart & Tracy Ewing

Cuisine:
Rustic Bohemian

Price Range:
$1.50 to $10.00

Hours:
Wed. & Th. 11am to 9pm,
Fri. & Sat. 9am to 9pm

Location:
20 North Main Street

Wi-Fi:
Yes

Contact Info:
(717) 667-6084,
www.reedsvilleseafood.com

Vegetarian Offerings:
Yes

Supports Local Farmers:
Yes

**Locally Owned
Accommodations Nearby:**
The Briar Rose B&B
(717) 667-6795

Things To Do Nearby:
Reedsville/Belleville Market
and Belleville Sale Barn on
Wednesdays, Antiquing,
Touring Big Valley

Jack's take AND had breakfast there and said it was "amazing!" Amazing? I've had some very good breakfasts in my day, but very few would I rightly call amazing. The timing was perfect – it was Friday morning, it was a beautiful day, I was hungry, and desperately trying to come up with something to get me out of the breakfast rut of egg sandwiches or cereal I had gotten myself into. Barely taking time to close my laptop, I immediately packed my stuff, jumped on the bike, and took off for Reedsville.

At the corner of Main and Railroad streets, I came upon an old building with those big, classic picture windows through which I could see folks milling about inside. I walked into a lovely space with original wood floors, plastered walls of Mediterranean colors, and cases and shelves containing local, imported, and exotic foods, cases of some of the most fresh and deelicious seafood you can imagine, and a sweet little bistro among it all. No more did I get in the door, when I was greeted by a very friendly guy who told me I could sit down wherever I wanted. I took a seat by a window and quickly settled in.

Once I looked at the menu, I realized the folks that bought my book and emailed me were right! The breakfast menu is kinda short, but sweet – down-to-earth, but kinda exotic. It was also pretty amazing. Here's what I had to choose from: Breakfast Stacker, a variation of a Cyprus breakfast featuring garlic-rubbed toast topped with ham, beefsteak tomato, roasted red pepper, basil, brie, poached egg, and a drizzle of imported olive oil, served with home fries; Traditional Eggs Benedict, an English muffin, ham, Hollandaise sauce, and poached egg; Seasonal Tomato Stuffed with Herbed Egg & Seafood, made with fresh seafood, vegetables, and herbs delicately paired with cream cheese and egg, stuffed inside a fresh tomato topped with Hollandaise sauce and served with a sausage link; Smoked Salmon Platter, classically prepared fresh smoked salmon, served with a bagel, cream cheese,

tomato, red onion, capers, and fresh dill; and
Reedsville Breakfast, including two eggs, bacon
or sausage, home fries, toast, and coffee.

I ordered the special – Orange Blossom French Toast:
Two slices of thick toast served with home fries and
a sausage link. But what was really cool, and fit the
"exotic" description, was a beautiful edible flower
placed on top. I even ate the flower, and it was all
sooo gooood! Amazing, in fact.

While I ate, I had the chance to look over the lunch
and dinner offerings. Besides some amazing Appetizers
and Salads, a few of the 19 Sandwiches and Wraps
include: Summer Ham & Gruyere, made with sliced ham,
grilled apples, and Gruyere cheese, served on a
toasted ciabatta roll with Dijon mustard; Maryland
Crab Cake, a house-made crab cake served with lettuce,
tomato, red onion, and choice of tartar or cocktail
sauce; and the Vegetarian Wrap, made with Mediterranean
spread, roasted red pepper, olives, lettuce, red
onion, tomato, and herbs. The Entrées include: Fish
& Chips, beer-battered fish served with house-cut
fries; Taiwanese Grilled Tuna, served with sweet
Thai chili sauce; Steamer Platter, a pound of snow
crab legs, a half-dozen clams, a half-dozen mussels,
and a half-pound of Gulf shrimp, served with butter;
Italian Chicken Breast, two chicken breasts served
with fresh basil, garlic, and salami and ham, then
topped with Parmesan and Provolone cheese; and an 8
oz. Filet Mignon. Wow!

After breakfast, I introduced myself to the guy who
greeted me. He turned out to be the owner, so I asked
if I could chat with him about his place. He told me

he started in the food service industry at the age of 12, working at a local grocery store. From there he dabbled in food service until he and his wife Tracy decided to try a catering business. After some research, they found out how to start importing stuff internationally as well as domestically. When that worked, they realized it was only a matter of time before a specialty shop and bistro combo would happen.

Their specialty is seafood, and here is where you separate the real from the fake – the already-prepared frozen crap you get at Lobster Trap from what you get here at Reedsville. Bart has researched and figured out how to get seafood right from the docks of Boston, Cape Cod, down south, and primarily Baltimore. He and Tracy hit the road early every Wednesday morning to go to the Baltimore Fish Market and then hurry back with a truckload of treasures from the sea. "Nobody was doing this," he said. They tried it and it worked!

Bart reasons that because of things like the Food Network, print media, and the internet, people's tastes have gotten more sophisticated, or at least they're more open to new and different things – even in the rural areas. The Ewing philosophy is "Good quality products, trying to represent them well, and taking care of people and building relationships."

The two recommendations I received for the Reedsville Seafood Company were right on. It was "Amazing," and it was "Fantastic." After my experience, I would only add this – Awesome!

Enjoy!

Note: *If you want the seafood at its freshest, come Wednesdays after 3...it's practically right off the boat.*

Boiling Springs Tavern

BOILING SPRINGS, CUMBERLAND CO.

I try to ride The Steed (my trusted Harley Sportster) to just about every place I go for my books. But when I want to take a friend, and that friend isn't too keen on bikes, but owns a super sweet Mini Cooper named Foxy, and offers her car along with her own personal company, I am all in!

Cici is a fellow adventurer and seasoned traveler. The fact that she drives a Mini Cooper just made the decision to keep my bike in the barn an easier one. She showed up on a warm summer Saturday afternoon sporting a new 'do, wearing a cute outfit, and ready to hit the road, and that road would put her and her little Foxy to the test – the winding and challenging PA Rt. 74 south over the mighty Tuscarora Ridge.

Actually, Cici must have racing blood in her, and she did the curves, hairpin turns, and ascents and descents like a pro. We rolled into Carlisle in about the same time as it would have taken me on the bike. Once in Carlisle, we hit Rt. 34 south, and then caught the tiny country road of Rt. 174 east into Boiling

JUST A TASTE

Locally Owned By:
Geoff and Debi Keith

Cuisine:
American

Price Range:
$5 to $24

Hours:
Tues – Sat 11:30am – 2pm,
5pm – 9pm, bar open all day

Location:
1 East 1st Street (at the corner of 1st and Front Streets)

Wi-Fi:
No

Contact Info:
(717) 258-3614,
http://www.boilingspringstavern.net/

Vegetarian Offerings:
Yes

Supports Local Farmers:
Yes

Locally Owned Accommodations Nearby:
Gelinas Manor 219 Front St.,
(717) 258-6584

Things To Do Nearby:
The Village Artisans Gallery & Studio, Appalachian Trail, Foundry Day in June, Fly Fishing

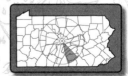

Springs. There, as it's been since 1832, and standing
majestically at the crossroads and across from the
"boiling" spring, was the Tavern. Cici whipped Foxy
into the big parking lot, and before we headed in,
we took a look at the beautiful Children's Lake
across the street. This sweet body of water was made
by partially damming a stream fed from 30 natural
springs! At one end, the water bubbles up from one
of the springs like boiling water. It is one of the
largest springs in the United States, yielding
24,000 gallons of water a day from a lake that must
be several acres in size. We almost went for a dip,
but the road rally-type driving had us both starved,
and we headed straight to the Tavern.

We were greeted by the Tavern's general manager, Kevin,
who was very gracious and welcomed us in. The dining
room to our right was big, with lots of tables and
lots of folks enjoying dinner. To our left was the
older part where the bar was. There were several
tables for two along the wall, and a couple of those
were by windows with 20 inch thick stone window
sills. Cici and I decided that was where we wanted
to be, and Kevin guided us to one at the far end.
From here, like most of my table choices, I could
watch the goings-on of the place. Our waitress
arrived and introduced herself and asked us what we
wanted to drink. I noticed they had Tröegs Sunshine
Pils on tap, and went with that. Cici ordered a glass
of Pinot Grigio and we settled in.

The menu at BST was really nice, and if you choose,
as we did, to sit in the old tavern, they offer a
sandwich menu as well. Their lunch menu has things
like Seafood Bisque, French Onion Soup, Coconut Fried
Shrimp, and Buffalo Chicken Wings as apps. Salads
include Boiling Springs Special Salad, mixed greens
topped with lightly-fried chicken breast, avocado,
and bacon with poppy seed dressing; Cobb Salad; Steak
and Potato Salad; Louisiana Caesar; Baked Salmon
Salad, salmon filet topped with spinach, artichoke

hearts, and cheese served over a mix of greens with balsamic vinaigrette; and a simple Tossed Salad.

Sandwiches cover everything from a Grilled Salmon BLT to the Tavern Cheesesteak; a Roasted Vegetable Stack of grilled portabella mushroom, roasted peppers, grilled eggplant, grilled onion, fresh tomato, and eggplant tapenade with Fontina cheese on multi-grain bread; to the traditional Tavern Burger, a ground sirloin burger garnished with lettuce, tomato, and onion on a kaiser roll.

Lunch entrees, served with house salad and crusty rolls, include offerings such as Scallops Mediterranean, sea scallops sautéed with tomatoes, Kalamata olives, feta cheese, garlic, and butter; Veal Medallions; Spaghetti Carbonara; Pecan Crusted Chicken Breast; and a Roasted Vegetables & Ziti, roasted portabellas, onions, sweet peppers, and eggplant, tossed with ziti, olive oil, roasted garlic, and spinach. Yum! And that's just a sampling of the lunch menu, my friends. Dinner offers a bunch of wonderful stuff, but those you'll have to discover for yourself, or visit their online menu at their website. Cici and I ordered and shared Seafood Bisque, Oven Roasted Portabella, sear-roasted marinated portabella mushroom with house bruschetta and field greens, Chicken and Polenta, grilled chicken and polenta with shiitake mushrooms, roasted peppers, garlic, and demi-glace, Peanut Butter Pie, and Crème Brûlée.

Needless to say, the Mini was a bit heavier on the way home, but her passengers were very happy. As we drove, we recounted our adventure – the twists and turns of an Allegheny Mountain pass, the vibe of a sweet historic town with its own bubbling spring, our great meals, and now a new place to share with fellow adventurers. The Boiling Springs Tavern is a great place in a wonderful town. Take the journey, dip your toes in pure spring water, walk the town, and then settle in, as we did, to a wonderful meal in a wonderful historic tavern.

Enjoy!

Pomona's Woodfired Café & Gettysburg Baking Co.

BIGLERVILLE, ADAMS COUNTY

I don't say this very often, but thank goodness for the internet. While trying to narrow down a good place in my 5 o'clock region, I found myself stuck. I had a few ideas and recommendations from people who bought my first book, but after much debate, inquiries, and research, I came up kinda empty. However, right when I was ready to give up, I did a Google search of the Gettysburg area and came across this:

Pomona's - Biglerville, PA
☆☆☆☆☆ 3 reviews - Price range: $$
Nov. 6, 2009 ... 3 Reviews of Pomona's "Superb food. An amazing restaurant in an ... Gettysburg, PA. Reviews of Biglerville American Restaurants on Yahoo! ...
www.yelp.com/biz/pomonas-biglerville

What caught my attention was not only a five star rating, but the word "Superb." Plus, the Google link indicated Yelp.com as the source of the reviews. I know that site and am a contributor myself. Granted,

JUST A TASTE

Locally Owned By:
Marc Jalbert

Cuisine:
Wood Fired, Spanish-Influenced Cuisine & Artisan Breads

Price Range:
$4.00 to $30.00;
Breads: $2.65 to $5.25

Hours:
Brunch/Lunch, Fri. & Sat. 10am to 3pm, Sun. 10am to 2pm; Dinner, Wed. & Th. 5:30pm to 9pm, Fri. & Sat. 5:30 pm to 10pm, Sun. 5:30pm to 9pm; Bakery: Tue. – Fri. 9am to 6pm, Sat. 8am to 2pm

Location:
213 East York St.

Wi-Fi:
Yes

Contact Info:
(717) 677-7014,
www.gettysburgbakingco.com/pomonas

Vegetarian Offerings:
Yes

Supports Local Farmers:
Yes

Locally Owned Accommodations Nearby:
Canter Berry Tails Apple Ranch
(717) 677-8900, www.farmstay.us

Things To Do Nearby:
Gettysburg Civil War Battlefield, Gettysburg National Cemetery, Apple Festival, Music and Art Festivals, Wineries, ABC Brewing (Gettysburg).

three reviews aren't much, but five stars AND "Superb food"? That's rare. I clicked the link and read the reviews. Here are samplings from all three.

"Superb food. An amazing restaurant in an unlikely place. This is a 'slow food' restaurant at its best so don't expect quick service, the food is served when ready. The wood oven baking added a little something to every dish. This is a BYOB, and reservations are a must."

Samiam H. Camp Hill, PA, 5/9/2010

"My uncle shared this gem with me while I was visiting over the summer. It was probably the meanest thing he could ever have done to me, because now that I'm home, I've been craving that food… Everything at Pomona's is locally grown and produced, the bread is baked in a stone oven in the back by [Marc], and the chef, Shaun, is the greatest gift to cuisine. …every single thing I tried was the most adoringly delicious thing I have ever eaten. Sometimes I fall asleep at night thinking about the grilled peaches with prosciutto on top."

Erin B. Seattle, WA, 11/6/09

"Originally opening as Gettysburg Baking Company with great artisan breads never seen in this area, they have opened a small, limited eatery called Pomona's. Wood fired pizza, grilled fish and meats, and fresh salads. A great bang for your buck and BYOB. What a jewel!!"

Tom R. Aspers, PA, 1/13/09

Wow, this place sounded like something I needed to check out further, and again the internet came through. I was able to get to Pomona's own site and read this:

"Adams County is an ordinary place with an extraordinary collection of growers and food producers. Almost all of our entrees are prepared to capture the magic of our wood-burning oven and to take advantage of our local bounty. Much of the produce and meat we use, save for the fish, comes from dedicated growers and producers who care as much about the "how" of what is grown, raised, produced, and ultimately served at your table. We operate in a way that gives you more than just a meal away from home. Instead, Pomona's offers a casual dining experience which celebrates the harvest of Adams County.

Relax, bring some friends and a bottle of wine or two. The convivial atmosphere you will find at Pomona's has its roots in European-style dining, where food and eating is a shared experience. It's a practice we hope will invoke a stronger sense of community. Pomona's importance of community begins with the ingredients you will experience in our dishes. Particular flavors coming together to reflect the diversity of the Adams County farming community, our food purveyors, only to return to you, as a patron, who, in your support, helps to complete the connection of land, food, and place."

That was it. I had to go. So, on a beautiful sunny Sunday morning, I took off on The Steed for brunch at Pomona's!

I arrived right at the 10am opening time, and as soon as I walked in, I knew I was going to love this place. I took a seat next to windows that look into the kitchen and the wood-fired oven, where I was able to see the chef create his masterpieces. This is cool for two reasons – one is the oven itself, which is fired by oak and apple wood, and the other is you can watch your food being prepared if you want. Their menu changes a lot, as they use as many fresh ingredients as are available. Here are the amazing offerings I had to choose from that day.

Breakfast: Tortilla Espanola, slow-baked eggs, arugula salad, and baguette; Churros, cinnamon sugar fried dough served with hot [dipping] chocolate.

Soup & Salads: Local Vegetable Gazpacho, served with fennel, orange, and basil breadcrumbs; Summer Salad, greens, watermelon, olive, and manchego, with gazpacho vinaigrette; Grilled Squash, grilled baby squash, stewed red pepper, basil, and grilled bread; Ensalada Cerdo, pig head, lomo, pancetta, grilled peaches, sherry, and greens; Beef Heart, wood-grilled beef heart, warm fava bean salad, radish, and baby greens.

From the Oven: Gambas al Ajillo, shrimp sautéed with garlic, lemon, and Aleppo (a dried crushed chili pepper native to Syria with a sweet smoky robust heat). Handcrafted Sausages, Spanish Flatbread con Tomate, Oven Roasted Fruit, wood-roasted peaches, mint, cinnamon, and turbinado sugar.

Vegetables: Vegetable gazpacho with basil breadcrumbs; Char Grilled Scallions with romesco; Local Green Salad; Pickled Vegetables.

After much debate, I went with the Tortilla Espanola and Oven Roasted Fruit. I watched as the chef prepared it, and when it arrived fresh and hot, I savored every bite and even used the bread to soak up the mint and cinnamon-infused peach juice. Wow, superb (just like Samiam wrote)! I was in heaven. That was an awesome breakfast! I can't imagine how awesome lunch or dinner would be there. I guess I'll just have to return to find out. When I do, I want to be sure to come on a day when the bakery is open.

Gettysburg Baking Company (within the same building) has been baking crusty artisan breads for the Adams County community since 1996 in the tradition of crafted European village-style baking. They offer sourdough bread, called Adams County Sourdough, using organic rye yeast that was started from a culture there in Adams County years ago. Their French bread uses a traditional "poolish" which is a type of starter using baker's yeast. This dough is used to make baguettes and their famous Seeded Twist, but this is topped with poppy, sesame seeds, and kosher salt. Other breads are Levain Batard, Multigrain, CiderHouse Rye, and a Deli Loaf. They also have an array of pastries and cookies, all made from scratch. All this is for takeout normally, but they do offer seating just for breakfast time called The Baker's Breakfast that includes some egg-based dishes as well.

So what started out as a simple Google search ended up as one of *the* best finds in this book! I'm so glad I visited and so will you. This place is what *going*

LOCAL! is all about. Owner Marc Jalbert and Chef Shaun Wolf are doing some amazing things there for their local community, as well as for foodies everywhere. The world-renowned Gettysburg Civil War Battlefield is just down the road, so if you're there visiting, you're in luck. And even if you're not, it's well worth the drive no matter where you're coming from. As one reviewer so boldly stated, and I now totally agree, this place is definitely "Superb."

Enjoy!

Note: The day I was there, I told my server Eric and Chef Shaun about my book and that I wanted to include Pamona's. I typically never accept a complimentary meal, but when I get a check like I did there, it's hard to say no.
Thanks Guys!

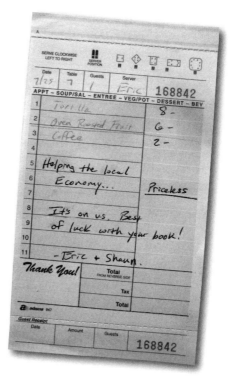

CHAPTER 6
6 O'CLOCK

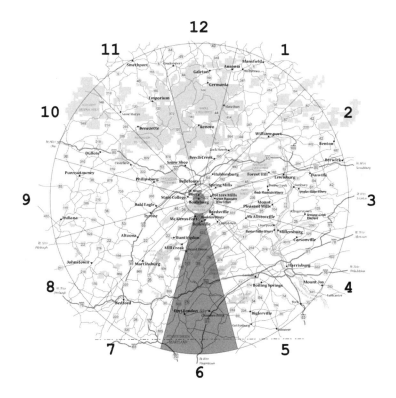

Couch's

MCALEVYS FORT, HUNTINGDON COUNTY

McAlevys Fort is not what you call a hub of excitement – unless a local farmer forgets to close his pasture gate and the cows decide to take a stroll through town. But there I was on a Friday night, scoping out a place for dinner, while State College was over- flowing with folks cutting loose at the end of the week. Restaurants were teeming with hungry patrons, and the bars overflowing with thirsty ones. But because I care about you, and want you to know about these little gems out in the hintermost regions of central PA, I selflessly chose work over excitement. Yeah, right. Seriously though, I did want to take a ride that evening, and I did want to find a place I remem- bered seeing signs for over in Huntingdon County.

My destination was a relatively new place. I had seen the signs on my way through McAlevys Fort over the past year but never took the time to investigate. The signs were cute enough, with a cartoon cow face licking its own nose, but they indicated only subs and gro- ceries there. I just wasn't sure what this place

JUST A TASTE

Locally Owned By:
Marylou & John Couch

Cuisine:
Country

Price Range:
$1.09 to 10.99

Hours:
M – Sat. 8am to 8pm,
Sun. 11am to 3pm

Location:
13605 Greenwood Road

Wi-Fi:
Yes

Contact Info:
(814) 667-2016

Vegetarian Offerings:
Yes

Supports Local Farmers:
Yes

**Locally Owned
Accommodations Nearby:**
Tranquil Lodge (814) 667-2001

Things To Do Nearby:
Antiquing in McAlevys Fort,
Greenwood Furnace State Park,
Belleville

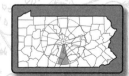

called Couch's was all about. Plus, I was kind of peeved because there used to be this cool little sub shop and general store right in the village, and I thought this new convenience store put them out of business. Little did I know, it was the same folks – they just wanted to spread their wings and offer the community even more in a bigger and better place. I thought I'd at least check it out, but really didn't know what to expect. What I didn't expect was what I found.

Couch's is really great! Yes, it's a convenience store selling subs and groceries, but its way more. It's an internet café, ice cream parlor, deli, pizza shop, video rental place, copy and fax service, UPS shipper, has an ATM, art and craft nook, AND a full blown restaurant! Oh yeah, and you can get lottery tickets. But be sure to check out the mini fridge with a very organized and well-kept supply of worms. Obviously they were for fishing, but as nicely as they were displayed in little Styrofoam boxes (like mini Omaha Steaks) they just as well could have been for medical purposes, OR maybe they were for some foreigners who had a camp nearby, that considered worms a delicacy and couldn't survive the summer without them. Either way it was funny, but local, and I loved it!

This place is really nice, very clean, tidy, and friendly – and there's no shortage of goods or goodies. Breakfast, lunch, dinner, dessert...you name it. Morning offerings are the usual suspects – eggs, bacon, hot cakes, sausage, oatmeal, etc. Specialties of the house are the Country Breakfast, the Big Country Breakfast, and Creamed Chip Beef w/ Gravy. They even offer a Breakfast Pizza. Lunches include Cold Subs, Hot Subs, Cold Sandwiches, Hot Sandwiches (everything from hot dogs to hamburgers), plus Salads and Soups. Dinners include Salads and Soups, along with Fish & Chips, Hot Roast Beef or Turkey Sandwiches served with Mashed Potatoes,

Chicken Tenders, and homemade Meatloaf with Mashed Potatoes or Fries. Matt's (the owner's son) Medley offers Wings (he won the Wing Off at the Huntingdon Co. Fair!), the "Holy Cow" Burger, and the Tavern Burger. They also offer pizza and a bunch of sides/appetizers. For dessert, they have Soft and Hand-Dipped Ice Cream, Single Serve Pies, Milk Shakes, Floats, Soda Fountain Drinks, Sundaes, and more (as if you could want any more).

That night I had the Fish & Chips and I was surprised how much I got for the price. I've paid as much as 17 bucks for the same thing at other places. While I sat there enjoying my dinner, I watched the flow of local folks go in and out, and it was clear to me that this place is a vital community business. I thought about it and guessed that it was 20 miles in any direction to something similar. The town needed Couch's and Couch's needed them. I've seen a lot of places come and go, and the main reason they go is lack of business. Fortunately this place doesn't have to worry — I hope.

While I was there I had a chance to speak with the owner, Marylou Couch, who told me that she had dreamed of having a place like this of her own. When the original store (that I mentioned earlier) in the village came up for sale years ago, she and her husband John decided to give it a try. After a few years, they wanted to expand but the store was too small and the parking even smaller (and dangerous). John and Marylou both grew up in farming families, and John's parents had a big farm just around the bend from the village on the way to Greenwood Furnace State Park. The parents agreed to sell the kids 10 acres to build Marylou's dream.

Now, instead of risking life and limb along the busy road trying to make your way into a tiny, dimly lit store, you can pull into a big, safe parking lot and into a big, beautiful, well lit place with big

windows all around, plenty of indoor seating, and
even a flower-covered (in summer) wraparound porch
with café tables and picnic tables. I like to take
my ice cream out into the adjacent field to watch
the sun set in the evenings.

Now instead of passing through McAlveys Fort on my
way to somewhere else, I set a course for there just
to go to Couch's. Here is a place that offers not
only good food at great prices and a nicely stocked
grocery/convenience store, but has ice cream, internet,
deli meats, pizza, videos, copiers, does faxes for
you, has UPS pickup and drop off, an ATM, an art and
craft nook, and all with a very friendly, down-home
atmosphere and the coolest display of live worms
in mini Omaha Steak boxes ever! This is excitement,
country style!

Enjoy!

Marge's Lunch at the Belleville Market

BELLEVILLE, MIFFLIN COUNTY

Belleville is tucked away in an area called Big Valley, parts of which are like a lost world. The Amish folk who live there are uncomplicated and hard working. Others live there too, with their

modern conveniences and occupations, but the Amish live off the land, and their commitments to God and family are notable, as their choice not to conform to the modern world is, too. Their means of transportation, by horse and buggy, are in stark contrast to the rushing of cars and trucks that fly up and down Rt. 655. But once a week this "lost world" comes alive as Amish mix with "others," and horses mix with cars, trucks, and even motorcycles. People from far and wide flock here by the hundreds, maybe thousands, to partake in a cultural experience that blends animal, vegetable, mineral, and even man-made together in a festive outdoor market.

All around, you'll find vendors selling just about everything – and I mean everything! Here, the saying

"One man's trash is another man's treasure" couldn't be more true. I've seen stuff there that you couldn't pay me to take, yet I've seen things I've had to put a poker-face on because the vendor had no idea the value of the vintage item he or she was practically giving away. There are also produce stands, food vendors, and even clothing of all kinds – including underwear in either camo or day-glo green!

There are a couple of buildings within the market grounds – one even houses an auction arena where man bids on beast, and chickens, pigs, sheep, goats, and cows parade around a packed house of farmers and curiosity seekers. In another building are vendors selling everything from baked goods to jewelry, house-wares to gum and candy, and cat food to old Matchbox cars. There's even a deli counter with a selection of meats. One end of this building has a live auction going on, but instead of animals, it's produce. Here, everything from blueberries to zucchini are auctioned off to folks sitting in little wooden folding chairs. But at the other end is where the real action is, and where folks have been coming to hang out, chat, laugh, and fill their bellies with good ol' home cookin' for 44 years.

Marge's Lunch, aka Marge's Restaurant, aka Marge's, is the best food at the Belleville Market. Serving only breakfast and lunch though – once a week, Marge's place is packed, and the smell of her home cooking fills the market, keeping the customers filling her little six-table place. Only six tables? Don't worry, these are six farm style tables that seat at least eight adults each. The thing about these tables are, you're almost obligated to at least say "hi" to the stranger sitting next to, or across from you.

I love this! I'm a people person, so I'm into it, but for those of you less extroverted, it's still a great way to allow you to meet new people and maybe make some new friends. Food is more than just fuel for the body, and eating is more than the act of refueling. The table, since the beginning of time, has been a place for families and even strangers to gather, refuel, reconnect, and get to know one another. Here at Marge's, it's like one big family. Family, in fact, is what Marge's is all about.

It all started back in 1966 when Marge and her mom, Elsie Peachey, started their little restaurant at the market. Marge was only 25 then but as a partner, worked right alongside her mom. Even her daughter Janell, who was 2 at the time, helped out. Then her husband came on board after he retired as a truck driver to "drive" the cash register. When he passed away a couple years ago, her brother Bob took over the register and is there to this day. Janell, now in her 30s, still works there. In fact, she lives and works a regular job in Hershey, PA, but takes every Wednesday off to drive up and help her mom! Janell is very skilled in the kitchen and represents the third generation to provide such wonderful home cooking to the market.

Jenell's childhood friend Carla works there too, as a waitress. Carla is super nice and buzzes around the restaurant with coffee, food, and plenty of banter for the regulars. Helping Carla is a girl named Angie. Providing needed help in the kitchen mixing pancake batter, washing dishes, prepping food, and keeping mother and daughter in check is Katie. She's a very kind-spirited Amish woman who's been working there for over 30 years.

With that "family and friends" way of doing things, Marge's is a place where, even if you enter as a total stranger, you'll most likely leave feeling like another member of the family, or at least a friend. Good food and good company abound here. Big tables filled with folks with big appetites and big hearts fill the single open room. Home cooked (from scratch) breakfasts and lunches fill stomachs and spirits without emptying the wallet.

Marge's Lunch, in a "hidden" valley, in the middle of a somewhat chaotic outdoor market, is a place where traditional mixes with modern, and both get along like old friends. The food is great, the prices are super affordable, and you'll feel like you're back home at your mom or grandma's house every time you visit. But remember, you can only visit on Wednesdays, and then only for breakfast and lunch. That's OK, because the experience will stay with you until the next time you visit. Marge's has been keeping folks coming back for 44 years now, and I suspect it will continue well into the future. What a sweet little place.

Enjoy!

Milky Way
FORT LOUDON, FRANKLIN COUNTY

The Milky Way is a little restaurant in mountains of southern PA, and a great stop if you're traveling east or west along the historic Lincoln Highway, also known as Rt. 30, or south or north on Rt. 75. The town of Fort Loudon is also historic. It was the site of a fort in colonial Pennsylvania, and one of

several in colonial America named after John Campbell, 4th Earl of Loudoun (1705 – 1782), a British nobleman and army officer. The fort was built in 1756 during the French and Indian War by the Pennsylvania Militia, and served as a post on the Forbes Road during the Forbes expedition that successfully drove the French from Fort Duquesne in modern day Pittsburgh. In 1765, the fort was evacuated, but a replica was built on the original site in 1993.

Fort Loudon is also a very special place because it's the birthplace of a very great man – my dad. President James Buchanan, Jr. (1791 – 1868), was born there too, but I bet he was not nearly as awesome as my dad is. However, my dad left there

JUST A TASTE

Locally Owned By:
Roger Dinsmore

Cuisine:
Diner

Price Range:
$.40 to $7.25

Hours:
Mon., Wed. – Sat. 6am to 9pm,
Sun 8am to 9pm, Closed Tues.

Location:
99 Path Valley Rd

Wi-Fi:
No

Contact Info:
(717) 369-3070

Vegetarian Offerings:
Yes

Supports Local Farmers:
No

**Locally Owned
Accommodations Nearby:**
Fort Loudon Inn, (717) 595-0065

Things To Do Nearby:
Fort Loudon (replica),
Cowans Gap State Park

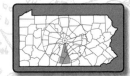

when he was just a little boy and way before the
Milky Way, so he never had the chance to eat there
or even know of it.

Since I always wanted to take a trip to my dad's
hometown anyway, and since my book career requires
me to scour the state for eateries, I went to the
web for any info on eateries in Fort Loudon. A Google
search yielded a site called Insiderpages.com. There
I found one place, The Milky Way. A couple of reviews
had great comments like this one: *"Since the early
60's my family and friends have been eating at the
Milky Way, and is our first stop before entering
Cowans Gap State Park. The Dilly Burgers are great
and you must have a soft serve for dessert. I love
the fresh strawberry sundaes! Step back in time and
dine at the Milky Way!!!!"* by Tina O. And this one:
*"I have been eating at the Milky Way Restaurant for
over 40 years now. I currently live 2 hours away,
but when I am in the area (about once a month), I
make a special trip to the Milky Way and treat myself
to one of their delicious ham hoagies and French fries
with a vanilla milk shake! They are conveniently
located along Rt. 75 in Fort Loudon, PA. Many tourists
stop there on the way to and from Cowans Gap State
Park, which is nearby. It is also a favorite haunt
of the locals. It is very clean, and the wait staff
is very friendly. If you're in the area, you must stop
in and see for yourself!"* by Janice G. With that, I
packed up the bike, and on a beautiful fall day, took
the scenic trip south along Rt. 75 to see where my
dad was born, and to try lunch at the Milky Way.

I arrived to what seemed to be a roadside ice cream
stand turned into a full scale sit-down restaurant.
I walked in and it was packed with folks having a
late breakfast or early lunch. Everyone looked like
they were enjoying themselves, and even the girls
behind the counter taking orders were smiling and
chatting with the customers. You see, similar to an
ice cream stand, orders here are taken at a counter.

There's a huge back-lit menu board behind the counter where you can choose from Breakfast, Breakfast Sandwiches, Sandwiches, Hoagies, Platters & Baskets, Specialty Sandwiches, Side Orders, Soft Drinks, Breakfast Beverages, and Dessert. You place your order, pay, and then one of the nice girls behind the counter brings your food to the table.

Even though the Diliburger (cheeseburger with lettuce, tomato, mayo, onion, and pickle) was recommended by one of the reviewers, I was really hungry and went for a Galaxiburger (which has the same toppings, but with two burger patties) and fries. I didn't have the vanilla milk shake, but I did have a hot fudge sundae for dessert. All was oooh sooo good!

I got a booth by the window and started taking notes while I waited for my lunch. In the booth in front of me were two older cats who were obviously regulars and locals. Figuring they wouldn't have known my dad, I politely asked them if they had ever heard of Lester Hull (my grandfather). They thought for a minute, and the one guy said he knew of a Mason Hull. My eyes lit up, and I said excitedly, "That was my great uncle!" Wow, these guys knew my grandfather's brother! Great uncle Mason lived his whole life in Fort Loudon and I only met him once or twice – he passed away when I was young. He was my dad's favorite uncle, and he loved my dad. They told me some really cool stories about Mason, but the best was that his only child, a daughter named Wanda, was still living and lived right down the road. After lunch I went to find her and had a really nice visit with her and her husband Jim.

This had been a wonderful day! The ride down was beautiful with the mountains blazing with color, I visited my father's birthplace, met guys who knew his uncle Mason, met Mason's daughter and her husband, learned some history, and found a great little place to eat at the intersection of two scenic byways.

For some of you, Fort Loudon may be a hike, but it's worth it. It's a lovely little town surrounded by mountains, and with a replica fort from the French and Indian War days. Plus, you'll get to enjoy a really nice meal or a sweet treat at a very sweet place – The Milky Way.

Enjoy!

CHAPTER 7
7 O'CLOCK

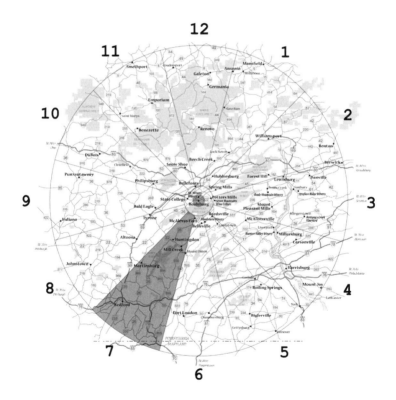

Standing Stone Coffee Company
HUNTINGDON, HUNTINGDON COUNTY

It was a cold gray day in mid-February when I found myself passing through Huntingdon, PA, in the afternoon. I was not only in need of a hot cup of coffee, but needed lunch as well - hopefully in a cool place where I could chill and warm up. I had heard about a place near Juniata College and drove around town near the campus. Thank goodness my sense of direction was on track that day because as I pulled up to the stop sign, I looked catty-corner and there it was - Standing Stone Coffee Co. It looked cool, with big picture windows on either side of a center door in an old classic structure with a narrow front and deep profile. From where I was, it looked warm and cozy inside. I could see small lights hanging from the ceiling, and the walls were painted burnt sienna. People were inside, and a big table by the window was filled with older ladies. I spotted a parking lot to my right and pulled in.

As I walked over, I saw a big van from Westminster Woods (a retirement community nearby) parked out front, which explained where the ladies were from.

JUST A TASTE

Locally Owned By:
Greg & Jessie Anderson

Cuisine:
Coffees, Light Breakfast, Lunch and Sweets

Price Range:
$1.15 to $5.95 (coffee by the pound $8.50 to $10.50)

Hours:
Mon. – Th. 6:30am to 10pm,
Fri. – Sat. 6:30am to midnight,
Sun. noon – 7pm

Location:
1229 Mifflin St.
(corner of Mifflin and 13th)

Wi-Fi:
Yes, Free

Contact Info:
(814) 643-4545,
www.standingstonecoffee
company.com

Vegetarian Offerings:
Yes

Supports Local Farmers:
Yes

**Locally Owned
Accommodations Nearby:**
Inn at Solvang, (888) 814-3035

Things To Do Nearby:
Shopping, Campus, Raystown Lake,
1,000 Steps

That's cool, I thought; it's definitely not just a student hangout. Just as I walked in, my impression of warm and cozy was pleasantly confirmed and punctuated by the sun that had broken loose from the clouds, and the whole room filled with sunlight. The smells of coffee mixed with baked goods and lunch smells caressed my nose as light conversation and hip music fell softly upon my ears. I couldn't help but smile.

Yeah, this place was cool alright. As I stood there looking around I noticed even more stuff, like a small comfy couch in the other window and two high top tables, each with a Dell desktop computer on them. Wow, not only free Wi-Fi, but two free PC's to use it with! Around the room were an assortment of different sized tables, and in the middle of it all was a really nice bar with stools. Behind that where the coffee and food are prepared, and to the left of the bar is where you order. That space was abuzz with activity, so I thought I'd just keep looking around until things slowed a bit.

I walked beyond the counter and noticed what looked like washing machines in the very back. As I headed for a closer look, I stopped dead in my tracks in a small middle room. There next to me was a sweet little red coffee roaster. Awesome, they roast their own (it just kept getting better, I thought). I looked to my right and saw a nice setup of whole bean dispensers of about eight varieties – all "relationship-based," fairly traded, and environmentally friendly, with two grown organically. I thought, "I'd like to return some day when they're working that little roaster," because unlike old ones I've seen, this was "new school" with some kind of funky electronic gizmo next to it and a laptop on top of that. Once in awhile I like to give technology a chance.

Noticing the empty counter back in the main room, I headed there to order a coffee and lunch. I decided to go for a no-nonsense good ol' cuppa joe to get the real "flavor" of the place. I was given an artsy

ceramic mug, and to my very pleasant surprise, it was preheated. Nothing chaps my behind like hot coffee poured into a cold ceramic mug. Within minutes the heat of the coffee is absorbed away and I have to ask for a blast in the microwave. Not this time – the mug was already hot, and my coffee was delicious and stayed hot till almost the last sip. Other coffee drinks include the usual espresso suspects like cappuccino, latte, etc. Mine, a drip brew, was offered along with a French press option. They also have tea, chai tea, cider, hot chocolate, bottled drinks, and a nice selection of fruit smoothies.

The menu included Soups, Panini Sandwiches, Deli Sandwiches, Salads, Breakfast Items, Desserts, and Baked Goods. Since it was cold out, a grilled panini sounded great. The Montana Mountain Climber seemed like a good choice, especially because it's "adventurous!" Here's the description: "This Standing Stone favorite is an adventurous combination of grilled turkey and bacon with melted Colby-Monterey Jack cheese on Sourdough with a brilliant avocado-ranch spread." Not so keen on the avocado business, but since they described it as "brilliant," I couldn't say no.

I took my coffee and continued my exploration all the way to the back. Yes, they were washing machines I saw earlier – eight washers, eight dryers, and one commercial machine, all brand new and the latest models. There was a nice lady there drinking coffee and reading a magazine. I asked if she was doing laundry and she said "Yes, and what a nice place it is versus the sometimes dingy, old laundromats." She was right, the place was spotless – just like the coffee shop. We chatted a moment, and then I returned to the main room and noticed a big deck alongside the building. It looked like a wonderful space on warmer days. But alas, that was not today.

I took a seat on the couch, and chilled out and warmed up as I had hoped for. I flipped open my PC to check if they had a website. Sure enough, and when I read what SSCC is all about, I was hooked on that place. They write that they're committed to creating a unique space for anyone to come, have quality and creative food and drink, share some thoughts, listen and learn, and be in community with their neighbors. They go on to write that they want their customers to have a valued experience every time they step in the door. Whether it's watching them roast coffee, catching up with an old friend, trying a new daily special, tackling the laundry over the lunch hour, or simply having space to read or study, from the minute you walk in they want you to feel like you have found a second home.

I sat and enjoyed my coffee and panini, and took in the vibe of this very sweet place on what had now become a beautiful sunny day. Was it that the clouds gave way, or was it just that I had discovered an awesome new coffee shop? It was both. And although the sun was soon to set, I hoped this place would shine bright for a long time. Owners Greg and Jessie are doing a wonderful thing here and I want them to succeed.

If you live in Huntingdon, you've got a great community gathering place that offers amazing coffee, food, live music, and a super nice staff. If you don't, you should take a drive and check it out. Bring your laundry and make an afternoon of it if you want. Your taste buds, heart, and senses, as well as your socks, will thank you.

Enjoy!

Top's Diner
MILL CREEK, HUNTINGDON COUNTY

When I was a kid, every other weekend or so my folks would load me and my sisters in the car for a trip to my Grandma's place in Franklin County down south. Though it was only about a two-hour trip, for a kid this was an epic journey and seemed to take an eternity. But the anticipation of our breakfast stop was huge and something I really looked forward to. It was always the same place too, a place that I loved as a kid and still love to this day — a place of great memories, great food, great atmosphere, and friendliness — Top's Diner.

The current Top's location was originally a fruit market, but in the fall of 1959, it was turned into the diner as we know it today. In 2006, it was sold to Rick Walker and his good friends Tracy and Deb Coover. Being a native of Huntingdon, Rick was very familiar with the Top's reputation and could remember visiting Top's when he was a little kid like me.

Rick didn't change the place much. You can still enjoy fresh baked pies, homemade meatloaf, fresh cut French fries, and real mashed potatoes and gravy. But what

JUST A TASTE

Locally Owned By:
Rick Walker

Cuisine:
American

Price Range:
$1.29 to $14.99

Hours:
Mon. – Th. 6am to 8pm,
Fri. & Sat. 6am to 9pm,
Sun. 7am to 8pm

Location:
12151 William Penn Hwy, 3 miles
east of Huntingdon along Rt. 22

Wi-Fi:
Yes

Contact Info:
(814) 643-4169, www.topsdiner.net,
rick@topsdiner.net

Vegetarian Offerings:
No

Supports Local Farmers:
Yes

**Locally Owned
Accommodations Nearby:**
Mill Stone Manor, (814) 643-0108

Things To Do Nearby:
1,000 Steps

he did change was adding several new sandwiches and salads to the menu, along with bread bowls, new soups, new desserts, hot wings, outside dining during the summer, and even free wireless internet! You can still stop in on Wednesdays for All U Can Eat Fried Chicken, Fridays for Baked or Fried Icelandic Haddock, and Sundays for delicious Filled Chicken Breasts.

As a kid I didn't really care about all that stuff, all I cared about was two "dippy" eggs, bacon, and pancakes (some things never change). Besides a killer breakfast, Top's does pretty much the whole gambit of restaurant fare. Their extensive menu includes just about everything. After we had our fill, it was off again and heading south to Grandma's.

Since those days, I've stopped at Top's countless times. Now, wanting to promote this wonderful place and help them continue to provide meals and memories for generations to come, I stopped in recently to talk with Rick, the new owner and the new blood of this vintage and classic roadside diner. It's funny how times change, when once I stopped in as a kid they were fiddling with an old school non-electronic cash register trying to get the drawer unstuck. This time Rick was on his cell phone talking with his IT support trying to get the internet up and running. I sat down in a booth that I was probably in 200 times as a kid, and with a digital recorder running, got the skinny on what this young restaurateur is up to here in the heart of central PA.

Although there are changes, Rick's not out to change everything – more like just improve on what has been successful for years, but also introduce the locals to a higher level of gastronomic consciousness. When I asked him why he does it (the restaurant biz) he replied "I ask myself that over and over again," but then he said simply "It's in my blood." All the way back to high school, Rick remembers wanting to be in the food service business. Even in college he worked at a restaurant in hopes of honing his skills for the future. Now at the helm of his own place, he has the ability to express his passions and live the life he was meant to live it – in service to others, filling their bellies with food and their hearts with joy.

When I asked him what they do best at Top's he said without hesitation "French fries." A fun fact that Rick told me is that when he took the place over, they (the diner) went through 400 to 500 lbs. of potatoes a week . . . now they go through 1400 to 1500 lbs. a week! When I mentioned that the Spruce Creek Tavern in my first book claimed to have the best fries, Rick said confidently "They haven't tried ours yet." Speaking of fresh, Rick mentioned that he's a stickler about not using pre-frozen foods or stuff like instant mashed potatoes. He admitted that some things come in frozen, but he tries to keep those things to a minimum. Rick is fresh too – he's a fresh spirit in an old and loved place. His passion for the new, as well as maintaining the old, is obvious in his current menu and in his plans for the future, which include expansion and more outdoor seating.

Top's represents a wonderful memory for me, but also gives me hope for the future and for the wee lads and lassies who can experience what I did then, and still do to this day. It's a shame that kids even know of places like Mc Diarrhea. In my day, places didn't have to entice children with toys in a box or factory made food-like meals. At Top's you get a "happy meal" every meal. This is a time-tested place that in my opinion is getting better with age!

Enjoy!

Kitty Hawk Restaurant
MARTINSBURG, BLAIR COUNTY

I always thought it was a cool thing to pull up to a restaurant, pub, or café aboard The Mighty Steed. His sleek steel, black and chrome frame on two wheels, stylin' looks, fast and powerful motor, and a rumble that makes the girls go "mmmm." However, my esteemed bikers, I one-upped myself the other evening, and it was on three wheels and not two, made of aluminum and fabric, not a speck of chrome, out-rumbled The Steed, and could literally fly in comparison. When I stepped out onto the tarmac of the Altoona Blair County airport from a Cessna Skyhawk for dinner, I felt like a movie star. My pilot and good friend Francois deFromont and his lovely wife Anne-Sophie treated me to a dinner ride courtesy of his flying club's plane, and I must admit it was awesome!

The Kitty Hawk is awesome too! Model planes suspended from the ceiling, murals depicting flight and pilots, and just a very clean, comfortable, and nice place, not to mention the view of the airfield. This was a sweet place to be whether or not you're a "fly-in movie

JUST A TASTE

Locally Owned By:
MaryJo W. Donaldson &
AmberJo K. Donaldson

Cuisine:
International

Price Range:
$2.10 to $17.95

Hours:
Mon. – Fri. 6am to 8pm, Sat. 7am
to 8pm, Sun. 8am to 8pm

Location:
Altoona Blair County Airport
310 Airport Drive Suite 5

Wi-Fi:
No

Contact Info:
(814) 793-9445

Vegetarian Offerings:
No

Supports Local Farmers:
Yes

**Locally Owned
Accommodations Nearby:**
Spring Garden Farm B&B,
(814) 224-2569

Things To Do Nearby:
Lake Raystown,
Horseshoe Curve in Altoona

star" or a local just wanting a great meal in a great setting dedicated to air travel. Yes, you can arrive by car. In fact, most customers do.

They offer breakfast, lunch, and dinner — and a lot of all! The menu is five and a half pages! They even have nice titles for their categories. Here are a few: From the Granary (French Toast, Hotcakes, and Oatmeal), Raiding the Henhouse (egg dishes), Appealing Appetizers, Delicious Favorites, Sumptuous Salads, and Side to Side (sides, duh). The usual suspects are Breakfast Specials, Daily Specials, Traditional Dinners, Kitty Hawk Menu (kids), Burgers, Beverages, and desserts. They also feature small ads for local businesses who, I suppose, help with the cost of the menu — locals helping locals — another reason to love this place. Another thing about the Kitty Hawk menu is that they have creative names for some of their dishes. I love this! When you have the creativity and willingness to give your menu items a special name, that's cool, and I usually always go for one of those.

That evening I chose the Mile High Burger. I figured I might not ever make the actual club, so a burger was the next best thing. When I told that to Francois and Sophie, Sophie didn't get it and Francois said he would "explain it" to her later. Plus it came with "propeller sauce" which doubled the cool creative name thing. Francois ordered the Western Omelet, which answered the question about what time they stop serving breakfast, and Sophie went with the Mushroom Swiss Burger. When they arrived I became a little worried that the Cessna's payload capacity on the trip home would be compromised. My burger was HUGE! I have a big mouth sometimes, but there was no way I was going to bite that burger and be graceful - I went for the knife and fork approach. Francois' omelet was huge too, and Sophie's burger was bigger than she is.

Several times during our wonderful meal our waitress came by to make sure all was good, and it certainly was. You see, if you've ever traveled (especially out of Philly) you know that airport food can be, uh, less than what you might call "home cooking." The Altoona Blair County Airport in my humble opinion has the best airport restaurant ever - including ones in France and Italy.

Since air travel is down, the Airport Authority discontinued some prime flights, and the restaurant relies a lot now on local travelers, so more and more locals are finding out about this great place for food and flight. School kids come just to view the incredible collection of model planes which were donated to the restaurant by a local woman, whose husband hand-built each one to exacting standards. Pilots and passengers, as well as airport staff, come for the food of course, and you and I can come too! So whether you fly or drive to the Kitty Hawk, you will at least be fed like a movie star, and treated like a king. Our waitress, Amber Jo, was probably the friendliest and most accommodating waitress/manager I've encountered in a long time. Even at ground level, this place flies high.

Enjoy!

Jean Bonnet Tavern
BEDFORD, BEDFORD COUNTY

I heard about this place from so many fans of my first book, and how wonderful it is, that I knew if I did a second book I would be making a trip to Bedford. Then, while doing a book signing at a beer festival, a really nice couple approached my table and asked if I'd ever been to the Jean Bonnet. I said I hadn't but heard a lot of good things about it. They went on and on about how great it is, how beautiful the old building is, how delicious the food is, and how they try and have as many craft brews as possible on their 18-tap system. Then something happened that never happens.

This young woman said very kindly "Hey, we're the owners of the Jean Bonnet, I'm Melissa and this is my husband Shannon. We would like to make you an offer. We'd like you to come to our place and check it out – and we'll even put you up in the B&B there for free. You come, eat with us, try our beers, stay over, and go home. If you loved your visit, would you consider us in your next book? If not, at least you got a little time away for free." I was totally taken aback, and very honored. For the first time I

JUST A TASTE

Locally Owned By:
Melissa & Shannon Jacobs

Cuisine:
Eclectic American Tavern

Price Range:
$5.00 to $30.00

Hours:
11am to 11pm, seven days a week

Location:
6048 Lincoln Highway

Wi-Fi:
Yes

Contact Info:
(814) 623-2250,
www.JeanBonnetTavern.com

Vegetarian Offerings:
Yes

Supports Local Farmers:
Yes

**Locally Owned
Accommodations Nearby:**
B&B on premises

Things To Do Nearby:
Old Bedford Village, Historic Downtown Bedford, Shawnee State Park, Fort Bedford Museum, Museum of the American Coverlet, Flight 93 Memorial.

felt like a famous writer or something. I've never had this happen and I accepted Melissa and Shannon's gracious and generous offer. Plus, they seemed so passionate about their place and were so cool, that I figured there was no chance I wouldn't love it. But it wasn't until a year later that I would make the trip and be totally blown away by this amazing historic tavern in Bedford, and the young couple who own it.

I arrived at the Jean Bonnet wet and cold after 60 miles of pouring rain. Because I'd made a call a couple weeks earlier, Melissa was there to greet me. She and her manager helped me get all my gear unpacked and up to my room on the third floor of the tavern. But since it was late in the day and a fog that was settling, I barely looked at the grand limestone structure on the way in. Plus I just wanted to take a hot shower and get a hot meal. Oh, and one of those craft beers that Melissa and Shannon told me about the beer festival.

Most of the time with accommodations in old taverns, "old" is usually the key word. Not at the Bonnet. After the Jacobs took over the place, and when they were able, they did a total B&B makeover. They have four rooms, with a couple that can accommodate several people. My room was beautiful! It had a lovely four-post canopy bed, a walk-out balcony, and the best part (for me at the moment), a completely renovated in-suite bathroom with a shower. As soon as Melissa and her manager were out of there, I was in the shower with the hot water flowing.

After my wonderful shower, I walked down to the second floor (the main floor) and scoped the place out. Even though this whole place is a tavern, this level is the "official" tavern. Here's where the bar and most of the action is - and was the very place I planned to park my butt for the rest of the evening. On my way to a booth in a corner, I perused the taps that Melissa and Shannon told me about. They weren't kidding, and I was impressed. They even offer one that's brewed by Marzoni's in Duncansville, PA, exclusively for them – Jean Bonnet's Forbes Trail Pale Ale. I try to go with the house beer whenever possible, especially when said house beer is a pale ale or IPA. Plus, this place is so historic that anything reminiscent of its history seems appropriate.

So what about the history? It's packed full! The Jean Bonnet was built in the 1760s and is a historic landmark. Due to its location, it became an important haven for early settlers and travelers. It was built on the only road connecting eastern Pennsylvania with the Ohio River and territories beyond, at the junction of the Old Forbes and Burd Roads (Rts. 30 and 31). In 1794, Pennsylvania farmers, angered by the federal excise tax on whiskey, met there and raised a liberty pole in protest (and most likely a bottle or two). Then in October 1794, troops summoned by President George Washington camped there on their westward journey to quell the insurrection.

The building, made of native limestone and featuring massive fireplaces and chestnut beams, was built by Robert Callender, an Indian trader, in 1762. The namesake, Jean (John) Bonnet, and his wife purchased the property in 1779. In October 1780, Bonnet was issued a license reading in part "Petitioner lives at the Fork of roads leading to Fort Pitt and the Glades with everything necessary for keeping a Public

House." It changed hands many times after that, and then in 1979 it was placed on the prestigious National Register of Historic Places.

Relaxing and sipping my beer, I took a look at the menu to see what I was going to have for dinner. The Bonnet's menu is as varied as it is complete. Appetizers included Grilled Ahi Tuna and Wings. Soups offered were Tavern Onion Soup, Tavern Chowder, and the Chef's Soup Du Jour. Sandwiches included the Jean Bonnet French Dip, a Battered Fillet of Cod Sandwich, and a Locally Raised Ground Bison Burger. A few Entrees offered were Steaks, Grilled Portobello over Mediterranean Couscous, Wiener Schnitzel, Chicken Parmigiana, Tavern Crab Cakes, Lobster Ravioli topped with Seafood Newburg, and Teriyaki Glazed Atlantic Salmon. They also offer some really nice salads and desserts, of course. Keeping with house beer theory, I chose the Bison Burger because it was a local.

As I enjoyed my lovely beer and delicious local Bison Burger, Melissa joined me for a chat. I asked her the question I ask just about every owner "So what inspired you and Shannon to get into the restaurant biz?" Melissa is like me, she is so passionate and so excited to tell her story that we sat for almost and hour and talked. Some highlights of their wonderful story are that they both worked for Hoss's Corporation, and they met at the opening of a new Hoss's in West Virginia.

But the best part was when Melissa had a corporate meeting in Bedford, and Shannon called and asked her out for a date. He told her he'd heard of a nice place in Bedford and said for her to "wear something nice." When they arrived, he had a dozen roses on the table with a bottle of champagne waiting. Then and there, he proposed to Melissa. Then was 1994, there was the Jean Bonnet! In 1999 they ended up buying the place, and the love that was flowing the night they got engaged is still flowing now.

After a great night's sleep, I awoke to crystal-clear blue skies and warmer temps. I got a cup of coffee from the coffee station in the B&B's hallway, and walked out to the other balcony at the back of the place. Looking across the fields, a little fog remained, but the sun was shining bright against the old limestone exterior and bathed the whole eastern side with warm, pinkish light. Wow! This place is beautiful! I just sat on a rocking chair and took it all in.

After I got dressed, I had a really nice breakfast in a dining room on the ground level of the tavern. This area is very nice too - more intimate and cozier — even more of a historic feel. Both Melissa and Shannon were there, and I had a chance to thank them both for one of the most wonderful experiences I've had while researching my book. They were so gracious and kind (they even provided me with hot, soapy water and a garden hose to wash my filthy bike before I headed home) and asked me to return sometime soon.

Eats, drinks, accommodations, beautiful architecture, history, super nice owners, and even a log cabin gift shop, mini petting zoo, and just a fantastic vibe, the Jean Bonnet has it all. Yeah, I was "bribed" in a way, but you know what? If I wouldn't have loved it, you wouldn't be reading about it. There are many places absent from this book because I just didn't like them or didn't have a good experience. But not here. I would have gladly paid for my stay. In fact I'm already thinking of another trip, and this time roses and champagne might even be involved.

Enjoy!

CHAPTER 8
8 O'CLOCK

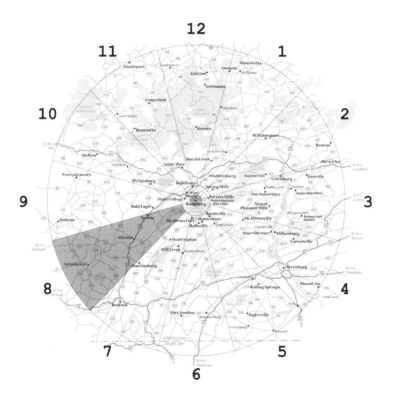

East End Hoagies, aka East End Pizza

TYRONE, BLAIR COUNTY

I first heard about this place from my beer geek friend Mark Dellinger, a savvy traveler and foodie like myself, who traverses the commonwealth for work, and eats on the run a lot. He, like any seasoned traveler, knows it doesn't take long to get sick of (or sick because of) chain restaurants or those mega gas stations that disguise themselves as a place to eat. Mark is also somewhat of a gourmet, so chain or gas station food is not something he even considers – he goes real and local as much as possible.

Since he covers more area on a daily basis than I do, he's become one of my trusted scouts. A few years ago he told me about East End Hoagies and raved about it. He said people travel great distances to eat there or get hoagies to go – to go around the block and all over the country, apparently. He also mentioned they have weird hours, are hard to find if you're a first timer, and close early sometimes.

JUST A TASTE

Locally Owned By:
Louise, Judy, and Kay Sweitzer

Cuisine:
American

Price Range:
$3.00 to $8.00

Hours:
Tues. – Sat. 11am to 7pm
(Closed 2 weeks over Christmas
and 3 weeks in August through
Labor Day)

Location:
1600 Columbia Ave.

Wi-Fi:
No

Contact Info:
(814) 684-2981

Vegetarian Offerings:
No

Supports Local Farmers:
No

**Locally Owned
Accommodations Nearby:**
Laurel Ridge Bed and Breakfast,
(814) 632-6813

Things To Do Nearby:
Walking tours of Tyrone;
Horseshoe Curve, Altoona

This was all very intriguing to me (it reminded me of when I had my combo art gallery and café). Of course, the fact that he raved about it and it was so popular piqued my interest too. So back when I was doing recon for book one, I decided to head out and check out this enigma for myself.

Since I don't do GPS (I personally think it's for wimps) and it wasn't on any map, I had a really tough time finding it, just like Mark indicated. After roaming the streets of Tyrone on The Steed with no luck, I finally spotted a bunch of construction workers on the outskirts of town and thought I'd ask them. Not only did they know about it, they knew exactly where it was and all of them said the hoagies there were the "best ____ing hoagies around." Funny thing, they all had onion breath. Hmm, what was that all about? I chalked it up to yet another piece to this enigmatic puzzle. They also told me I was only a couple blocks away so I took off and was glad to be breathing fresh air again.

Sure enough, as I rolled up to East End (which by the way is...let's just say...well, not the Taj Mahal) it was totally dark inside and a Closed sign hung in the door. "Yeah, this IS weird" I thought. It was Friday, and OK, its 1:30 by this time, but still within the realm of lunch. Hmm, Mark was right on two counts so far - hard to find and weird hours. How can a place be closed at lunch time? The other thing adding to the "enigma" reference was that East End Hoagies is actually East End Pizza. The big red sign hanging from the building clearly reads "East End Pizza." However, everyone I've talked to, including Mark, calls it by what they do best, sell the most of, and are famous for - their hoagies! What's up with this place?

Then, just recently, I was out one night with some friends and one of them, Tara, was talking with me about my book. She was so excited to tell me all the good places she had been to around her hometown of

Altoona. She said "Have you ever been to East End
Hoagies (see, not East End Pizza) in Tyrone? I love
that place! When I go home to visit I always stop
there on the way to pick up hoagies for the family.
Then on the way back, I stop again and pick some up
for my friends here in State College." I said "Yeah,
I was going…" She cut me off and said "Oh, they have
weird hours so if you go you might want to call first.
And do you like onions?" Onions? What? OK, now I've
got to get to this place!

A day or two later I jumped on the internet to see
if East End Pizza/Hoagies had a website. Of course
they didn't, but my Google search yielded an address
and phone number. The next day I tried calling again,
and finally at 9:30am someone answered! I was told
the hours were 11am through 7pm and I thought to
myself, "That's not so weird, but why were they closed
last time?" I did a few things around the house,
packed my gear, and by 10:30 I was on the road.

With the memory of my failed first attempt, and not
wanting to repeat that, I remembered the correct
route through Tyrone. Turning right on to the main
drag (Pennsylvania Ave), I just followed Rt. 453
north past the Rite Aid, then left at the first light
onto W. 14th St. I rolled over the train tracks, veering
right near the park and the American Legion on Lincoln
Ave., and I knew I was close. One more left on to W.
15th (still on 453 N.) and a short right onto Columbia,
and I thought I could smell onions again...but no
construction workers were in sight.

Getting close, I noticed a couple of pickups and a
PennDot truck parked nearby with construction dudes
sitting inside. As I pulled up to the curb right at
11am, the lights where bright inside and a woman was
just unlocking the door. All of a sudden guys were
pouring in, and a line at the counter had formed. I
walked in and was quickly greeted by the strong smell
of onions and a sweet woman behind the counter. I was
asked what I wanted and had no idea. I was, as usual,

taking it all in, and politely said I would let her know. I looked around the small restaurant and watched the guys who had come in before me leaving with brown bags stuffed with hoagies.

When they cleared out I was able to see the menu board, and once again the sweet lady behind the counter asked if she could get me something. "Actually, do you have a public restroom?" I said. She said "No, but just go straight back there (pointing to the back) and it's the first door on your left." I walked back through the supply room and into the little bathroom. It was an ordinary bathroom, but what was funny was they must have had 73 rolls of toilet paper stacked up in the corner! On my exit I joked with a woman working on supplies about their stock of TP. She joked back that if I needed some to go, they could help me out. The sweet woman who greeted me got in on the banter and we all had a good laugh. That seemed to set the tone for my next 2 ½ hours at this wonderful little restaurant, because if I thought our banter was fun then, the best was yet to come.

Laughing aside, I figured it was finally time for me to actually order something. I told the woman that it was my first time there and I heard the hoagies are famous and I'd like to try the one they're most famous for. She said that was their Original (an Italian), so that's what I got. As she turned to go make it, I said, "Oh, no onions please." She stopped dead in her tracks and the whole place went silent. The banter of construction dudes, the chatting of the women working there, the chit-chat of folks waiting in line, and I think even the traffic out front – everything stopped and all eyes were on me! If I was ever a "deer-in-the-headlights," it was now.

Being very cool and not making me feel like an idiot, this sweet woman gently informed me that the "Original" comes standard with onions. "You can have it any way you like, but the original does come with onions." My indecision hung in the air like the heavy smell of the onions I was debating over. "I never get onions," I thought, but it is the "Original" and you know the old saying, "When in Rome..."

So, I went completely Roman and said, "Yeah, go ahead with onions, I want it just like it's meant to be." Like on cue, the place returned to its former vibe of friendly banter, chatting, and hoagie-making bliss - even the cars outside went on their way. I was off the hook and instantly accepted into the fold. I broke precedent and it paid off. The woman formerly referred to as "the sweet woman," introduced herself as Judy. I asked Judy what they had to drink. She pointed to a cooler filled with bottled drinks and said those were my choices. As she walked back to make my hoagie she suggested the chocolate milk which was exactly what I was thinking. By the time I grabbed it, Judy had my hoagie ready. As I took it, I felt eyes watching me, and when I looked at it I knew why.

East End either has a deal with the onion guy, or they're just crazy about onions! What I thought would be a light sprinkle of onions turned out to be a literal PILE of them atop my hoagie. I wisely rolled with it and took a table by the window. I confess I  had a moment of remorse but, "When in Rome..." I picked up my onion-laden hoagie and took a big bite. I could feel the tension in the room - heck in all of Tyrone for that matter. Then something amazing happened. Like an uncontrollable sneeze, a smile came to my face and I audibly made an "Mmm" sound. Wow, what does East End do to their onions?! Wow, what does East End do to their hoagies?! The construction

workers were right, this was by far the best ____ing
hoagie I've ever eaten! The tension in the room
instantly vanished. I was in! I was an East Ender!

I could go on – I have so much more I could write.
Like the hilarious conversations I heard and was
involved in, the history of East End provided table-
side by a visit from Judy, how they opened in Tyrone
in '56, served 89 dozen hoagies on their 50th anniversary, how Judy's mom at 89 still comes in everyday, and how with Kay (her sister), they make the
family operation complete (dad passed away some time
ago – he's the true "Original"). I also found out
about the "weird" hours.

Seems since forever (including when I made my first
visit) the hours were 11am to 1pm, then 5pm to 9pm
or 10pm. (Ah yes! I was there the first time at
1:30!) Since then, they went to 11 to 7 to simplify
life and avoid missing hungry traveler like myself.
But still to this day, if they happen to run out of
hoagie-making stuff, they close early. Why? Well,
it's simple – everything at East End is fresh everyday – meats, cheeses, and veggies (including those
delicious onions) are sliced and prepared daily. Even
the rolls come fresh each day, and in a limited amount.

This place is so worthy of the trouble it took to
pay a visit. I'm hooked! It's no longer an enigma,
and I totally get it. And I understand what Mark and
Tara were talking about. I also get why people even
ask Judy and Kay to ship hoagies via overnight express
delivery all over the country. You gotta try these
hoagies and you gotta go Original. Even if you don't
normally take onions – go for it! However, if you
do, make sure your sweetie goes Original too – those
onions stay with you ALL day and then some!

Enjoy!

Tom & Joe's
ALTOONA, BLAIR COUNTY

My *going LOCAL!* philosophy has a lot to do with the experience, not who's food is  better or worse. So if I had any hope of being true to that in this book I had to include Tom & Joe's – it's an experience and then some. Even without the "experience" part, it's a must-visit place! Great food, authentic décor and atmosphere, "interesting" clientele and personnel, tons of locals/regulars, food cooked out in the open before your eyes, AND free entertainment – all contained in a corner diner that's been doing business since 1933 in the heart of downtown Altoona. You just don't get this kind of stuff in many places anymore.

It all started back in '33 when Tom and Joe Batrus opened a small place they called Tom & Joe Lunch. The name was painted on the windows, as were their features of Sandwiches, Steaks & Chops, Orange Juice, Tomato Juice, and Booth Service. Joe sold his share in the late '40s to Tom, and in 1950, Tom moved the operation to a bigger location across the street and

JUST A TASTE

Locally Owned By:
George Batrus Jr.

Cuisine:
Diner

Price Range:
$1.35 to $7.95

Hours:
Mon. – Fri. 8am to 2pm., Sat. 7am to 1pm., Sun. 7am to noon

Location:
1201 13th Ave.

Wi-Fi:
Yes

Contact Info:
(814) 943-3423,
www.tomandjoes.com

Vegetarian Offerings:
Yes

Supports Local Farmers:
Yes

Locally Owned Accommodations Nearby:
Sebastiano's Hotel, (814) 943-9839

Things To Do Nearby:
Railroaders Museum, Shopping

tweaked the name to just Tom & Joe's. But instead of old-school painted lettering, he went with the latest cool thing of the time, neon. In 1956 he renovated the place, and sometime after that Tom's son George took over the family business. Then around 1989, George Jr. came on board to help his dad and learn the ropes of the diner biz. George Jr. worked alongside his dad until his dad passed away in 2008. Now George Jr. has become the third generation Batrus to run Tom & Joe's.

Working with his dad, and the lifelong relationship the father and son had, is beautifully documented at tomandjoes.com under the heading "A Final Tribute." Here, George Jr. pays homage to his dad with a touching story and the eulogy from the funeral. It's clear that he loved his dad and respected him highly. Now he's able to continue the legacy that his dad left behind, but he's still under a watchful eye. At age 74, Angie Batrus, George's mom, and wife of the late George Sr., still works there and keeps the till running smooth while the rest of the staff whizzes back and forth and in and out of a hungry crowd and a full house. This is where the fun is, if you have a sense of humor and aren't thin-skinned.

Things can be calm one minute, and the next a little dicey if you don't watch yourself, or if a scrap occurs behind the counter. This is where the "experience" and "free entertainment" come in and believe me, it's a T&J's tradition. Way, way back when I was training for a job with Mid State Bank circa 1980, I had to spend a week in downtown Altoona and the word on the street even then was that T&J's was the place for what the Altoona Mirror so accurately described as "Homestyle cooking with a side of sass." (Man, I wish I had come up with that!). And if you think oh, how sassy can they be? How about this quote from waitress Kimberly Rosenberry: "You get what you get, you eat it, you like it, and you shut the hell up." Sassy? You bet!

A lot of folks come to T&J's for the sass as much as for the food. But if George Jr. learned anything from his dad, mom, and short order cook bloodline, it's really the food – and cooking it with love, skill, and speed that keep the customers happy and coming back for more. To master a grill and a cast iron frying pan that's bigger than a car wheel is one thing; to manage a whole restaurant, staff, unruly regulars, AND have the entire menu and all its prices memorized, while flippin' cakes, cookin' bacon, folding omelets and frying homefries is another. George Jr. does all that and still has the capacity to banter and joke with the customers just like his dad used to.

If you go, and I know you will (how can you not?), and if you go on a Friday or Saturday morning for breakfast, be prepared to wait for a table. But, don't do as I did on my first visit and wait to be seated. Donna and crew have no time for such formalities – it's seat yourself or go hungry. And, if you see a table open and you're next in line, you better run for it because I might beat you to it.

Tom & Joe's specialty is breakfast and lunch, but once a week, on Saturdays, they stay open until 1 am. I guess this gives the evening/nighttime crowd a chance to "experience" what the rest of us have come to love and expect from this icon of "Home cooking with a side of sass."

Enjoy!

Texas Hot Dogs
ALTOONA, BLAIR COUNTY

This place was originally called Texas Hot Wieners and has been an Altoona tradition since 1918. The tradition continues, and  the loyalty is still well represented here at Altoona's original Texas Hot Dog. Go there any day of the week (except Sundays) and at any hour, and you will most likely be sitting next to, or standing in line with, someone who has been coming in for dogs for perhaps the past 50 years. I'm not kidding.

One day I was there, Bob (owner/master hot-dogger) didn't even have to be given a verbal order from many of the customers that walked in for takeout. He simply greeted them, chatted for a minute or so while he skillfully prepared their order, and with a few rolls and folds of wrapping paper, their dogs were bagged and they were out the door. I asked him about this and he said that most of his customers are regulars and get the same thing every time. "That last guy has been coming in here for probably the past 30 years," he said.

JUST A TASTE

Locally Owned By:
Bob Lamont

Cuisine:
Hot Dogs

Price Range:
$1.40 to $2.25

Hours:
Mon. – Fri. 9:30am to 7:45pm,
Sat 11am to 7:45pm

Location:
1122 12th Ave

Wi-Fi:
No

Contact Info:
(814) 942-6381

Vegetarian Offerings:
No

Supports Local Farmers:
No

Locally Owned Accommodations Nearby:
Sebastiano's Hotel, (814) 943-9839

Things To Do Nearby:
Railroaders Museum, Shopping

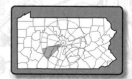

Talk about regulars, every Wednesday the railroad
workers at Norfolk Southern call in an order of
between 160 and 180 hot dogs! These are the "Texas"
style, or regular dogs with the works - chili sauce,
mustard, and onions. I asked Bob how in the world he
keeps 180 hot dogs hot. His reply: "Do it real quick,
wrap 'em up real tight, get 'em done as fast as you
can, and get 'em down there." That one order takes
half an hour to get ready.

Being a master hot-dogger, one of Bob's skills is
lining buns filled with hot dogs up his left hand and
forearm to "dress" them. He can do eight, but 180?
That's more than he can handle, he said with a chuckle.
After that bit of info, I just had to ask the question. I asked Bob how many hot dogs he goes through
in month. "400 to 500 lbs. a week," he said! When I
commented that his hot dog supplier must love him,
he chuckled again and just said "Yeah, probably."

Bob Lamont has the hot dog gig in Altoona locked up,
but he's a mild mannered and modest guy. When I told
him about Lock Haven's claim to have the best Texas
hot dogs, he just chuckled once again and said, "I
don't claim that I'm the best. Every town has a place
they like, and that they're used to. If I'd move to
Florida and try this I might go broke." I hope he
doesn't go to Florida, because Altoona would be
missing a landmark and the regulars would spend way
too much on gas and airfare to get there.

Actually, that may not matter. Regulars and/or locals
don't necessarily have to live in Altoona anyway. Bob
said that many former residents who live out of town
or out of state come in every time they're back in
town. Holidays are big for returning THD-ophiles - I
guess you just can't match an original anywhere else.
And they don't even have to be regulars, locals, or
have ever been to THD before to make a pilgrimage.

In the spring of 2008, then presidential-candidate
Barack Obama stopped in to Bob's place for a Texas

Dog. Bob said that for a week prior to his visit he knew but couldn't tell anyone – not even his mom (who, by the way, was really peeved about that). Not even his staff knew until minutes before Obama's arrival. How did the now-president of the United States of America get to Texas Hot Dog in Altoona, PA? A local who was a lifelong fan worked for the campaign.

But it's not just tradition that brings in the locals and seekers of Texas style hot dogs, it's that a filling hand-made, fresh-off-the-grill lunch can cost as little as a couple bucks and change! Seriously, my lunch, which is pictured with this piece, cost $3.80 ($1.40 per dog and $1.00 for fries). I didn't ask Bob, but I wonder if he would allow BYOB? A cold beer would make that lunch just about perfect.

THD offers many great items at great prices. If you're so bold as to ask for something other than the original, they have everything from naked dogs to those with Cheese and Sauerkraut. They have Burgers, Ham Sandwiches, Fish Sandwiches, Chicken Strips, Mac & Cheese, Chili, and Soups. Sides include Fries, Onion Rings, Cheese Balls, Fried Mushrooms, and Baked Beans. The usual suspects of drinks are offered, but Bob has a "Best Kept Secret" that's not made known on the menu, but the locals know – Draft Root Beer. Draft root beer? What's so secret about that you ask? "It's all in the barrel," Bob says.

He asked if I checked out the big old root beer barrel next to the end of the lunch counter. I did, but thought it was just a prop (many places like to display antiques). However, this was no prop. It was a functional antique that was almost 70 years old and still working like this was its first day. Bob said that it was in the back for years in non-working condition. He had wanted to rehab it, but had no idea how to find parts or instructions, so it continued to sit, but it was always in Bob's heart to bring it back to life. Well with the advent of the internet, and the ability to "Google" most anything, Bob found some old cat in Michigan that knew all about that model of root beer barrel, and even had all the parts he needed to get it up and running again.

Bob tried to explain to me the complexities of the system and how it yields the "best-tasting root beer and birch beer you'll ever have." He even pulled over a chair for me, took off the top, and let me look into the inner workings. I admit, it was an impressive system, and Bob was beaming as he told me all about how he rehabbed it and how cold it keeps the "beers" – he was like a proud father.

I hung out for a while longer and watched more regulars flow in and out. With every one of them it was more than just hunger that brought them in. It was tradition, loyalty, AND the reassurance that the owner is there every hour of every open day, greeting customers and proudly doing a job that his grandfather started almost 100 years ago.

It's all about *going LOCAL!* my friends. And what goes around comes around. Locals, travelers, ex-pats, and even the president support Texas Hot Dog of Altoona. And if WE don't, we'll lose it and every place like it. The motto at THD is, "It's all fun and games until someone loses their wiener." Let's hope that this wiener is never lost. Because what's a guy to do without his wiener? This wiener is a winner!

Enjoy!

Tulune's Southside Saloon
JOHNSTOWN, CAMBRIA COUNTY

"Oh Tulune's, how can I describe thee?" Well, read on, as their website answers that question.

"Well, I can start off by stating that you may be 106 years old, but you look as fresh as ever. You have the area's Largest Selection of Imported and Craft Beers hiding in your cellar, over 200 tasty morsels from 20 countries covering almost every style that a Brewmaster can dream up. Your Staff is as helpful as they are knowledgeable about your many brews and your Food is absolutely Scrumdiddlyicious!

Your atmosphere is as Cool and Eclectic as the myriad of musical styles flowing from your speakers and is a direct reflection of your customer base. You have the type of bar where the Hipsters, Geeks, Jocks, Alternatives, Nerds, Yuppies, Hippies, Baby-Boomers, Emos and Punks collide in a blender of mellowness under a flag of beer appreciation. It seems everyone is friendly and understands that we are all just trying our damndest to have the best possible time. This nirvana is main-

JUST A TASTE

Locally Owned By:
"Founded by" Todd A. Holbay & Michael Pilot

Cuisine:
Pub Food

Price Range:
$3.00 to $9.99

Hours:
Tue. – Sat. 4pm to 2am

Location:
36 Bridge St (Rt. 403)

Wi-Fi:
Yes

Contact Info:
(814) 536-1001,
www.southsidesaloon.com

Vegetarian Offerings:
Yes

Supports Local Farmers:
Yes

Locally Owned Accommodations Nearby:
Stone Ridge Bed and Breakfast, (814) 288-3931

Things To Do Nearby:
Oktoberfest (3rd weekend Sept.) Worldwide Beer Mung (3rd weekend in May), Thunder in the Valley, Music Festivals

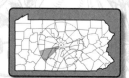

tained through your strict No Jerks Allowed policy, which we all appreciate.

Last, but not least, I must mention your legendary events. Sure, you get in awesome bands every month that know how to throw down some great tunes, but I really look forward to your other events, such as your Anti-Valentine's Day, Helloweenie, Christmas Eve Bash, '70s and '80s Night, Dead Actor Delight, an Oktoberfest with real German Beers and, of course, your amazing Beer Mung that rivals the best beer tastings in the country.

Hands down, THE BEST place to be!"

As a writer, sometimes you just have to admit when you've been bested. I try to be creative, fun, and use unusual words when I write – heck I even make words up, but I don't think I ever used the words scrumdiddlyicious, myriad, or nirvana, and I don't even know what "Emos" means. So after reading that, it was clear that something cool was going down in J-town and I had to check out "THE BEST place to be."

It was an awesome summer afternoon when my friend and fellow artist and biker John Ritter and I took to the road. I knew the route to J-town and we did it in record time. However, I forgot the address and the printout from Google Maps so we were a bit lost when we arrived in the heart of this little city of steel.

Being the atypical man, I looked for the first guy on the street that might be a local and pulled over to ask directions. Turns out this guy wasn't from J-town either, but from Lewistown (near me). He too had ridden his bike there to visit some friends and had no idea where Tulune's was either. However, this cat was so cool that he called his friends to get directions for us. At that, John and I ask him to join us, but he said he was to meet up with his friends and couldn't come. We thanked him, committed the directions to memory, and headed to the old factory district of Moxham.

The factory area of Moxham is not in the most upscale locale in J-town; the surrounding neighborhoods seem cool though. And Tulune's? Well, it's certainly not in the most attractive building I've ever seen and you can easily blow right past it like we almost did. But hey, it's not always the outside that counts, is it? Once inside, I knew in a millisecond that I was going to love the place (and that's before I saw the tap lineup!). We took a table in the barroom because I wanted to be right in the mix of the great groove that was going on – the place was jumpin' and John and I settled in and soaked it up.

John, being an artist himself, instinctively knew what was happening in my head. He knew I was really there for "work," so he just sat back and let me sink deep into Tulune's vibe, and a fine vibe it was. English pub feel actually, with lots of folks enjoying themselves. It has authentic décor with an awesome original tin ceiling above. The food menu is simple pub fare that's designed to be easily made and easily enjoyed. They have all kinds of appetizers, and headings like Burgers, Chicken, Sea & Shore, Pastas, and Platters. All looking very tasty. However, when we looked at the beer menu, the only words I had were those from the book of Revelation.

"Then I saw a new heaven and a new earth, for the first heaven and the first earth had passed away" (Rev. 21:1).

Wholly (not Holy) crap, the website piece was right, there must have been over 200 beers listed! Sometimes I'm actually anal enough to count beer lists, but not this night. Plus it's far too laid-back at Tulune's for such things. I went for a draught of Delirium Tremens and John picked one of my favorites out of the cooler - a most lovely but strong Unibroue La Fin du Monde. I then ordered their Tulune's Crab Cake Platter, and John chose the Bacon BBQ Cheddar Burger. Both our beers and our dinners were as the web writer claimed they would be - "absolutely Scrumdiddlyicious!"

Then, in the middle of my Tulune's "nirvana," John broke protocol and told the waitress who I was and why I was there. I could have killed him! But, if I thought things were going well at this point, when the waitress returned with the owners, it just ramped up a hundred fold.

If you were to pass Todd Holbay and Mike Pilot on the street you would have no idea they even ran a saloon, let alone an awesome one. And you would have no idea they were two of the biggest beer geeks in central PA, AND two of the smartest and most rogue businessmen in the beer biz. They're also two of the most fun, interesting, and nice guys I've ever met. They had John and me laughing so hard a couple times I thought I was going to have a French fry come out my nose! But they also told us stories of how they got where they are today, and it was with a lot of guts, ambition, and good ol' Johnstown grit. These boys have a wonderful story to tell and I encourage you to stop in, have an amazing beer, some great eats, and meet them - you'll be very glad you did. Oh, and be sure to ask them what their old boss said to them when they told him they were quitting so they could introduce craft beers from around the world to the J-town market.

"Oh, Tulune's how can I describe thee?" I think I just did, and then some. However, the story is far from over, and I do encourage you to go there and hear it from Todd and Mike yourself. After a session at Tulune's Southside Saloon, you'll agree, it's "Hands down, THE BEST place to be!"

Enjoy!

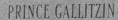

PRINCE GALLITZIN

BORN DEC. 22, 1770, IN HOLLAND.
DIED MAY 6, 1840, IN LORETTO, PA.
FR. DEMETRIUS AUGUSTINE GALLITZIN,
WHOSE PARENTS WERE FROM PROMINENT
RUSSIAN AND AUSTRIAN NOBLE FAMILIES,
ARRIVED IN BALTIMORE, MARYLAND, IN 1792.
HE WAS ORDAINED A ROMAN CATHOLIC PRIEST
MARCH 18, 1795, AND SEVEN MONTHS LATER
HE VISITED THE McGUIRE SETTLEMENT
WHERE HE LATER FOUNDED THE TOWN OF LORETTO.
HE WAS MOST INSTRUMENTAL IN
THE SETTLEMENT OF NORTH CAMBRIA COUNTY
WHERE HE PROMOTED AGRICULTURE,
TRANSPORTATION AND EDUCATION.

CHAPTER 9

9 O'CLOCK

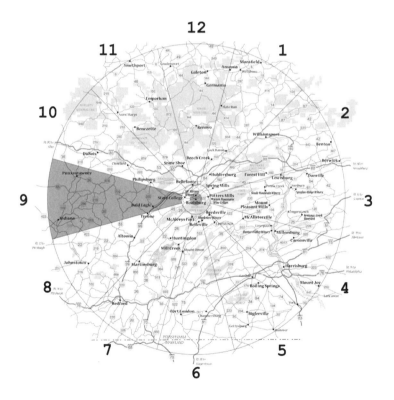

The Family Chill & Grill Restaurant
BALD EAGLE, BLAIR COUNTY

I'm not the only one out there with a passion for riding to out-of-the-way, indie-owned, unique eats. It seems that you don't need a Harley to do it, either. In fact, I was one-upped on this place by a Vespa rider! Like me, Steve Williams  scoots all around central PA doing pretty much what I do, but instead of writing a book about it, he writes his adventures in blog form on the internet. It was there that I found this little gem - The Family Chill & Grill Restaurant.

While perusing Steve's blog, I came across his entry about a little place he seemed to love, shown by the photo of his empty breakfast plate. The caption read something about the food being so good and him being so hungry that he forgot to take a picture before he ate it all. That was OK because he had been there before and had a great photo of a full plate along with one of his scooter outside the place. After looking at the photos and reading about his great review of the place, I just had to check it out for myself. I remember the day well. It was a beautiful

JUST A TASTE

Locally Owned By:
Scott and Juanita Illig

Cuisine:
American

Price Range:
$3 to $16

Hours:
7am to 8pm, seven days a week

Location:
1767 Old Business Rt. 220

Wi-Fi:
Yes

Contact Info:
(814) 684-1990, be3601@aol.com

Vegetarian Offerings:
Yes

Supports Local Farmers:
Yes

Locally Owned Accommodations Nearby:
B&B Tyrone

Things To Do Nearby:
Ridge Soaring Gliderport,
Walking tours of Tyrone

sunny spring day with temps climbing to the '60s, which after a long, cold, and, gray winter, was just what The Steed and I needed. Life was good.

Going over Skytop Mountain is a lot easier now that it's an interstate, but I still prefer the groove of Rt. 45 for destinations west. On that day I chose a path off 45 through Baileyville and then hooked up to a road that dropped me into Warriors Mark. From there I could shoot over the mountain to 220 and into the community of Bald Eagle. I spotted the place Steve raved about on his blog by the photo he'd posted. Honestly, I'm not sure if I would have stopped on my own, as it kinda resembled a convenience store, but on Steve's recommendation I was committed. And from the moment I stepped through the door into this place, I knew I was going to love it. Thanks, Steve!

I know I write this a lot, but you just know a good place when you find it – there's something about the vibe, décor, sound, and clientele – the smell of bacon cooking and coffee brewing sure helps, too. This April morning the place had it all going on and I was smiling from ear to ear. The vibe was that of a classic family restaurant, the décor was wood paneling and memorabilia (authentic, not kitschy). The sounds were of the TV, radio, and locals bantering, as well as the sweet sound of cutlery against porcelain.

The locals were in great form too, especially the older cats at the counter. That day they were ripping on the presidential race while watching the 700 Club and I had to hold my tongue – I was concerned that a newbie donning a "Stop the Insanity" button on his jacket and sitting directly under a signed photo of "the insanity" himself, might cause a stir. My concerns were unfounded though, and the old guys seemed very cool. I was really enjoying this place already, but then the scale tipped a little more.

As I was looking over the menu (which, by the way, was like a 14 year old boy looking at a girlie magazine, as hungry as I was) my waitress, Evelyn, walked up and said, "Would you like some coffee sweetie, while you're looking over the menu?" (Ah, she called me sweetie - the mark of a classic old-school waitress - I loved it!) I said that I would, but was ready to order, too. I went for the works - eggs, toast, bacon, home fries, and pancakes, decaf coffee of course, and water with lemon and no ice. Life was good, for sure, and this day was starting out even better.

It's not just breakfast at The C&G - they offer the whole Kahuna - everything from breakfast to dinner. Here's just the headings to all they offer. From The Griddle, Breakfast Special, Omelets, Breakfast Sandwiches, Breakfast Extras, Lunch Specials, Daily Specials, Subs, Hot Subs, Italian Specialties, Appetizers, Soups, Salads, Burgers & More, Specialty Sandwiches, and Dinner Platters. There's also a very nice pizzeria attached to the place called Firehouse Pizza Shop. But since I don't really write about pizza places I won't get into this one too much, but if you like pizza and like a cool place to enjoy it, this is a great spot. There's a beautiful outdoor patio off to the side and I was told you can get the restaurant fare there too.

The Family Chill and Grill is a great place with great food, atmosphere, and nice waitresses like Evelyn. Hopefully by now they've taken down the photo of what's-his-name but, you know what, even if you're a tree-hugging liberal like me, you're gonna love this place. It's a great destination and drive as well. And if Vespa riders dig it, anyone will. Ha, ha!

Oh yeah, I just realized I didn't write about the "Chill" part of The Chill & Grill. On the opposite side of the restaurant from the Firehouse is a tiny ice cream stand. I think you can go inside but unless you have a peanut body like me, don't expect to get in there with a lot of friends. The true way to do it is to stand outside and order at the window. This side is only open spring through summer and makes use of the patio out back.

Now go and get some Grillin' and do some Chillin'.

Enjoy!

Nick's Corner Lunch
PUNXSUTAWNEY, JEFFERSON COUNTY

I intended to include Nick's Corner Lunch in my first book but just didn't have the time to complete it or the room for it. The funny thing is, part of my book's title reads "Unique Eats," and I admit that not every place I included was that unique. Yeah, I really liked the places I wrote about, or they had lots of other merits, but when it came down to the pure definition of "unique," well maybe some weren't so much. So when Nick's got bumped, I was bummed because this is certainly one with "Unique Eats" and I'm so happy he's still at it so I can feature his place here and now in Volume 2.

I first heard about this place from a woman who works at the North West PA Great Outdoors Visitors Bureau. She emailed me with this simple bit of info *"Old style lunch grill, three types of foods - that's it - hot dogs, hamburgers, and sausage, ALL on hot dog buns."* With my curiosity piqued, and on a beautiful summer day, I fired up The Steed, and the quest for the *Ménage à Trois* of the hot dog bun was on.

JUST A TASTE

Locally Owned By:
Nick & Barb Gresock

Cuisine:
Old School Lunch

Price Range:
$1.00 to $2.10

Hours:
Mon. – Sat. 11am to 7pm

Location:
265 N. Findley St.

Wi-Fi:
No

Contact Info:
(814) 938-4020

Vegetarian Offerings:
No

Supports Local Farmers:
No

Locally Owned Accommodations Nearby:
Pantall Hotel,

135 East Mahoning St.
(800) 872-6825, (814) 938-6600

Things To Do Nearby:
Groundhog Day, Groundhog Zoo, Weather Museum, Historic Smicksburg

I found Nick's on the north side of Punxy, on the left going up Findley, just on the other side of the train tracks. It was a huge brick building and must have been an old railway warehouse or something. It was very beautiful and had a hand-painted façade on the south side with giant letters spelling out Lauderbach-Barber Co. Wholesale Grocers, making Nick's a place you can't miss.

When I walked in, I was immediately impressed by the cleanliness and the simple and uncluttered décor. Some places fill every nook and cranny with stuff, but at Nick's, it's clean and efficient. At the far end was Nick himself wrangling dogs, burgers, and sausages on the grill with the skill of a seasoned short-order cook. But when I took a closer look, I noticed something else on the grill that totally messed up the *Ménage à Trois* idea (which I personally thought was clever if not hilarious). There was ham on the grill!

Turns out Nick's been grillin' ham, and ham & cheese sammies since the beginning, when he started at a little neighborhood grocery and grill place called Carlino's in 1959 (they had been in business in Punxy

since '26). Actually back then he worked mostly with the grocery part, but in the mid 1980s started working at the grill. He worked there perfecting his skills and eventually took over the place when the last of the Carlino brothers passed away in '97. By 1999, the property that Carlino's occupied for 73 years was torn down, which brought Nick to the railroad warehouse in 2000.

So why is everything served on a hot dog bun? Well believe it or not, back in the day (1926) the only type of bun was a long-style bun. There were no round buns then. That stinks for one obvious reason (probably just obvious to me of course), all the "bun" or "buns" jokes and comments had to wait. Imagine life without "Bun in the oven," or "Whoa, nice buns!" According to Nick, round buns didn't come out till sometime in the 1930s. I guess I could have tried to Google that, but let's just go with it. Nick said when they came up with hamburgers (long after the hot dog) as we know them today, they used sliced bread. Prior to the round hamburger they just cooked hamburger meat and laid it in a regulation hot dog bun.

Think about this for a minute – serving any meat, whether tubed or not, is best in a hot dog-style bun because you can add your condiments without said condiments running out on all sides. Only the two ends become escape routes and the one side should be mostly in your mouth – leaving the other to be carefully tilted up so as to not allow for a mess on your clothes. Brilliant! Nick knows what he's doing *and* is saving you time and money at the cleaners.

Another interesting fact Nick shared with me, is that "back in the day" it was just dogs and ham sandwiches. In fact, Punxy had five hot dog shops back then. Dogs ruled, and ham was right there to fill in the gaps. Nowadays, save the little hot dog shops scattered around, and kids menus, it seems the hamburger has taken the lead in our quest for meals on the run, or meals you can eat with your hands. But at Nick's

Corner Lunch, all meats get equal billing and all
are as they used to be - served on a long, regulation
hot dog bun. And you know what else is as it used to
be? The price! Dogs here cash out at $1.10 ($1.00 w/
out bun - for kids) and the most expensive item (not
counting the beer), the hot sausage, cashes out at a
whopping $2.15! Did I just mention beer? Yes my friends,
beer! Nick (God love him) knows that, other than
pizza, the good ol' American hot dog, hamburger, hot
sausage, and ham sandwich are best enjoyed with a
cold beer.

So, right there in all its glory, right in the middle
of the place, is a big cooler filled with beers. And,
for a somewhat small town, with what is probably a
small, if any, beer snob population, Nick carries
some pretty good beers. At last check he had the
usual suspects *but* also had some fine ones like Harp,
Guinness, Pilsner Urquell, and Anchor Steam! He was
also quite the jokester, never missing an opportunity
to tell a good one, whether clean or a little "dusty,"
never dirty - he's a quality dude.

Nick's wife, Barb, is a sweet woman and kinda like
Nick's "straight man." She didn't joke, but you knew
she loved it when Nick did, but acted like she didn't
(that in itself was funny). But, she was very easy
to talk to until I whipped-out my digital recorder
to make sure I got all the history and happenings of
Nick's place. I guess not too many bikers come in
asking so many questions, then whip out a recorder
to boot. Once we started chatting again though, she
didn't seem to mind and even took the lead to help
me with the "Just a Taste" section. She and Nick
made a good pair, and she was very efficient as the
sole waitress and cashier.

When Barb asked what she could get me, I said without
hesitation, "A *Ménage à Quatre* and a beer!" Kidding.
I said "All four, and a beer!" She gave the order to
Nick and he started putting my gastronomic love fest
together. When I asked Nick what beer he'd recommend,

he told Barb to go to the bottom right side of the cooler and grab the one there. I didn't know what was going to appear, and honestly I was a bit scared. What if she pulled out a Coors Light or something? I wouldn't want to insult Nick or Barb by refusing it – I would just have to drink it. Well, as I wrote earlier, Nick takes his beer selection pretty seriously. Barb opened the cooler door, reached down to the bottom right side, and pulled out a Leffe Blonde – a most wonderful Belgian ale that I first fell in love with while in France.

Before I knew it, there before me at the counter was a hot dog with everything, a hamburger with everything, a ham & chesse with everything, a hot sausage with everything, AND a super cold and most wonderful Belgian beer! Wow, all was super good, and all for under $10.

Now get yourselves to Punxsutawney and check out Nick's Corner Lunch. He and his partner/wife Barb run a really nice little place that is like it must have been "back in the day." Go for the *Ménage à Quatre* (please don't call it that – they'll have no idea what you're talking about)! Seriously, go for one of everything, with everything! Ask for a good quality beer from the cooler (Nick will joke that a glass will cost extra) and enjoy a great lunch or dinner all served on hot dog buns! What a find! What a great place!

Enjoy!

Caffe Amadeus
INDIANA, INDIANA COUNTY

How often do you hop on your bike or get in your car and travel 100 miles for a cup of coffee? Probably not very often. But when you're writing a book that includes Cozy Cafés, and you hear of one that's in a town you wanted to visit anyway, and it's a brilliant sunny summer morning, it seems like a good idea to at least make one trip to check it out. That was my thinking this morning when I got up. Once I plotted out a course for Jimmy Stewart's home town of Indiana, PA, to check out a place called Caffe Amadeus, I fired up the bike and took off.

Yeah, 100 miles seems like a long way to go, but isn't this book about adventure? Doesn't the title read in part, "An Adventurer's Guide?" So what's 100 miles? And yes, I realize my radius is 75, but that's as the crow flies - cars and motorcycles have to follow set paths, and by my odometer, the path to Indiana took exactly 100 miles. And like I predicted, as soon as I walked in though the door of Caffe Amadeus, I knew it was worth the trip! I'm sitting here now in a big, super-soft couch, and in front of me on a

JUST A TASTE

Locally Owned By:
Bill, Andi, and Alex Szep

Cuisine:
European Style

Price Range:
$1.45 to $5.50

Hours:
Mon. – Fri. 7am to 5pm, Sat. 9am to 5pm, Sun. 9am to 2pm

Location:
628 Philadelphia St.

Wi-Fi:
Yes

Contact Info:
(724) 349-0540,
www.caffeamadeus.com

Vegetarian Offerings:
Yes

Supports Local Farmers:
No

Locally Owned Accommodations Nearby:
Heritage House Suites,
(724) 463-3430

Things To Do Nearby:
Jimmy Stewart Museum, Indiana University Museum, Covered Bridges, Fairs and Festivals.

coffee table are a beautifully prepared latte and a sweet slice of cranberry apple cake. I'm sooo glad I made the trip! Speaking of making a trip, it's been a long journey for this place too – one that's taken them around the world.

In 1993, Bill Szep made a trip to Seattle where he was amazed by all the cool coffee shops there. Because of that trip, he got a job at La Prima Espresso, where he learned how to be a barista. Later he even learned to roast coffee. In 1998, he volunteered for a peace-keeping mission in Hungary where he discovered his Hungarian roots. He was also "out to eat every pastry and see every coffeehouse!" he said.

It was at a coffeehouse that he met a Hungarian woman named Andi. With his limited Hungarian vocabulary and trusty English/Hungarian dictionary, they met every day for coffee. Within a short time, Andi and he were married in a former palace and began their life together. "Andi is my hero!" Bill exclaims. "Andi learned English, got her citizenship, and learned to drive!"

Andi's a creative woman and needed a creative outlet. She got a job at Aldo Coffee Company in Mt. Lebanon, and the owner sent her to Chicago for training at Intelligentsia Coffee. She mastered latte art and soon became Aldo's trainer. Andi even participated in the Millrock latte art competition at the 2005 CoffeeFest in Washington D.C. and was a finalist! Andi now knew her creative passion: creating latte

 art. She's come all the way from Budapest, where she once worked in a pastry shop, to Indiana to own of her own world-class café!

Caffé Amadeus opened in 2007, and Bill and Andi's daughter Alex works there too. In fact, Alex is giving Andi a run for her money, as she is an upcoming latte artist too!

Not only is she the youngest competitor at the Millrock latte art competition, but has competed in Chicago, Seattle, and in 2010 broke into the finals with her overall 4th place finish in New York. This kid is good!

Bill's not at the café much, as he now works full-time with the Pennsylvania Air National Guard. He himself has done some pretty cool stuff, having served his country in the military since 1984. The Guard has also given him and his family a lot of opportunities and experiences, and his employment there brings in "the daily bread," as he says. Bill is very proud of his service, though especially his services during the Lockerbie disaster, the 1998 Bosnian relief effort, and the 1999 Kosovo campaign. Many people thank him for his service, but he really thanks all of them for their support and work to make America a safer place. He is also grateful for all those who support him and his family's coffeehouse too.

Wow, 100 miles is nothing compared to what Bill has traveled and what lengths Alex and Andi have travel-led to bring this wonderful place and their coffee making skills to Indiana. Sitting here now, and after enjoying my coffee and cake (which Andi makes from scratch), I had the absolute joy of meeting Andi and Alex. What a sweet woman and girl! And what a passion for perfection and authenticity from a 17 year old! Her mom beamed as she spoke of Alex, her husband Bill, and the life they've created and work so hard to maintain there in Indiana. I have no doubt this wonderful family will succeed.

Please make the trip. Whether 1, 10, 100, or more miles, Caffe Amadeus is worth the drive. You will experience and taste there what a true European coffee shop is like. And just think, even 100 miles is nothing compared to a trip abroad for the same thing. You "Rock me, Amadeus"!

Enjoy!

CHAPTER 10
10 O'CLOCK

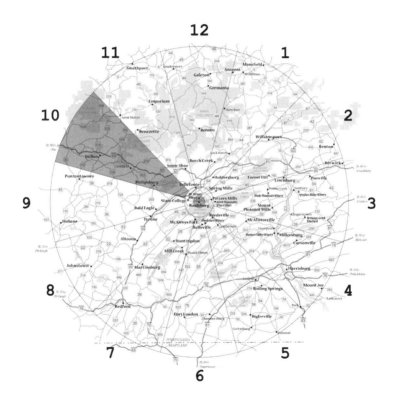

Hogs Galore
PHILIPSBURG, CENTRE COUNTY

I had first heard about Hogs Galore at a number of local eateries when, while looking at their menus, I read that they exclusively use Hogs Galore for their pork. I wondered what the heck Hogs Galore was, but figured places like Otto's Pub and Herwig's Bistro knew what they were doing. Plus, whenever I had a meal or sandwich involving pork at any of these places, the taste was amazing. After some inquiries, I found out that Hogs Galore was a farm, a butcher shop, and a restaurant. Restaurant? At that, I thought I better check this place out.

It took some doing, but I finally found the place on the outskirts of Philipsburg in the Moshannon Valley Regional Business Park near the top of the mountain. It was a really nice place with a small eatery on one side and a full-blown butcher shop on the other. I walked into a place that was bustling on both sides. Customers were lined up waiting for a young guy to custom cut their meat, while others gathered pre-packaged portions. Everywhere you looked it was pork, and folks where buying it up!

JUST A TASTE

Locally Owned By:
The Mathis Family

Cuisine:
All Pork, All the Time

Price Range:
$2.99 to $13.25

Hours:
Mon. – Th. 11am to 7pm,
Fri. & Sat. 11am to 8pm,
Sun. noon to 6pm

Location:
330 Enterprise Dr. Philipsburg,
PA, at the Moshannon Valley
Business Park

Wi-Fi:
Yes

Contact Info:
(814) 342-7060

Vegetarian Offerings:
Are You Kidding?

Supports Local Farmers:
Yes (they ARE the farmers)

**Locally Owned
Accommodations Nearby:**
The Philips Hotel, (814) 343-5582

Things To Do Nearby:
Bowling

Seriously, this place is like a tribute to pork. In the butcher shop they have Pork Chops, Pork Loin, Pork Shoulder, Pork Roast, Pork Hocks, Pork Shanks, Butt Steak, Butt Roast, Ground Pork, Neck Bones (yikes!), Pig Legs, Pig Feet, Baby Back Ribs, St. Louis Ribs, Ham, Bacon, and a lot more. Then there's the Smoked Loin Ends, Smoked Hocks, Smoked Feet, Smoked Ears (yikes!), Smoked Sausage, and more. Speaking of sausage, they offer Hot Italian, Mild Italian, Breakfast, Maple Breakfast, Wisconsin Style Bratwurst, Kielbasa, Garlic Kielbasa, Bologna, Pepperoni, and... But since I wasn't in the market for pork to go, and I was getting really hungry looking at the stuff, and smelling what was going on in the restaurant, I decide it was time to taste what I was seeing.

Over in the small restaurant they offer St. Louis Style Ribs, Baby Back Ribs, Pulled Pork Sandwiches, Pork Chops, Sausage Sandwiches, Wings, and BBQ Chicken. Hey, how'd they get in there?! I ordered the large pulled pork sandwich, and luckily just the small order of fries. The sandwich was HUGE and came with BBQ sauce and so much pork that I had to ask for a fork to get all that fell out of the bun. I struggled to finish the last fry (not a common occurrence, my friends), and when I paid the bill it was $5.28! Granted, I only had water because they have no alcohol license, but guess what? They allow BYOB! So you might be thinking "Hey Ken, there are BBQ places everywhere, and we can buy any pork product we want at the grocery store. (Well maybe not pig ears)." I say, eat any of that stuff for a while and eventually you'll either be sick, glow in the dark, or both – probably both. Why? Because you wouldn't believe the crap (putting it mildly) industrial meat producers put in your food. Plus you don't even want to know how the animals they raise are housed and treated. Do yourself, your kids, and perhaps your grandkids a favor and stop buying industrially produced food – especially meat. Do yourself another favor and check out www.themeatrix.com.

The Mathis family are also farmers (livestock only), and have what is called a Farrow-to-Finish farm – the pigs are bred there, born there, grow up there, and go to market from there. This allows for complete control of the animal's genetics. These folks are so sensitive about the health of the livestock (and yours) they even mix all their own feed for the pigs which makes sure that absolutely NOTHING gets into the animals except the purest of ingredients. Did you know that the digestive system of pigs is very similar to ours? They're not ruminants – not able to digest grass like cows or sheep so they don't "free range." They basically can eat what we eat, and for the tastiest pork, it's a diet based on corn and soybeans.

Do you think I knew all this? No way (well, I do know about the whole industrial meat corruption system and I do not buy ANY meat other than from sources like Hogs Galore or other local health-minded farmers). But Garfield Mathis does, and he's the one who spent almost an hour with me after my meal.

He told me this all started – the farm, the shop, and the restaurant – because his mom and dad were given one little piglet as a wedding gift in 1979! Both of them are actually successful doctors. Dr. Jeanne Beyer is still practicing, but Dr. James Mathis retired when the Philipsburg hospital closed in 2006. Now he and his son have one of the most renowned hog farms around. Their attention to quality control, animal welfare, and a passion for bringing healthy meats to you and me is outstanding. Their meats can be enjoyed at quality-minded local restaurants, and at their own shop and restaurant. I encourage you to visit their place outside Philipsburg and taste for yourself. Hogs Galore, for me, represents where I hope the future of food production and food service is headed now and in the future.

Enjoy!

American Diner

PHILIPSBURG, CENTRE COUNTY

I've stopped at this place many a time over the years, so I consider it a sure bet – you probably won't ever find  it listed in the updates page of my website due to closing – let's hope not anyway. Most, actually all of my stops there have been aboard The Mighty Steed, and not just for food. One time my pal Mike and I stopped for more than breakfast.

(For The Rest of the Story go to **www.goingLOCALpa.com/TRS**)

JUST A TASTE

Locally Owned By:
Dave & Dee McClure

Cuisine:
American

Price Range:
$1.50 to $11.35

Hours:
6am – 7pm

Location:
1841 Philipsburg/Bigler Hwy.

Wi-Fi:
No

Contact Info:
(814) 342-5304

Vegetarian Offerings:
No

Supports Local Farmers:
No

Locally Owned Accommodations Nearby:
Whispering Sisters B&B, (571) 233-8606

Things To Do Nearby:
Shopping, Outdoor Activities

Luigi's
DUBOIS, CLEARFIELD COUNTY

This might be the best authentic Italian place I've been to this side of Rome, and it is most definitely the most welcoming and friendly  place I've been to anywhere. That's a big boast, because I've been to many places here and abroad, and have been treated very well. At Luigi's though, it was like I walked into a big family reunion or was some sort of long-lost friend of everybody – from the customers to the cooks! But the welcome and attention I got from Eddie Tate, the owner, well, it was like none other. By the time I left his place, not only was my belly full and very happy, but my heart, soul, mind, and spirit were filled to capacity as well, and I can't wait to return. And here's how it all happened.

It was 6pm when I rolled up Brady Street in downtown DuBois. I turned into the parking lot of a huge old building with a massive sign on it reading "Luigi's Ristorante and Catering." I got off the bike and headed in to find a bunch of folks hanging out, talking, laughing, and drinking, all with lots of smiles.

JUST A TASTE

Locally Owned By:
Eddie & Heather Tate

Cuisine:
Italian

Price Range:
$3.25 to $22.95

Hours:
Tue. – Th. 11am to 9pm, bar till 10pm, Fri .& Sat. 11am to 10pm, bar till 11pm, Sun. 12am to 8pm, bar till 9pm

Location:
32 N. Brady Street

Wi-Fi:
Yes

Contact Info:
(814) 375-9113,
www.luigisristorante.com

Vegetarian Offerings:
Yes

Supports Local Farmers:
Yes

Locally Owned Accommodations Nearby:
Narrows Creek B&B

Things To Do Nearby:
DuBois Harley Davidson, Punxsutawney, Straub Brewery in St. Marys, Allegheny National Forest

And why not? It was Friday, it was summer, and life was beautiful! As I walked farther in, I noticed a table set up in the middle of the outdoor patio area filled with a bunch of appetizers – all well prepped, and presented on silver platters with linens underneath. I also spotted a temporary bar at the far end attended by two young women dressed in formal attire. Right away I thought it was some sort of private party or something, so I just kept walking, wishing I had been invited.

As I passed a group of very attractive, well-dressed women, one of them stopped and asked "Are you here for the party?" Not wanting to lie, but not wanting to be overlooked as a possible guest of this great event, I sheepishly said, "Maybe." Then she said, "Well, are you?" Now I picked up on a little bit of banter starting, so I replied, "Well, if you want me to." She didn't miss a beat and came right back with, "So you're here for the duck farts?!" I said, "I have no idea what that is (it's whiskey, amaretto, almond liqueur, and Bailey's). I'm from out of town and it's my first time here, but if you want me to be here for duck farts, I'm all in." Then one of her posse said, "This is the owner." I smirked and responded with, "You don't look like a Luigi." She fired back, "I'm his wife, and his name is Eddie." I thought, "You idiot! You were just bantering with the wife of an Italian guy named Eddie!" Now, what I thought was just playful banter was going to end with me at the bottom of the Treasure Lake!

Just then she looked to the door of the restaurant and said "There he is!" I looked to see a guy coming out who was neatly dressed with a crisp white shirt, black pants, black apron, jet-black slicked-back hair, and with a face of the quintessential Italian restaurant owner of every "mob" type movie ever made. Then to my surprise she enthusiastically said, "Eddie, this guy's from out of town and it's his first time here!" Eddie made a beeline right to me with an outstretched hand and ear-to-ear smile. He shook my hand, looked me straight in the eye and said, "What's your name?" I told him, and he said "Hi Ken, I'm Eddie Tate, welcome to Luigi's!" Whew!!!

Before I knew it, I was getting a tour of the place! This guy knows and practices the Holy Grail of running a business - customer service and attention. On my tour, Eddie must have greeted and shaken hands with 20 other people. Those he knew, he introduced me to, and they all seemed genuinely happy to meet me! As we made our way through the two large dining rooms, Eddie told me that the building used to be a department store. I swear the walls were 20 feet high and covered with photos till they reached the ceilings, which were the old antique decorative tin type. Practically all the tables in the dining rooms were filled, and again, the vibe was like a big family reunion. Everyone was smiling, eating, talking, laughing, and just having a wonderful time. Once Eddie guided me around to the front of the place and then into the bar area just off the entrance, I had to pause a moment. I then said to Eddie, "Wow, this is where I'm hanging out for dinner."

I've been in a lot of barrooms, my friends, and this one ranks among the very best. Just like the dining rooms, this too had a beautifully restored and painted tin ceiling overhead. The walls were also nearly covered with photos, posters, a vintage DuBois Budweiser Beer sign, and a big Italian flag, among other things. Behind the bar was a beautiful hand-carved back bar with the classic huge mirror in the center. Bar stools allowed for both drinking and dining at the bar, but what I thought was the best were about five or six booths for two along the walls. Luckily for me, the last one was just clearing and I snagged it. From this very cozy vantage point, I could not only clandestinely write about the place, but observe, soak it all in, and EAT! By this time I was getting hungry, and like clockwork my waitress arrived with a menu.

Luigi's menu offers a wonderful selection of choices from Appetizers to Desserts, but a few things set this menu apart from others and are worth noting. The Luigi Sampler is an appetizer for six that includes Stuffed Mushrooms, Stuffed Hot Peppers, and Bruschetta; Skip's Tomato Salad is a popular feature ("Skip" was Eddie's dad); Luigi's Tuscany Collection comes with either grilled vegetables, chicken, or shrimp scampi, and is served on a bed of Luigi's own vegetable spaghetti made from julienned carrots, zucchini, and yellow summer squash. Luigi's House Specialties include their Famous Spaghetti, made with their homemade sauce, which is also sold by the jar; Elise's Tour of Italy, lasagna with a meatball; Chicken Maria; and Gnocchi with Alfredo; Polenta; Cod Romano; Portabella Ravioli; and Italian Style Steaks, served with house garden salad, vegetable, and pasta or potato. Luigi's also offers a variety of sandwiches, pizzas, and stromboli.

Not long after I got settled in, Eddie came by to check on me and I asked him what he recommended. This was like somebody asking me what my favorite place is that I've written about (happens all the time). Eddie was gracious and highlighted several selections. It was Friday and I thought fish would be appropriate, so I went for the Cod Romano and a glass of house Chianti. Eddie said the cod would melt in my mouth, and it did. What I didn't read from the menu or apparently didn't hear from him, was that it came with pasta topped with a delicious clam sauce. Nor did Eddie tell me how big the cod was - it was HUGE! Between the salad, large fillet, and pasta, I couldn't finish my meal. I tried, mind you, but no - I got the remainder to go.

This had been an awesome evening. From the time I arrived at Luigi's and stumbled unwittingly into a Duck Fart Party, mistakenly and unintentionally (honestly Eddie) bantering with Eddie's wife, meeting Eddie himself (and not being fitted with a pair of cement water wings for a "dip" in Treasure Lake), getting a personal tour of the place, meeting a bunch of new friends, having a wonderful meal, and just hanging out in a first class, totally authentic, and totally casual restaurant, I considered myself a very blessed man and a much-appreciated customer. But then I did something that would elevate the evening to epic status.

Typically I do not do or say anything when I'm visiting a potential place for my book. For one thing, I don't want to be treated any differently than when you visit. The next is that maybe I won't like the place, and I sure don't want to hurt anybody's feelings when they find out I didn't include them. But this place was a done deal from the time I met Eddie and he shook my hand and welcomed me to his place. Plus, production time on this book was coming fast and I had to get the facts of Luigi's for the Just a Taste section.

I found Eddie (where else) hanging out with the locals, still enjoying the summer's eve and shots of duck farts on the back patio. As I shook his hand, I leaned in and told him about my book and my plans to put his place in book 2, and I needed some info. Well you would have thought I was a famous writer or personality from the Food Network or something. He put his hand on my shoulder and took me directly over to meet his wife. I cringed a bit, but Heather was so gracious and actually apologized to ME for not being a better hostess when I came in. I apologized to her profusely and she and Eddie had a good laugh. Eddie then whisked me off again for another tour - this one was ALL ACCESS!

I got the basement tour and then learned all about the building's past, I met John, his manager, was introduced to more guests (but this time like a celebrity), and then got the prized tour of his massive and bustling kitchen operation. As soon as we walked through the double swinging doors, Eddie called out to the entire kitchen "Hey everybody, say hi to Ken!" Like it was totally scripted (and I guarantee it wasn't), EVERYONE (like a dozen or more), in complete unison, stopped what they were doing and shouted "Hi, Ken!" I actually felt like a celebrity. Eddie pointed out how everything runs to make his place work as well as it does. He sung great praises of his staff and even gave me a loaf of his homemade bread AND a jar of his famous spaghetti sauce!

His arm across my shoulder, he walked me back out to the patio. He gathered more guests and friends and told them about my book. We chatted a bit more, and as I walked out to my bike, I heard Eddie say "Hey everybody, say goodbye to Ken!" Again, like it was scripted, everybody in unison yelled out "Goodbye, Ken!" They all waved as I pulled out of the parking lot, and I truly felt as though I had met some lost relatives, or at least made some great new friends.

As I cruised home on Rt. 80 with a wide open road ahead and a big yellow moon shining over me, I thought "Wow, I'm so blessed, and so happy to have visited Luigi's." My head and heart were so overflowing from the experience that I practically wrote this whole story in my head on the way home. That night was truly epic, and one I'll never forget.

Thank you Eddie and Heather!

Enjoy!

251

CHAPTER 11
11 O'CLOCK

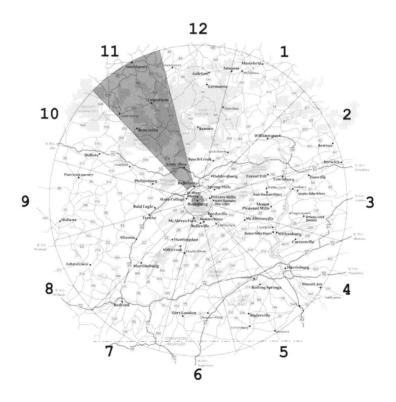

Snow Shoe 22 Restaurant

SNOW SHOE, CENTRE COUNTY

I came about this place because they don't discriminate. What I mean is, they don't discriminate on what you want to eat, or when you want to eat it.

I woke up to a beautiful day, hungry and wanting to ride somewhere for breakfast, but as usual, didn't get going on time. I ended up at a little restaurant craving breakfast but arrived a half an hour after they stopped serving it. I admit I was a bit annoyed and my stomach grumbled, as I did, under my breath. I walked out of the restaurant, hopped back on the bike, and decided to head north to a truck stop I remembered from years back. Truck stops are one of those Americana icons of good ol' home cookin' that most of the time serve all meals at all times. I bet you, at one time in your life, you had breakfast for dinner. Remember that evening when nothing seemed better to you than pancakes, or waffles, or eggs, or some kind of breakfast food? So thank God for the great American truck stop, which has based their business model on the fickle cravings of the human palate at any time of day.

JUST A TASTE

Locally Owned By:
Rees Family

Cuisine:
Truck Stop

Price Range:
$1.50 to $10.95

Hours:
7am to 11pm Everyday

Location:
Exit 147 on Interstate 80 &
Rt. 144, 516 East Sycamore Road

Wi-Fi:
No

Contact Info:
(814) 387-4288

Vegetarian Offerings:
No

Supports Local Farmers:
Yes

**Locally Owned
Accommodations Nearby:**
Mountainview Farms Bed and
Breakfast, (814) 345-6185

Things To Do Nearby:
Riding the "Ridge Road"
Rt. 144, PA Wilds

After a fun and rather fast ride up Rt. 144, I arrived
at the Snow Shoe 22 Restaurant even hungrier and later
than before. I walked in and headed straight for the
lunch counter, or in my case, breakfast counter. Since
I was neither a trucker, interstate traveler, or local,
I wasn't quite sure what kind of a reception I'd
get, but my waitress was very gracious and welcomed
me with a smile. Nervously, I asked her if they were
still serving breakfast and she replied "Sweetie, we
serve breakfast all day," and handed me a menu. I was
sooo happy, plus she called me Sweetie! Love that –
totally old school.

I perused the menu and found exactly what I wanted –
the "Mountain Top," two pancakes, two eggs, and two
strips of bacon. After I told my nice waitress what
I wanted, she walked away and I drifted into a daydream
of me running across a beach with my arms open wide
while a big ol' pancake and strips of bacon were
running towards me.

"ORDER!"

What?! I snapped back into reality when my mild-
mannered waitress shouted that through the tiny window
separating our space from the kitchen. I thought she
was mad at the cooks or something, but when the other
waitresses came and did the same for every order, I
figured it was just standard protocol. It was funny
too, and was another old school thing. In my opinion,
if truck stops and diners aren't old school in at least
a few ways, and the waitresses don't call you Sweetie
or something, it's not a real truck stop or diner.

I swear, no more did I hear "ORDER!" than I heard my
waitress say "Here ya go, Sweetie." There before my
eyes was the most wonderful plate of steaming hot
yummy breakfast bounty I could have dreamed of (and
obviously I can dream up a pretty awesome breakfast).
I tore into it so fast I forgot to take a picture
first. I did after the first bite, but now my delicious cakes of fluffy goodness looked more like a

syrupy golden brown Pac-Man, but Pac-Man never tasted sooo deelicious!

Once done with my afternoon breakfast, while sipping my coffee, I finally took a closer, more serious look at the menu, and it must have had around one hundred different items! Rather than list them all I'll just list the headings. They have Dinners (including seafood), Platters, Sides, Sandwiches; Hoagies, Soups & Salads; Dessert; and of course Breakfast all day. After that, I gathered my things and asked for my check.

At this place you pay your bill at a little area between the main restaurant and the lunch counter. There I noticed something I didn't on the way in (probably because I was too focused on getting breakfast). This place has a tiny gift shop with a very "eclectic" array of stuff (for lack of a better word). Things like knives, chewing tobacco, cigars, gum, Necco Wafers, radios, angel key chains, lottery tickets, rolling papers, and romance novels just to name a few. There's also some "interesting" video games in the entrance that you might want to shield the kids from.

Hey, this is a Truck Stop, not an upscale frou-frou place. It's simple food done well, and at very reasonable prices. So it has some quirks...most of the best places do. This one's been around a long time and has seen a lot of different folks from coast to coast walk through the door. So whether you're an old scruffy trucker (not that there's anything wrong with that), world traveler doing a road trip across America, a local looking for a good meal, or a motorcycling scout of unique eats like me, this place welcomes all. They're really friendly here and don't discriminate with people, or what time of day you can get breakfast. Snow Shoe 22 Restaurant is a Must Stop Truck Stop!

Enjoy!

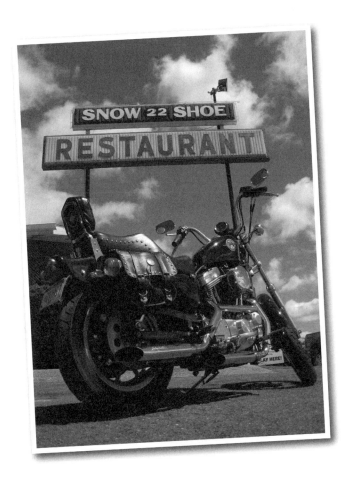

Benezette Hotel
BENEZETTE, ELK COUNTY

I had heard about the Benezette Hotel from lots of folks over many years. I don't know why it took me so long to get there, but once I made the trip I was so glad I did! It's the kind of place, like many old-timey hotel/taverns, that have that *Je ne sais quoi,* that certain something I just love. And like many of its kind, it's not the outside that makes it, but the inside. No chain, no matter how hard they try, can replicate a place like this. The Benezette's the real thing. Not only that but the food is great, the owners are local, it's community supported, and wild elk roam the property from time to time. They even roam the menu too!

That's right, The Benezette Hotel offers an Elk Burger — real elk for real people, and that's what I had for dinner on my first visit, along with a very nice Straub Special Dark. The burger was really good and is good for you. It's low in fat and not pumped with nuclear waste like industrial beef. It comes from a local farm down the road and is one of the most popular menu items. They offer lots more than that -

it's a full-service restaurant offering great food at reasonable prices in a friendly, casual atmosphere. It's that atmosphere that makes for a nice opportunity to mix it up with tourists and locals both. The night I was there I met a guy who's in construction and is a fellow biker. He rides a BMW and treated me like a friend. We talked about travel, life, and of course, motorcycles. He's been all over the country but calls Benezette home. It seems like this tiny, remote mountain village has that effect on others.

Brian Kunes, one of the owners, is one such "other." This dude had an engineering job with the government in DC when he decided to quit and buy the place. I had the pleasure of meeting Brian, but he didn't really elaborate on his previous job or exactly why he left. I can only imagine it's one of those "If I tell you I'll have to kill you" things, and since I hadn't paid my bill at that point, he'd be out an elk burger, fries, and a beer. He did say that he bought the hotel in '06 and for the first three years commuted to Benezette from DC. Only recently did he move his family there full time, and is now a full-time restaurateur and hotel manager.

Brian runs the front of the house and hotel, and his partner Matt runs the back of the house and is the chef. Matt was really busy that night so I didn't get a chance to meet him, but I hope to on another trip. He's doing a good job too because there were a lot of happy faces there that night. And the menu reflected his cooking prowess.

Matt doesn't offer just one menu either — he offers a Breakfast Menu, Dinner Menu, a Late Night Menu, and even a "Mexican Night" Menu. Breakfast includes: Eggs, Steak and Eggs, Omelets, Pancakes, Waffles, Home Fries, and all the other usual breakfast suspects. The Dinner Menu offers plenty of stuff for dinner and lunch, too. Here's a sampling: Nacho Platters, Onion Rings, Cheese Sticks, Quesadillas, Deep Fried Veggies & Ravioli, Wings, Pizza, Soups,

Chili, Salads, and a bunch of burgers including the Elk Burger, Bugle Burger (which isn't elk, believe it or not), and a Turkey Burger. For sandwiches there's Fish, Meatball, Grilled Steak, Reuben, Grilled Chicken, Tuna Melt, Club, Tuna Salad, BLT, Grilled Ham & Cheese, Grilled Cheese, and Hot Dogs.

The dinner entrées offer up some deelish dishes like Steaks, including Prime Rib, Delmonico, and a Black Diamond Steak, an 8 oz. marinated sirloin cooked to order. There's Smothered Chicken, Pork Chops, Deep Fried Haddock and Baked Fish, Roast Beef, Roast Turkey, Meat Loaf, Liver & Onions, Deep Fried Chicken, and Ham. Italian Dishes include Spaghetti and Meat-balls, Chicken Parmigiana, Veal Parmigiana, and Chicken Alfredo. Then there's the Late Night Menu.

As I was reading the menu, I found this on the back, and it's something that Brian takes to heart. It's the story of The Mayonnaise Jar and The Beer.

"When things in your life seem almost too much to handle, when 24 hours in a day are not enough, remember the mayonnaise jar and the beer.

A professor stood before his philosophy class and had some items in front of him. When the class began, he picked up a very large, empty mayonnaise jar and proceeded to fill it with golf balls. He then asked the students if the jar was full. They agreed that it was. So the professor then picked up a box of pebbles and poured them into the jar. He shook the jar lightly and the pebbles rolled into the open areas between the golf balls.

He then asked the students again if the jar was full and they agreed it was. Then he picked up a box of sand and poured it into the jar. Of course the sand filled up everything else and he asked once more if the jar was full. The students responded with a unanimous 'Yes.'

He then produced two cans of beer from under the table and poured them into the jar. 'Now,' he said 'I want you to recognize that this jar represents your life. The golf balls are the important things — your family, children, health, friends, and your favorite passions – things that if everything else was lost and only they remained, your life would still be full. The pebbles are the other things that matter too like your job, house, or car. The sand is everything else – the small stuff. If you put the sand into the jar first, there is no room for the pebbles or the golf balls.

The same goes for life. If you spend all your time and energy on the small stuff, you will never have room for the things that are important to you. Pay attention to the things that are critical to your happiness. Play with your children. Take time to get medical checkups. Take your partner out to dinner. Play another 18. There will always be time to clean the house, and fix the disposal. Take care of the golf balls first, the things that really matter. Set your priorities. The rest is just sand.'

One of the students raised her hand and inquired what the beer represented. The professor smiled. 'I'm glad you asked. It just goes to show you that no matter how full your life may seem, there's always room for a couple of beers with friends."

It might have taken a long time for me to visit the
Benezette Hotel, but hopefully there will be many
more visits to come. And I'm sure, no matter how full
my life may seem, taking the time and back roads to
get there for a great breakfast, lunch, dinner, late
night snack, or just a cold Straub on draught will
be worth it. This is one of those places the chains
or cookie-cutters places can't replicate. Do you have
a cookie-cutter life? I hope not. But if you do, fill
it with real stuff, fill it with places like this.

Enjoy!

Aroma Café & Restaurant

EMPORIUM, CAMERON COUNTY

After the release of my first
book, I got all kinds of
recommendations from folks
all over the state on where
to go if I needed places for
a second book. One of those
folks was a woman from
Cameron County – a county I might describe as being
in the "hinterlands." Seriously, I was told (how
accurate this is I don't know) Cameron County has
only 6,000 people in a county of 400 square miles,
that's like 15 people per square mile. But, if you
go there, you'll see right away that there's tons
of land where not a soul lives – wildlife galore,
but no humans. Why? Because like many northern-tier
counties, Cameron is blessed with some of the most
intense and beautiful mountain land in the state,
leaving only a handful of towns and villages to provide safe haven and work for the humans. One of these
towns, and the county seat of Cameron, is Emporium,
the place that drew me to this remote but gorgeous
region of the state.

Access to Emporium is limited. There are only three
routes into town 46 and 155 from the fabled and

JUST A TASTE

Locally Owned By:
Jill & Kirk Gibbs

Cuisine:
Café (full restaurant fare)

Price Range:
$2.99 to $19.99

Hours:
Mon. – Sat. 8am to 9pm,
Winter Mon. – Th. 8am to 8pm

Location:
51 E. Fourth St. (Rt. 120)

Wi-Fi:
Yes

Contact Info:
(814) 486-7662,
aromacafe7662@yahoo.com,
www.aromabakeryandcafe.
weebly.com,
Facebook: Gibbs Aroma Café

Vegetarian Offerings:
Yes (upon request)

Supports Local Farmers:
Yes

**Locally Owned
Accommodations Nearby:**
Buttonwood Motel

Things To Do Nearby:
PA Wilds, Elk Watching,
Hiking, Fishing

historic Rt. 6 to the north, and then 120 from either Driftwood to the south or Saint Marys to the west. Rt. 120 is my preferred access, simply because it's the most accessible coming from the south. Rt. 120 is accessible via the absolutely amazing Rt. 144 (Ridge Road) out of Snow Shoe. Or, if you want another beautiful drive of epic proportions, start in Lock Haven and take 120 north along the West Branch of the Susquehanna River, then west and north again.

However, if you take the western-routes combo of 153, 255, 555 and then hit 120 at Driftwood, it just may be as "epic." The easy start to this route is Interstate 80 at the Penfield Exit 111 but you can find a more adventurous way. But wait, if you do 879 from Moshannon to just beyond Karthaus, and then turn right on the Quehanna Highway (State Rt. 1011) to either Wyckoff Run to Sinnemahoning, or continue on to Rt. 555 at Medix Run you won't be disappointed either – in fact this is my favorite route! If you haven't figured it out yet, to me, the journey is just as important as the destination. But no matter the journey, by the time you get to Emporium you'll most likely be hungry, and do I have a place for you!

Aroma Café and Restaurant has been around for awhile but was recently acquired by Jill and Kirk Gibbs, a local couple who thought they'd try their hand at owning and running a restaurant. Jill had worked in the food biz most of her life but never as an owner, and Kirk, not at all. In fact it took quite a bit of talking and a poor economic scene there to convince Kirk to take the plunge. But now that he's in, the two are working well together and Kirk's even getting along pretty well in the kitchen, from which they offer a full breakfast, lunch, and dinner menu.

Once she got deep into it, Jill realized that all her years of working at a restaurant didn't really prepare her for owning one. The hours are long and the respon-sibilities great, but that's fine with her. She loves it and is looking forward to more improvements.

Some of the improvements already made include: Friday
Night Fish Fries, an Open Mic Night on Tuesdays, and
book signings. Fish Night is a real crowd pleaser
that packs the place! Jill uses fresh (not frozen)
haddock and a "secret" ingredient for the batter.
I was able to guess it, and I'll only write that it
comes from St. Marys, is Special, Dark, and makes a
very refreshing drink on its own. Their Open Mic Night
is an opportunity for locals to showcase their talents.
Jill told me that some nights are "interesting," but
there are plenty of nights when some really talented
folks show up. She said that two teenage brothers
from St. Marys come in who are "awesome" (in her own
words). The town really supports this event week after
week and it's the only Open Mic session in town.

Something else Jill told me about was what might be
called the Old Cats' Coffee Club (my title, not
hers). These are local dudes who come every day to
discuss, argue, spin tales, complain, and give Jill
and her staff a hard time, but mostly just to have
fun and add that great local color to the place.
Aroma also hosts a Monday wing night and Wednesday
Italian day, Thursday is Two Eat for $20, and Satur-
day is Steak Night.

Oh, two more things; street parking costs 25 cents
for two hours, and Cameron County is chain-free! That's
right, only locally-owned places! In today's world
of cookie-cutter feed troughs, this is refreshing,
and you'll find Aroma Café & Restaurant a refreshing
place, too. Deep in the heart of the "hinterlands"
this is one destination well worth the journey.

Enjoy!

Hull's Lounge & Restaurant
SMETHPORT, MCKEAN COUNTY

My first visit to Hull's Lounge & Restaurant was in August of 2003 when my buddies and I decided to ride the length of Pennsylvania on the historic Grand Army of the Republic Highway, more commonly known

as Route 6. I like the formal name, as it invokes an era of travel that I like to think I live - when a trip, no matter the distance, is an adventure. For me and my friends, the trip was an adventure of epic proportions and I remember it well.

On the middle leg of the trip, we made a stop in Smethport, where I first discovered Hull's. We had a great time that day enjoying some good eats and some cold beers. I can't remember what we had, but the place stuck in my mind so much that when I was look-ing for places up north for this book, I knew right away I wanted to include it. That also meant another trip north and another grand ride along the Grand Army of the Republic Highway!

This time I walked into Hull's Lounge in July of 2010, and also into some fun and lively banter between the

JUST A TASTE

Locally Owned By:
Waverly Hull

Cuisine:
American

Price Range:
$1.00 to $37.95, Cash Only

Hours:
Lounge: Tue. – Sat. 9am to 2am,
Dining Room: Fri. & Sat. 5pm to
9pm, Closed Mondays

Location:
103 E. Main St.

Wi-Fi:
No

Contact Info:
(814) 887-5063

Vegetarian Offerings:
No

Supports Local Farmers:
Yes

**Locally Owned
Accommodations Nearby:**
Rooms on Premises

Things To Do Nearby:
Hiking, Biking, Lumber Museum,
Armory Museum, Eldred WWII
Museum, ATV & Snowmobile Trails

bartender and an older guy at the bar. I looked around for a table where I hoped I could eat, have a beer, write a little, and enjoy the free entertainment. I spotted the exact table the guys and I sat at back on the first Rt. 6 ride and took up residence there. The bartender stopped her part of the verbal wrestling match just long enough to ask me what I wanted to drink, and I ordered a draught and started taking notes.

As I looked around it was exactly as I had remembered. There was a big jukebox right next to me, the lighting was low, but the walls were bright and colorful with beer promo mirrors, posters, and memorabilia. But the most prominent feature was a display of old-fashioned beer trays. There must have been 50 attached to the walls, with names like Genesee, Pabst, Rolling Rock, Stoney's, and Fort Pitt.

The two at the bar were really going at it when the older guy turned and very politely asked if they were disturbing me. I said no and that I was actually enjoying it. Well, that was all it took, and now I was part of the scene. It was fun and I was able to meet and talk with Marsha Hull, the owner's daughter and the barkeep, and the older guy, Dick Renner, a totally awesome and interesting world traveler.

They were both funny and very nice. When I asked if I could take a copy of the menu home, Marsha went all the way downstairs and brought up a portable copier and made copies for me! Watch out though, she's a pistol and tells it like it is - I like that. Dick was an oil man who traveled the globe for some of the biggest oil drilling projects in history. He's absolutely fascinating and we talked at my table over a couple beers for an hour or so. He's long since retired and lives most of the time in far-off Paraguay. He's originally from the area and his kids live in Smethport, so he visits often. He also stops in Hull's when in town, not just for good banter, but for good meals and drinks at good prices.

Hull's has a nice dining area that offers Appetizers, a Salad Bar, and an Off The Charbroiler menu where you can get wonderful in-house cuts of steaks. The Seafood menu offers many items, including a great sounding Broiled Seafood Platter with Lobster Tail! Fridays they have an Icelandic Haddock menu, and one other unusual menu item is Frog Legs! The Lounge menu is simple, with Sandwiches, Soups, Sides, and Salads. I had an English Burger which came with bacon, lettuce, and tomato. It was HUGE and deelicious for only $4.25!

I really enjoyed myself there and was glad I had the opportunity to meet and talk with Marsha and Dick. Hull's is a nice and fun place, and Smethport is a really cool and historic town. After I got home that night I decided to check the web for information on Smethport. Turns out Wikipedia had a bunch of really interesting info, and some fun facts. Here's a sample:

It was in 1807 that Dutch land investors purchased this area from the Commonwealth of Pennsylvania, and named it in honor of the Dutch banking family, the De Smeths, who financed the investments.

During the 1870s through early 1900s Smethport was in an economic explosion that created some of the wealthiest entrepreneurs in the country. Financier and Smethport benefactor Henry Hamlin was reported to be the wealthiest private banker in the United States during the 1890s. Smethport is blessed with numerous exquisite mansions, and the Smethport Mansion District is one of the community's paramount attractions. Examples of Victorian-style architecture include Greek Revival, Queen Anne, Stick, and Italianate. Visitors can view these masterpieces through walking tours with the aid of the Smethport Mansion District walking tour guide.

The first magnetic toys in the country were invented in Smethport in 1908, one of which was the famous 1950s hit toy "Wooly Willy." It was created by Jim Herzog when he worked for the family-owned Smethport Specialty Co. Wooly Willy is celebrated by the town in June during Summer Fest when any Willy-want-to-be can enter the Wooly Willy look-alike contest. With more than 50 million sold, this toy is one of the largest promoters of Smethport.

And that's only a small part! Go to Wikipedia and read it all...it's fascinating. Better yet, go to Smethport! Even better than that, go to Smethport and stop in at Hull's Lounge & Restaurant and have lunch or dinner and something to drink. Marsha will most likely be there in the tavern side, and if you're lucky, Dick Renner will be in town. Don't forget, Marsha tells it like it is and is a lot of fun, and Dick can tell you story after story that will have you around the world and then some.

Smethport is a great stop along a Grand Highway, and Hull's is a great place to get a grand taste of it.

Enjoy!

CHAPTER 12
12 O'CLOCK

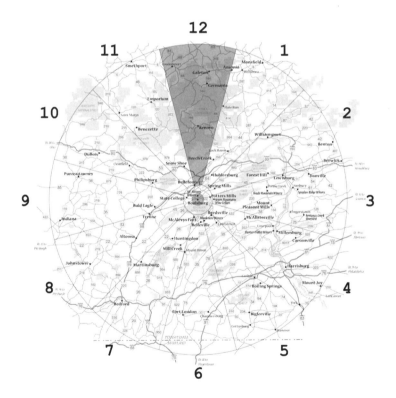

Darlene's Country Cottage
RENOVO, CLINTON COUNTY

It was a beautiful summer Saturday, and after I shed the traffic and hustle of State College, I could settle-in and get down to business. And that business was putting The Steed through his paces on one of the sweetest roads in central PA (maybe all of PA), Rt. 144. For me, it's like a highway to heaven. Here, I fly through twists, turns, mountain ascends and descends, and some of the most picturesque mountain plateau scenery in the state. Halfway along this amazing route is the remote river town of Renovo. Prior to this writing I didn't really know of any good food stops here but I was determined to find one. Plus, riding 144 at breakneck speeds makes a guy quite hungry!

I cruised over the bridge across the mighty West Branch of the Susquehanna and turned left towards Emporium. I rolled through town and saw an old cat walking his dog. I stopped and asked for a place to eat, and without hesitation he recommended a place called Darlene's. He said it was on the main street through the business

JUST A TASTE

Locally Owned By:
Darlene Mills

Cuisine:
Home-Made Country

Price Range:
.95 cents to $8.00

Hours:
7:30am to 4:30pm,
Weekdays Sat. 7:30am to 2pm,
Closed Sundays

Location:
500 Erie Street

Wi-Fi:
No

Contact Info:
(570) 923-1153

Vegetarian Offerings:
Yes

Supports Local Farmers:
Yes

Locally Owned Accommodations Nearby:
Tripps Motel

Things To Do Nearby:
Fishing, hunting, hiking, touring Rt. 144

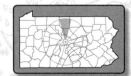

district and along the abandoned railroad works that was the hey-day industry of Renovo prior to WWII. He said to head down the street to 5th Street, make a right, and Darlene's was at the end on the right corner. This was good news, because if it panned out, I would not only get something to fill my growling belly, but guide you to a place to fill yours, too, when you have the pleasure of going up that way.

I found the little eatery right where cat said it would be. It was on the first floor of an old brick building with a huge old faded Mail Pouch ad painted high above on the 5th St. side. The front of the place was on Erie Ave., and hanging from the entrance was an old school RC (Royal Crown Soda) sign with "Darlene's Restaurant" written underneath. In the window below was little hand-painted sign reading "Darlene's

Country Cottage Restaurant." I managed to find enough space between the parked cars out front to park the bike. I gathered my stuff and walked in.

The place was buzzing, and the smell of home cooking picked me up and carried me to the only seat left at the little counter at the rear of the restaurant. This turned out to be a great spot because it was just off the kitchen and right within ear-shot of some great conversation between locals and also between them and the sweet young girl who was doing a great job keeping up with the orders. A few stools down was an older gentleman named Mr. O'Donnell who was a super nice guy and ended up telling me some history of the town, as well as some insider info on some great fishing spots nearby. This is one of the perks of eating at little local joints — you meet people, get some helpful info, and maybe a personal fishing guide if you're so inclined!

Even though I arrived around noon, and the menu had a lot of tempting lunch offerings, when I saw the home-made Belgian Waffle, I knew that was what I wanted. Plus, it was only $1.99! Accompanied with scrambled eggs, bacon, and coffee it would fill my hungry belly without draining my pocket. Two eggs, waffle, bacon, coffee, and tax for well under $5.00!

Besides all the usual suspects on the breakfast menu, Darlene offers specialties like Darlene's Campfire Breakfast, fried potatoes, eggs, onions, and ham all cooked up in a pan and topped with melted cheese ($4.75); and Darlene's Big Country Platter, two eggs, a waffle or pancake, hash browns, country ham or sausage, and home baked toast ($6.95)! Darlene added this after the description: "Get this & your coffee is on me!" I'll have to come back with my friend Mike - he'd eat that up, literally! She also does Breakfast Sandwiches, a Breakfast Burrito, Omelets, and Sausage Gravy with Home Made Biscuits.

The lunch menu is simple but enough to satisfy the hungry traveler. There're dogs, burgers, subs, salads, soups wraps, nachos, wings, and specials. All Darlene's dishes are made fresh and from scratch. She shops for all her ingredients and uses as many local supplies as possible. While I was there, Mr. O'Donnell was asking her how many tomatoes he could bring in for her.

Everyone at Darlene's is really nice, and it's a peaceful and pleasant place to be. I got the sense that Darlene was a Christian by the little sayings around the room. Her compassion and generosity sure came through when she told me that one of the reasons her prices are so inexpensive is because her clientele needs it and appreciates it. She said, "At the end of the month when many seniors receive their financial help, they come in and enjoy a time of socializing and dining out, without spending too much." I thought this was cool, and I really hope she can stay afloat in this tough economic time. It's exactly this kind of place that inspired me to write books about supporting local eateries.

I hope you're inspired to take the amazingly beautiful along Rt. 144 or even Rt. 120 north from Lock Haven to Renovo and stop by Darlene's. Tell her I sent you. She's an artist and writer herself, and will totally appreciate you coming to visit. It's a little place but with a big heart.

Enjoy!

Germania Store and Lodge
& Germania Hotel
GERMANIA, POTTER COUNTY

Introduction

Dropping into the village of
Germania, it's as though you've
come onto a tiny hamlet in the
mountains of Europe – Germany
to be more precise. There you'll

find an old hotel, store
and lodge, a few houses,
and the classic white
church with its steeple

as the highest point around. All
making this out-of-America experience seem real –
a pleasant and welcomed find as you travel through a
very isolated part of the state. Hey, this is Potter
County – God's Country, where wildlife outnumber
human life. Here too, modern conveniences are few
and far between so looking for nourishment not only
for me, but for The Steed wasn't easy.

As I rounded the curve and over the bridge into the
heart of Germania, I spotted a single solitary gas
pump outside the general store across the street
from the hotel and pulled in there first. I figured
I'd get the boy fed and then relax with a cold beer
and dinner at the hotel. I asked a guy standing out
on the porch of the store if the pump worked (I thought
maybe it worked at one time, but now was just a prop
or something) and he said, "Yeah, and it's ethanol
free." "Cool," I said, and proceeded to fill the boy
with high test.

As I was pumping gas, I took a look around – this
place is beautiful! The architecture and authenticity
of the store façade as well as the hotel and surrounding building was so out-of-the-ordinary – it

was like time stood still here back in the 1800s, yet other things made it seem like it started again in the 1960s or 70s, then stopped once more. The first was the gas pump I was using and the other was a phone booth – a phone booth! Where do you see a phone booth anymore? Well ya do in Germania,

and you see a lot of other things you don't see much anymore and some you don't wanna see. But even that would be all in fun, and this trip up into God's Country would end up to be a blessing for sure.

Germania Store and Lodge

Locally Owned By:
Lonnie Foltz and Roxana Divinie

Cuisine:
Sandwiches & Stuff

Price Range:
$2.50 to $9.00

Hours:
Mon. 7am to 7pm, Tues Closed,
Wed. & Thu. 7am to 7pm,
Fri. – Sat. 7am to 8pm

Location:
42 Constitution Ave.

Wi-Fi:
No

Contact Info:
814-435-6555,
jagergermania@yahoo.com

Vegetarian Offerings:
No

Supports Local Farmers:
Yes

**Locally Owned
Accommodations Nearby:**
Lodge on premises (5 rooms)

Things To Do Nearby:
Hiking, Snowmobiling, Skiing,
State Parks

The whole idea of time standing still was once again revealed when I walked into this old general store to pay for my gas. The inside was as period and authentic as the outside, with old wood floors, high wood-planked ceilings, shelves of goods running the length of the place, a wood stove in the back, old photos and "stuff" hanging from the walls, and a customer counter with a really cool old cheese box at the one end. Inside was a 1/4 wheel of cheese and a giant built-in knife hinged at the bottom for cutting. If all that visual stuff wasn't enough for me to feel like I was back in time, just the vibe of the place was sooo old school. Is it me, or everyone, but when I'm in a place like this, I feel good. There's something about the nostalgia, look, feel, smell, and vibe that just makes me feel good - something I definitely don't get or feel at a modern day mini mart. I paid the guy who was previously out on the porch for my gas, and when I asked him about the place he answered me in a southern accent. I would have been a little surprised by German, but southern, what was that all about?

The guy behind the counter turned out to be the owner and introduced himself as Lonnie. His dad was originally from Lancaster, PA, but he and his family lived in Key West. His dad's family had kept a camp up in Germania for years, and when his dad brought his mom there, she fell in love with the place and wanted to stay. So when they decided to retire, they sold their place in Key West and moved up. When Lonnie learned that the store, which had been in operation since 1884 was for sale, he decided to buy it. In 2004 he moved up as well to run it and be closer to his folks.

Like a general store should, this store has a little of everything - there's even a bucket by the door with huge smoked dog bones with meat still on them! You can look around for a while and see all kinds of stuff. Lonnie even offers some things you can't see like steaks and baby back ribs. He also offers sandwiches and hoagies, but more recently he's trying to offer some more interesting things. On weekends, Lonnie has introduced a Reuben, but instead of sauerkraut he uses a spicy slaw that he fries, and it's served with homemade potato chips. His new Meatball Sub is made from scratch as well as his Cheesesteak. He also does regular hot dogs and chili dogs with his own chili sauce that he says "has a little kick to it."

I asked Lonnie about the cool cheese box and he said it was super old and came with the place – it might even be original. He's a very nice guy with that southern hospitality thing going on, and cut me a slice to try. He said he goes through a lot of cheese and a lot of locals and camp owners stop in to get it. With that, I asked Lonnie if he had any interesting stories about his place, and he didn't. I then asked if he had any interesting customers that stop in and he said, "Up here, they're all interesting." I laughed.

It was getting close to closing time for him, and I thanked Lonnie for all the time he spent with me, the cheese sample and his hospitality. I thought to myself that I really wanted to come back there for lunch someday, or pick up meats and cheese or sandwiches to go before a camping trip or long ride. Heck, maybe I'd forgo the camping and stay at the lodge there above the store! It would be cool to use his place as a base to explore all the beauty of Potter County. Another day, I thought, it was late and I was in need of dinner, and that was only a walk across the street to the Germania Hotel.

Germania Hotel

Locally Owned By:
Marcie Drake

Cuisine:
American Tavern

Price Range:
$3.50 to $25.00

Hours:
Noon to midnight all week

Location:
1361 Germania Rd, Rt. 144

Wi-Fi:
Yes

Contact Info:
(814) 435-8851,
germaniahotel@yahoo.com

Vegetarian Offerings:
No

Supports Local Farmers:
Yes

Locally Owned Accommodations Nearby:
17 rooms on premise

Things To Do Nearby:
Ghosts on premise, Fishing, Anything outdoors

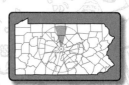

It was the middle of June, and on days like this, when the temps are warm and the sun is shining, I can't be inside – especially after a long cold winter. I know these folks up here love winter but give me summer, an old mountain village hotel, a porch, a beer, and some good eats, and I wish time would actually stand still – at least until next spring. So I dropped my gear at a table on the wrap-around porch and headed in to the tavern to see what this place was offering for dinner.

It was Friday night so the place was buzzing, the bar was full and I could barely squeeze in to ask for a menu. The young woman behind the bar was moving so fast she was almost a blur, but as soon as she saw me she kindly asked what she could get me. Unfortunately, they did not cater to my "Mr. Fancy Pants" beer tastes, so I opted for another one of my summertime favorites, Corona, and asked for a menu. In one seamless move, she handed me my beer with a lime wedge stuck in the top and their six page menu.

While I was standing there at the bar, a guy told me that they serve a "killer" cheese steak sandwich and he highly recommended it. However his recommendation came with a warning – "It's huge!" he said. Then he looked me over and added "If I were you I'd go for the half portion, and you might not even finish that." This cat had no idea who he was talking too (I can put it away), but I was in a new place far from home and far from a hospital so I thought I'd at least consider his advice.

I took my Corona and menu with me and sat down at my table on the porch. I squeezed the lime into the bottle then poked his little carcass through the opening. He splashed down like a kid doing a "cannonball" into a pool. I watched him fizz with delight as he floated happily in the golden sea of Mexican lager and realized I was way too into this moment. I threw back a good gulp and just smiled as I looked across towards the church steeple rising above and enjoyed the peace and quiet of this wonderful village.

Little did I know that the silence was about to be broken - and my eyes paralyzed.

(Remember back at the end of the introduction when I wrote "...you see a lot of other things you don't see much anymore — some you don't wanna see"?)

Just then, I heard a rebel yell from behind me. I turned and just stared. Honestly, I thought that I was caught in a bad nightmare or an outtake from Girls Gone Wild - it was like a train wreck - I didn't want to look but I couldn't help myself. There before me was the biggest pair of boobs I had ever seen. Apparently this flasher and her friend were celebrating a day without their hubbies and celebrating they were! Once I realized what I was seeing, I quickly turned back to my beer and church steeple.

Maybe because I was the new guy in town, maybe I seemed lonely, or maybe I was just in the right place but the wrong time, because she (shirt pulled down now) and her friend came straight over and sat down at my table and proceeded to tell me about all the fun they had that day. I tried not to encourage them, but to no avail; they ordered another round of drinks for themselves (not needed) and another beer for me (also not needed). It turned out that they were both hysterical and really nice, just two country girls blowing off steam. We talked for a few minutes and then they were on their way to meet up with said hubbies. Man, those guys probably have no idea.

Eyes now somewhat back to normal, I checked out what else the Germania Hotel had to offer. The menu is six pages with some really good looking stuff, but one thing I wasn't too sure about. Halfway into the menu, I saw a cartoon frog jumping up with legs flailing and a big smile on his face. Under him was written:

FROG LEGS
½ DOZ. 6.50
DOZ. 12.99

First I wondered why the frog was smiling, then I wondered why he had both his legs. Maybe it was his arch enemy that got caught and he was celebrating! Nonetheless, I wasn't too sure about that one. The front of the menu was titled "Sandwich and Fryer," and there they offer Burgers and Wraps, Cheese Steaks and Chicken Cheese Steaks with this below: *"Our beef and chicken cheese steaks are made just how you like them. They are piled high with meat and toppings and served on fresh home-made bread."* That was it, between the recommendation and description I went straight for the cheese steak, but only the half portion – when in Rome . . .

Other menu items were Clubs, Subs, Other Choices like the Huge Haddock Sandwich and Grilled Chicken Breast; Salads; Fried Fun, which was where the Frog Legs are offered along with Fish & Chips, Wings, Fresh Cut French Fries, Sweet Potato Fries and lots of others; Pizza; BBQ Baby Back Ribs; Appetizers; Steaks; Seafood; Pasta; Chicken; and Other Meat Selections including Pork Chops and a Huge Ham Steak.

It seemed like "huge" was a theme on their menu, but no mention of that for the cheese steak. However, when it arrived I realized the word "huge" must have been mistakenly omitted because even the half portion was HUGE! The fries were fresh cut and bountiful! I sat back, gave thanks, and enjoyed my Germania Hotel feast.

After I had finished my delicious cheese steak and fries, the busy bartender actually took the time to come out and asked if I enjoyed my dinner. I said yes, and asked her about the place and the owners. She told me she was the owner and her name was Marcie. She was super nice and so passionate about her place. She told me that she put herself through college working there, and when the place

came up for sale she went for it. She's been the owner operator for eight years as of 2010, and really cares about the place. She also cares about Germania and the history there. And when I asked about the village and said how much I loved it there, and that it reminded me of Europe and how it felt as though time stood still, she got up and disappeared. She quickly returned with a book.

Marcie handed me a hard cover book called Germania: Our Heritage 1855–1995. It was a wonderful book on the history of the area compiled by Connie Rawson, Ruby Welfling, Lois Gardner, and beautifully illustrated by Kimberly Neefe Scharr. And it was printed locally by Free Press-Courier in Galton, PA. I paged through it while I finished my beer, and even noticed that Germania had its own brewery at one time! I went in to pay my bill and return the book, and Marcie said I could keep it as a gift from the hotel. I couldn't believe it, and thanked her for her kindness and generosity (a picture or two from the book appear in this piece).

I walked back out to the porch and collected my things. I looked around one more time and saw that the old building was showing signs of age. Like any owner, Marcie must have a hard time trying to manage a business, let alone the upkeep and repairs on a historic building like that. But she's so positive about the place and just loves what she does. She said to me "I couldn't live without the place." And later she said "I wouldn't change my life for anything." Now that's a passion and commitment that's worthy of supporting.

I bid Marcie goodbye. And as I rode away from this wonderful little town where time seemed to stand still, I was happy to know that it would be moving forward by the passions, hospitality, and commitment of two young country proprietors for a long time to come.

Zum Wohl! *(Enjoy! in German)*

The Brick House Café & Deli

GALETON, POTTER COUNTY

So how and why does a couple go from working for corporate America and manufacturing in a major metropolitan area to owning and operating a sweet little café and deli in a remote sparsely populated region know as God's Country? In this case it's a few things – the economy, a need to get out while the getting was good, being motorcycle foodies like me, and the internet. What came along with that was a new place to call home, a new passion, a place for their family, and a community that welcomed them and supports them, and now a lovely place for you and me to come to and enjoy. This is the story of Cindy and Ron Pflug and the Brick House Café & Deli.

I met this couple a few years ago right after they opened their place in Galeton. I mentioned then that I was traveling around in search of cool places to eat, but I don't remember telling them of my book idea. Well, when I returned there in the summer of 2010, they remembered me! I couldn't believe it, but no more did I step up to the counter than a really friendly woman behind it said, "Hey, I know you. Weren't you here a couple years ago and wrote a

JUST A TASTE

Locally Owned By:
Rob & Cindy Pflug

Cuisine:
Upscale Soups, Salads and Sandwiches

Price Range:
$2.95 to $8.95

Hours:
Mon. – Fri. 9am to 7pm,
Sat. 9am to 4pm

Location:
4 West Main (Historic Rt.6)

Wi-Fi:
Yes

Contact Info:
(814) 435-2444,
Facebook (brickhouse deli)

Vegetarian Offerings:
Yes

Supports Local Farmers:
Yes

Locally Owned Accommodations Nearby:
(On premises coming soon)
Rough Cut Lodge,
(814) 435-2192

Things To Do Nearby:
Rt. 6 touring, Lumber Museum,
Cherry Springs Dark Park, Lyman Run State Park, Hiking, Fishing, ATV, Snowmobiling

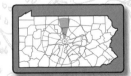

book about local eateries?" I said yes, and realized I must have told them after all. But that was good, because it gave me a great chance to tell them later after lunch about my new book I was working on and that I wanted their place to be in it. It was also an easy way to find out about their place and them, without all the covert tactics I usually employ.

Typically, I travel and scout incognito. This hopefully makes my visits and experiences what you would have and not something otherwise. If an owner and staff know I'm coming, they might treat me differently and I would write from a totally different perspective than what you would experience. But some places treat everyone the same – whether you're an adventurous author of eateries or simply a person out for a good and pleasant breakfast, lunch, or dinner. Here at the Brick House they don't show favoritism – everyone is treated like a valued customer or friend. But watch out for co-owner Ron, if you've been fortunate enough to become a regular or friend, he likes to have fun with you. That wasn't more clearly made than on this recent visit.

Before anybody even spotted me, and while I was just nosing around the place, Ron was bantering with two young women who were locals and regular customers. It had something to do with the one woman's salad or something, I just remember it was funny and continued until they left. When I got to the counter, I was ID'd by the woman working there alongside Ron, who turned out to be Cindy, his wife and co-owner.

She was sooo nice and remembered so much about my previous visit. I placed my order for the Brick House

Salad, which was a spinach salad with red onions, walnuts, craisins, feta cheese, and poppy seed dressing, and took a seat at a big wooden table with two other guys. The reason for that is, the Brick House is a wonderful place and the locals as well as those traveling along Rt. 6 support it well – it's not a huge place so it can fill up easily.

The guys were really nice, and I think one of them mentioned he had relatives in Boalsburg. As I was enjoying my amazing salad, I took the opportunity as I do often, to check out the other menu items. This is pretty much a breakfast, lunch, and early dinner place with a menu highlighting their features on the front and then detailed inside. Here are their features: Breakfast Sandwiches, Homemade Soups & Specials Gourmet Coffee-Cappuccino, Sliced Lunch Meats & Chesse Bakery Goods, Premium Salads, Hot & Cold Sandwiches Casual Catering – Just Ask, Smoothies – Iced Coffee

POTTER COUNTY

Formed March 26, 1804 out of Lycoming County, and fully organized in 1835. Named for Revolutionary hero, General James Potter. An early center of the lumbering and tanning industries. Coudersport, the county seat, was laid out in 1807; incorporated 1848.

PENNSYLVANIA HISTORICAL AND MUSEUM COMMISSION 1981

After my salad and after things calmed down, Cindy joined me to tell how this wonderful little eatery and deli in Galeton came to be. She told me that she and Ron came from outside Philadelphia where they had successful jobs – Cindy in the corporate world, and Ron was an engineer for a large manufacturer. Well, with the recent economic down-turn, corporate downsizing, and manufacturers going off-shore to places like China, they both feared for their financial future, plus neither one was in love with what they did anyway. Plus, now their property looked like it was going to start taking a dive in value.

The two are sharp people, and they thought of a plan that would free them from the uncertain high-profile business world, and give them a chance to relocate their lives and make a hobby/side business into a way of life.

Ron is a big-time biker and he and Cindy love to ride. They both also love doing what I do, and ride to restaurants, pubs and cafés to eat. When Ron landed a side job as a writer for a biker publication and his assignment was to do that and write an article about the places he visited, he and Cindy discovered a lot more than the ins and outs of eateries – they wanted one of their own. With all that was happening as mentioned before, this seemed like a way to step into a new and exciting life!

Cindy began to search the internet for places nearer to home, but the search results kept taken them north and west. Then one day a search yield-ed an old brick mansion built by a doctor in 1895 that had been already turned into a deli two years prior to

Cindy's search, so it was, as she put it, "a turn-key operation." When they made the trip to check it out, they fell in love with it and everything, including the town, environs, and the people there. They have totally been welcomed into the community and have grown so much in love with the area, way of life, and quality of life, that now both their children and their kids have moved up and live in Galeton too.

The Brick House Café & Deli is yet another example of something this book is all about – people like you and me, taking a dream or passion, and going for it; riding high and being forced to downsize, or choosing to downsize so you can break free and fly high with your own business; wanting to give your friends and neighbors the best you can offer and hope they will support you; keeping it local and embracing your local community and in turn having them embrace you back; putting your passion and talents out there for the world to critique, and hearing or reading rave reviews. This story of The Brick House Café & Deli is one such review. This place is as sweet as it gets with owners equally as sweet!

This also marks the last story in this book, and marks a long road to get here. I now write with tears in my eyes, these last and perhaps familiar words.

After I left this lovely place, I hopped back on my friend and most trusted traveling companion, The Mighty Steed, and pointed him south towards home. And as I rode away with my belly full and my heart ever fuller, I thought what a great day, and what a great adventure it's been!

Enjoy!

Central PA Wineries
THE SUSQUEHANNA HEARTLAND WINE TRAIL

OK, it's time for me to concede that the New York Finger Lakes region no longer holds the title for coolest wineries within driving distance of central PA. YES, it's no longer necessary to drive three hours to enjoy wineries where you can sip, taste, and buy local fruit of the vine! The Susquehanna Heartland Wine Trail offers you seven cool places to experience the flavor of central PA in a region that supports a climate not only good for the growth of hardy native grapes and premium hybrids, but also more delicate varieties such as Riesling, Chardonnay, Cabernet Franc and Pinot Noir.

The next few pages list all the wineries with a brief description of each provided by their own websites. All of them are easily accessible off major roads or interstates, and they're all include on the fold-out map in this book.

Enjoy!

Mount Nittany Vineyard & Winery

"Nestled high on the southern slopes of Mt. Nittany, above the historic village of Linden Hall and just seven miles east of State College, Mount Nittany Vineyard & Winery commands a breathtaking view of the distant Tussey Mountain Range. Come enjoy our handcrafted, award-winning wines in an idyllic setting.

The winery was opened for business in July of 1990 by proprietors Joe and Betty Carroll, who had been amateur winemakers for 20 years during Joe's career as a professor in the College of Business Administration at Penn State. Their purchase in 1983 of the sixty-five acre property was followed in 1984 by the first grape plantings. The entire wine making operation was initially contained in the original chalet-style building which now houses a state of the art bottling line. A spiral staircase leads upstairs to the tasting room and views of the adjacent pond, mountain range, and the five acre vineyard."

Phone: (814) 466-6373
Website: www.MtNittanyWinery.com
Hours: Tue. - Fri. noon to 5pm, Sat. 10am to 5pm, Sun. 12:30pm to 4pm

Seven Mountains Wine Cellars

"Tucked neatly into the side hills of the Seven Mountains region of Central Pennsylvania, our family-run winery is just 'LUCKY ENOUGH' to be located between two of the best places to visit in Pennsylvania, Happy Valley and Big Valley. So on your next trip through, come on back just one mile off the beaten path and have some Wine in the Woods! We can offer many services along with Great Wine.

Feel free to bring along you own picnic lunch and enjoy yourself in the spacious tasting lounge or on the deck. Schedule you private tour and take a peek at the only wine cave in all of PA. We hope to see you soon!"

Phone: (814) 364-1000
Website: www.sevenmountainswinecellars.com
Hours: Mon. & Tue. by appointment, Wed. & Thur. 11am to 5pm, Fri. & Sat. 11am to 7pm, Sun. 11am to 5pm. Please call for winter hours.

Brookmere Winery & Vineyard Inn

"Brookmere Winery & Vineyard Inn is located in a 19th century stone and wood bank barn in the beautiful Kishacoquillas Valley in the heart of central Pennsylvania's 'Seven Mountains.' The entire wine making process takes place on the premises. We invite you to visit and taste our wines made from premium Pennsylvania fruit.

You may stroll through the vineyards, bring a picnic, and enjoy a bottle of chilled Brookmere Wine. We offer a variety of quality wines which are affordable for everyday enjoyment."

Phone: (717) 935-5380
Website: www.BrookmereWine.com
Hours: Mon. - Sat. 10am to 5pm, Sun. 1pm to 4pm.
Call for winter hours.

Shade Mountain Winery

"Tucked away in the fertile Susquehanna Valley, our land offers ideal growing conditions for grapes. We are pleased to produce our own premium wines, from vine to bottle. The vineyard began on our family farm in 1989 and has grown to include 65 acres now known as Shade Mountain Vineyards and Winery. We grow all our own grapes, including varieties of Vinifera, hybrids, and native vines. These grapes are then fermented, aged, and bottled here on our farm.

Currently, our vineyard is home to over 40 different varieties of grapes, including the following: Cabernet Sauvignon, Merlot, Pinot Noir, Syrah, Sangiovese, Chardonnay, Pinot Grigio, Riesling, Traminette, Viognier, and the list does not stop there! We enjoy the challenge of growing grapes in the northeast, so we are always looking for new varieties to culti-vate successfully.

We welcome you to visit our renovated mid-19th century bank barn and sample our extensive list of wines — grown, produced and bottled on our family farm. Bring a picnic lunch to enjoy on our deck overlooking 60 acres of beautifully tended vineyards."

Phone: (570) 837-3644
Website: www.ShadeMountainWinery.com
Hours: Mon. - Sat. 10am to 5pm, Fri. 10am to 7pm, Sun. 12pm to 5pm

Hunters Valley Winery

"Our fine wines are ideally suited for your dining pleasure, casual events, family gatherings, holidays, and parties. Are you looking for a perfect wine for a wedding or a quiet dinner for two? Hunters Valley Winery has the wine you need for all your special occasions. With the charm and style of small town living comes wine with bold, beautiful taste at a price that anyone can afford.

Our 21-year-old winery moved to a beautiful new building in August 2006. The new site overlooks our vines and has a breathtaking view of the Susquehanna River. We welcome visitors to sit on the porch or have a picnic in the shelter from which they can watch the Millersburg Ferry cross the river in the summer.

Over the years our wines have won many awards. Our friendly staff welcomes the novice or experienced wine taster. Come enjoy the experience and the taste of our wines."

Phone: (717) 444-7211 or Toll Free: (877) 447-7211
Website: www.HuntersValleyWines.com
Hours: Wed. – Sat. 11am to 5pm, Fri. 11am to 6pm,
Sun. 1pm to 5pm

Spyglass Ridge Winery

"Spring of 1995 was the year that changed our family's lives forever. That was the year we decided to plant our vineyard of premium wine grapes. After years of supplying other Pennsylvania wineries with award-winning grapes, we decided to take that next giant leap. So begins the saga of owning a vineyard and winery.

Spyglass Ridge believes that life takes on a certain beauty; it's all how you view it. If you slow down, you'll find opportunities for a lot of simple pleasures.

Things like a glass of fine wine, good food, and friends to share it with. Spyglass Winery can enhance some of those pleasures. Lose yourself on our beautiful grounds as you savor a crisp Pinot Gris, or indulge in quiet conversation on our spacious deck with one of our fine wines."

Phone: (570) 286-9911
Website: www.SpyglassRidgeWinery.com
Hours: Wed. - Sun. 11am to 7pm

Benigna's Creek Winery

"It is the passion and desire of the entire Benigna's Creek family to bring to you the highest quality wine possible at a price that is affordable. Great wines can be produced all over the world, from the Champagne Province, to the Napa Valley, to the southern Australian Regions. As our international awards prove, great wines also can come from a small winery in the Mahantongo Valley.

Our wines are very approachable and fun to drink. We have created styles of wine that complement food as well as social events. You, our customer, are the ultimate judge of our efforts. Our philosophy of wine is for everyday enjoyment, in moderation, not just for special occasions.

With that in mind, producing a high quality and affordable wine will always be our goal. We will never rest on our laurels. We will always try to make our wines better for you. We realize that our success will be rooted in the excellence of our wines. We have started a life long journey of making great wine. If you have never tasted our wines, we invite you to start today.

The vineyard and winery overlook the beautiful Mahantongo Valley. Come enjoy the view from our porch and rear deck. Bring a picnic lunch, tour our wine cellar, and sample our wines. Choose from the many items in our showroom for the perfect gift."

Phone: (570) 425-3090
Website: www.BCWinery.com
Hours: Wed. - Sat. 11am to 5pm, Sun. 1pm to 4pm

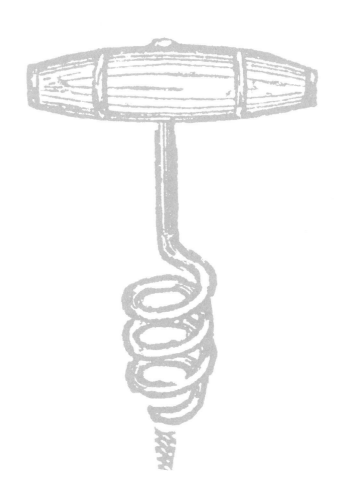

ACKNOWLEDGEMENTS

This started out as just a bunch of words typed, and photos loaded, into a laptop computer. It took the amazing talents and skills of graphic designers Bryan Benner and Rose Ann Hoover to make it into a book. Bryan's interior layout work took my 75,000 + word manuscript and hundreds of my photos and turned it into pages of art. Rose Ann not only took all my convoluted ideas for a cover design and created a second masterpiece that exceeded my vision, but was also a light of inspiration and encouragement to me from day one. RA, you're one of the kindest souls I've ever met. I thank you both so very much.

My writing skills are less than ok, so I would like to thank my volunteer editing team of Lisa Yoder, Sam Komlenic, Cici Cruz-Uribe, and Cecilia Mills. I am eternally grateful for your constant vigilance and patience while reading this Second Helping of *going LOCAL!* — eight eyes are better than two (especially my two) — thanks team!

In this age of technology it's essential to have a website - a great one is a bonus! Bien Concepcion has been my website designer since book one and he truly does great work. His knowledge and skills are amazing and I thank him for that along with his more than fair prices.

I would also like to thank my mentor and fellow author John Carr, whose years of knowledge, experience, and discipline were transformed into guidance, encouragement, and a good kick in the butt when I needed it - and I needed it a lot! Thanks too to Chuck Fong who volunteered his professional photography skills with the cover, and almost got run over taking photos of me in front of Zeno's.

A big thanks to all of my *going LOCAL!* fans who suggested so many great places that I didn't know about, but are now in this second edition. This book would not exist without the support of the communities that support local food and drinks.

I would also like to thank all of the awesome owners and employees of the unique eats, cool pubs, and cozy cafés here in central Pennsylvania. I have been so blessed to meet people from all walks of life who are out there trying to make it in a world full of chain restaurants and big box stores. To all of those folks, thank you so much for all of the hard work you've done that has made this book possible.

Finally, thank you for buying this book. Without your support, I would never be able to earn a living bringing these awesome adventures to you. I consider it a privilege and honor that you would think enough of me and believe in what I'm doing to part with your hard earned money so that I can do what I do. As a former artist and now an author, I am grateful for your support.

Thank you all so much!

INDEX

NOTES